Managing mental health in the community

The policy of community care for mentally ill people has had wide-ranging effects, some of which were not foreseen when the system was implemented. *Managing Mental Health in the Community* addresses the problems that affect the quality of care received by clients, and encourages the reader to think of ways of providing better services.

The anxieties and disturbances which distort the relationship between carers and clients may be understood and partially managed by adopting a reflective approach to practice. Creating the space to think about the inter-related systems which comprise care in the community is a way of providing the containment so crucial for this work.

Through the presentation and analysis of their own experience, the contributors show how to identify and understand the deficiencies of the 'triangular' relationship between user, carer and community. They illustrate that the common tendency to establish a two-way relationship, and disregard the perspective of the third party, obstructs the healthy functioning of the care system. Recognising the disturbance within individuals and within systems, and understanding why such disturbance exists, allows the establishment of systems in which it is possible to engage openly with clients without being hindered by undue anxiety and chaos.

Managing Mental Health in the Community is essential reading for practitioners, managers, policy-makers and students who have an interest in developing good practice in community care.

Angela Foster and **Roberts** work jointly as Foster Roberts Associates, offering and organizational development programmes in co related fields.

gs; Angela Foster; Lorenzo Grespi; Bob Hinshelwood; Caffrey; Helen Morgan; Jack Nathan; Trini Navarro; nael Wallbank.

Managing mental health in the community

Chaos and containment

Edited by Angela Foster and
Vega Zagier Roberts

London and New York

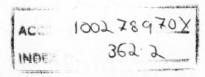

First published 1998
by Routledge
11 New Fetter Lane, London EC4P 4EE

Simultaneously published in the USA and Canada
by Routledge
29 West 35th Street, New York, NY 10001

Typeset in Times by Routledge
Printed and bound in Great Britain by
TJ International Ltd, Padstow, Cornwall

British Library Cataloguing in Publication Data
A catalogue record for this book is available from the British
Library

Library of Congress Cataloguing in Publication Data
Managing mental health in the community: chaos and containment
/ edited by Angela Foster and Vega Zagier Roberts.
p. cm.
Includes bibliographic references and index.
1. Community mental health services – Administration. I. Foster,
Angela, 1948– . II. Roberts, Vega Zagier, 1948– .
RA790.M327 1998
362.2'2'068–dc221
98–15339
CIP

ISBN 0–415–16796–5 (hbk)
ISBN 0–415–16797–3 (pbk)

To our clients – managers and workers dedicated to providing high quality services in community care – who have given us the opportunity to learn from experience with them.

Contents

Illustrations

Figures

Contributors

Simon Biggs is Senior Lecturer in Social Policy at Keele University. He has published widely in the areas of social work training, community care policy and social gerontology, and has consulted to health and welfare organizations in these fields. He is author of *Understanding Aging* (Open University Press, 1993) and principal author of *Elder Abuse in Perspective* (Open University Press, 1995).

Angela Foster is a psychoanalytic psychotherapist and an organizational consultant. She initially trained as a social worker, working mainly in therapeutic communities before moving into social work education. She developed training and consultancy in community care through the Adult Department of the Tavistock Clinic, currently teaches on the Tavistock Clinic and University of East London course 'Consultation and the organization: psychoanalytic approaches', and is an associate of OPUS (Organization for Promoting Understanding in Society). She has written many journal articles on her work in the mental health field and has contributed to *Therapeutic Communities: Reflections and Progress* (Hinshelwood and Manning, 1979).

Lorenzo Grespi is a consultant psychotherapist working for the Riverside Mental Health Trust in London. Before training in psychotherapy with adolescents and with adults at the Tavistock Clinic, he was a consultant community psychiatrist in Italy. He is also a visiting teacher at the Tavistock Clinic and has produced a number of papers in Italy and the United Kingdom on community care practices as well as training modules in community care.

Bob Hinshelwood is a psychoanalyst and Professor of Psychoanalysis at the University of Essex. He worked for many years in the NHS, particularly in the area of therapeutic communities, and at the Marlborough Day Hospital, and was Clinical Director of the Cassel Hospital. He has written widely on the psychodynamics of institutions, particularly care organizations. His books include *What Happens in Groups?*, *A Dictionary* *of Kleinian Thought, Clinical Klein* and a recent book on psychoanalysis and ethics, *Therapy or Coercion.*

Naomi Landau is a senior care manager with joint responsibility for a large multidisciplinary community mental health team in central London. She is also a part-time freelance trainer on mental health issues.

Tony McCaffrey comes from an academic background in social anthropology, after which he held several management posts in social work, particularly in the area of child and family work. Following a training at the Tavistock Clinic in adult psychotherapy and organizational consultancy, he worked for four years as an internal consultant with Surrey Social Services.

Helen Morgan is a practising psychotherapist and an independent mental health consultant and trainer. She has a wide range of experience in therapeutic communities and in managing and developing mental health services in the voluntary sector.

Jack Nathan is a case consultant on the MSC mental health social work course at the Maudsley Hospital and a tutor on the couples therapy course at the Institute of Psychiatry. He is also a practising psychoanalytic psychotherapist. His original training was in social work and he was formerly team manager in adult psychiatry at the Maudsley Hospital.

Trinidad Navarro is Director of Clinical Practice and Development at Tulip (Haringey Mental Health Group). Prior to this she was team leader of the outreach team where she developed the Tulip Team Approach. She is also a psychoanalytic psychotherapist in private practice. She has worked in the field of mental health for twelve years in NHS, local authority and voluntary sector establishments, and has extensive experience of therapeutic community practice.

Vega Zagier Roberts trained originally as a psychiatrist in the United States. Since 1984 she has worked as an organizational consultant in the public sector and as a psychotherapist in private practice. She is Senior Organizational Consultant at the Cassel Hospital, a member of the development group of OPUS Consultancy Services, where she has designed a series of courses 'Management and Leadership in Mental Health Services', a visiting tutor at the Tavistock Clinic and an associate of OPUS. Her past experience includes working as an internal consultant with the Riverside Mental Health Trust. She is programme organizer of the Tavistock Clinic Consulting to Institutions Workshop and co-editor with A. Obholzer of *The Unconscious at Work: Individual and Organizational Stress in the Human Services* (1994).

Michael Wallbank is a community psychiatric nurse, formerly team leader in a community mental health team in central London, a post from which he stepped down to return to clinical practice as a CPN. He also runs a small consultancy service for health professionals.

Preface

This book is aimed at all practitioners, managers, policy-makers and students who have an interest in developing good practice in community care. Although it draws mainly on experiences in the mental health field, we believe that the problems and dynamics described will be recognizable and relevant to people working in other areas of community care.

There are many excellent books on community care. In the main, these focus on policies and procedures, either suggesting 'how to' improve services and plug gaps, or arguing for or against community care. Here we try to examine the *actual experience* of the chaos and anxiety in the system, and different attempts to manage these, using psychoanalytic and systems theory to make sense of experience, and numerous case studies to illustrate these ideas.

While the case examples, legislation and contracting arrangements referred to in the book are British, the problems, challenges and dynamics described are similar to those in many other countries seeking to provide care in the community which was, until recently, provided mainly in institutions. The core challenges are, first, to create systems of care that can contain need, dependence and disturbance within the unbounded and multi-faceted setting of a community; and second, to maintain these systems as healthy structures in which it is possible to engage openly with clients and to think about the work without being overwhelmed by chaos and contaminated by destructiveness and despair. The additional difficulty of providing adequate care within ever-tightening financial constraints is also common to countries outside the United Kingdom.

In order to meet these challenges, we need to provide ourselves with a reflective space in which to examine the nature of the relationships between different parts of our care systems, and to work with the actual and potential chaos within and between these subsystems, at the same time as recognizing that – given the nature of mental disturbance and the nature of organizations – chaos will always be present. In this book, we invite readers to share with us a series of explorations of systems of care. We hope that it will provide support in thinking about their difficult and often very painful experiences and dilemmas – an opportunity for them to locate and use a reflective space within themselves.

Contributors

All the contributors are or have been mental health practitioners – from psychiatry, social work, nursing or psychology – as well as having worked as psychotherapists, managers, teachers/academics, or organizational consultants in this field. Herein lies a strength of the book – the first-hand experience of people working with mental illness (and other forms of disability), and their empathy with the struggles of others engaged in this work. The contributors share a concern about the quality of community care, and about the toll it takes. While trying never to lose sight of the intrinsic, unavoidable stresses of the work, we revisit some of the assumptions on which current systems are based and put forward some ideas about possible alternatives.

Plan of the book

This book looks at a number of key issues in the mental health field: the aftermath of the closure of the large mental hospitals, managing risk, the purchaser/provider split, multidisciplinary teamwork, the changing role of the voluntary sector, and strengthening the user voice. Inevitably, many other equally important issues are not addressed. We have not included anything that specifically addresses the issue of race and mental illness although we provide a great deal of evidence of the harmful effects of splitting and projection whereby an individual or a group of people become marginalized because they are not only struggling with their own difficulties but are also forced to 'carry' other people's despised and unwanted 'bits'.

Similarly, this book does not focus specifically on the politics of mental health care or on the more radical approaches to care in the community, although these are impressive where they exist (see K. Tudor, 1996, *Mental Health Promotion: Paradigms and Practice*, London: Routledge). Neither is it a book that goes into detail about different approaches to treatment. Instead, we have taken as our focus community care as it exists in all its variety and confusion. The vast majority of case illustrations are drawn from mental health, but on occasion we have used some from other 'neighbouring' fields such as physical health care or learning difficulties because the material they provided seemed particularly relevant.

The book examines current dilemmas in community care from various perspectives: social, systemic and psychoanalytic. The social perspective attends to changes in relationships and attitudes – for example, regarding the giving and receiving of care, and towards authority and control. It also considers some of our current experiences of care in the community – not only as professionals, carers and users, but also as citizens. The systems perspective draws on both open systems and family systems theory. The psychoanalytic perspective is based mainly on the work of Melanie Klein and its later applications, as described in the Introduction.

The book is divided into four parts. The first, 'The move into the community', comprises five chapters discussing different aspects of the move away from hospital-based care. The first draws attention to how the very deficiencies in care systems that prompted the move can be replicated in community-based agencies if they are not understood. Chapter 2 considers the impact of the move on ordinary neighbourhoods and citizens, and the impact of these citizens and communities on mentally disturbed people living in their midst. Chapter 3 explores some of the dynamics that contribute to personal stress and disillusion among those trying to implement the dream of community care. Chapter 4 examines some societal changes and how these affect professional as well as personal relationships. The final chapter in this section introduces a triangular model of community care as a way of thinking about dysfunctional aspects of current care systems, and also as a potential container of disturbance.

Part II, 'Managing anxiety in the system', looks at some of the structures and systemic defences used to manage the anxieties associated with mental health work – both the inherent 'task-related' anxieties, and the 'external' anxieties such as those about resources. The thesis of this section is that these anxieties need to be contained and managed. When they are not, structures and practices evolve to avoid anxiety which may then get 'passed around' different parts of the care system in counterproductive and even destructive ways.

The chapters in Part III, 'Learning from the experience of face-to-face work', are all written from the perspective of working directly with people with mental illness, or of managing first-line teams. In different ways, they challenge some of the assumptions underlying current policy and practice.

The final section, 'Initiatives for empowerment', opens with a chapter describing an alternative to more traditional approaches to user involvement and empowerment. However, it is not only users who can feel disempowered by the current structures and policies. The second chapter in this part describes a training model which has been used with both managers and front-line staff to facilitate their taking a more proactive stance in the wider systems within which they work. The last two chapters in this part consider how the capacity for reflection can be eroded or enhanced, and how this reflection can be translated into action.

Confidentiality

Throughout the book, we have used vignettes and case studies which we hope will bring the ideas to life by resonating with our readers' own experiences. The examples have been selected because they are typical of situations that recur throughout community care. Readers may therefore recognize – or think they recognize – some of the individuals or organizations described. However, all names are fictitious, and identifying details have been altered to preserve the anonymity of those involved.

A note on terminology

Workers in the mental health field use different words which then become associated in an emotionally charged way with their source. For example, very heated feelings can arise in response to the term 'mental illness' as suggesting a medical and derogatory point of view. Personal beliefs and political correctness have led to a plethora of alternative terms such as mental health problems or mental distress. In this book, we have opted in many cases to use the starker, more traditional terms in order to emphasize the severity of the mental state in question. As regards the equally heated differences in usage of the terms 'patient' and 'client', we have generally used the former to refer to people while they are in hospital, and the latter to refer to these same people while they are in the community.

Angela Foster and Vega Zagier Roberts
June 1998

Acknowledgements

Thanks and acknowledgements are due to the following organizations and people:

- The Tavistock Clinic for sponsoring Angela Foster's developmental work in the application of psychoanalytic thinking to the field of community care of the mentally ill. We especially want to acknowledge the part played by Julian Lousada, who coordinated the work at the Tavistock Clinic, for his considerable contributions to the thinking behind the work described in Chapter 5 and for the central part that he played in the community care workshops and in the forum for managers that were hosted by the Tavistock and are described in Chapter 16.
- The Riverside Mental Health Trust for its sponsorship of the later workshops and the provider forum.
- The Ealing, Hammersmith and Hounslow Health Authority for commissioning the user consultation described in Chapter 15.
- The *Journal of Social Work Practice* which first published the material that forms the basis of Chapters 4, 5, 6, 9, 14 and 16.
- The South Bank Press which published an earlier version of Chapter 17 in the book *What Makes Consultancy Work: Understanding the Dynamics* (1994).
- Nick Benefield for the diagram accompanying the section 'Note on the internal market and the purchaser/provider split in current funding arrangements for UK mental health services' in the Introduction.
- Ann Scott for help with Chapter 12.
- Sue Turner for help with Chapter 2.
- The scientific meetings, sponsored by OPUS Consultancy Services, and the Consulting to Institutions Workshop at the Tavistock Clinic – of which we are both members – for providing opportunities to reflect with colleagues on our work.
- To the many organizations that have commissioned the training, consultancy and research work that underpin the thinking in this book.

List of abbreviations and terms

ASW   Approved social worker. Local authority social service depart-
           ments have a duty to provide ASWs who are specifically trained
           to have statutory responsibility under the Mental Health Act.
           Their duties include ensuring that a careful social assessment is
           provided in the making of applications for guardianship or for
           compulsory admission to hospital.

Care   A social worker whose primary function is the assessment
manager   of a client's needs for social care and to design, purchase
           and provide an appropriate 'package of care' which will be inte-
           grated into the CPA (see *Building Bridges*, DoH, Nov. 1995).

CCETSW   Central Council for Education and Training in Social Work.

CMHC   Community mental health centre.

CMHT   Community mental health team: a multiprofessional team of
           mental health workers, generally including several care
           managers, many of whom will also be approved social workers
           (employed by the local Social Service Departments) and several
           community psychiatric nurses with one or more consultant
           psychiatrists, junior doctors, psychologists, occupational thera-
           pists, and possibly others employed by the local NHS Trust. A
           CMHT provides assessment, treatment and social care for severely
           mentally ill people who live within a specified geographical
           catchment area.

CPA   Care Programme Approach. Introduced in 1991 as one of the
           cornerstones of the UK government's mental health policy. It
           provides a framework for the care of people with severe mental
           illness outside hospital by introducing systematic arrangements
           for assessment and after-care to ensure that people being

treated in the community receive the health and social care that they need. By June 1996 all health authorities had reported that CPA was in place (*Developing Partnerships in Mental Health*, DoH, 1997). (For a fuller description see *Building Bridges*, DoH, Nov. 1995.)

CPN   Community psychiatric nurse.

DoH   Department of Health.

GP   General practitioner: a 'family' doctor. Most GP practices now include other professionals who collectively make up the primary care team. This team – which provides most physical and mental health care for patients – is usually the first point of contact with the health service. The GP may, however, refer patients on to a specialist service, e.g. for people with serious mental illness, to the local community mental health team. GPs who choose to become fundholders purchase a proportion of health services on behalf of their patients. For mental health this includes out-patient, day services and community mental health services (see *Developing Partnerships in Mental Health*, DoH, 1997).

NHS   National Health Service: established in 1946 and generally considered to be under threat now although most health (and mental health) care in the United Kingdom is still provided by the state, paid for by taxation and free at the point of service delivery. Private care is also available.

Section/   These terms come from successive Mental Health Acts and
sectioning   refer to the use of sections of the acts which give the criteria for the action(s) taken. Different sections of the acts provide the criteria for different forms of compulsory admission to hospital for psychiatric observation and/or treatment (often referred to as sectioning someone) and also provide the criteria for some discharge arrangements and other actions that are sanctioned by law. In order that a person can be compulsorily admitted to psychiatric care, an application must be made by an approved social worker or the nearest relative with a recommendation by one or more medical practitioners (see Gostin, *A Practical Guide to Mental Health Law: Mental Health Act 1983 and Related Legislation*, 1983).

SSI   Social Services Inspectorate.

Supervision registers   Introduced in 1994, they identify and provide information on service users with severe mental illness who are liable to be at risk to themselves (through suicide or serious self-neglect) or to others (through violence). The aim is to ensure that these people receive appropriate and effective care in the community (*Developing Partnerships in Mental Health*, DoH, 1997). (For a fuller description see *Building Bridges*, DoH, Nov. 1995.)

Trust   Refers to an NHS trust: an independent, self-governing health service provider which runs the hospitals, in-patient and out-patient services, as well as other provisions in the locality, employing (in the case of services for the mentally ill) psychiatrists, mental health nurses, community psychiatric nurses, psychologists, occupational therapists, etc. Mental health services may be provided by a mental health trust, or by a mixed trust providing general as well as psychiatric services. (For information on funding arrangements see the section on pages 8–11.)

For further information on the law relating to community care see M. Mandelstam and B. Schwehr (1995) *Community Care Practice and the Law*, London: Jessica Kingsley.

Introduction to the theoretical basis of this book

Angela Foster and Vega Zagier Roberts

Some of the theoretical concepts that underpin the thinking in this book are so central that, although they are explained by each contributor when they are used, we have decided to give an overview here. We will identify and acknowledge those writers whose work on the dynamics of systems of care has influenced our thinking, and briefly comment on the range of theoretical approaches to mental illness. Finally we will indicate how this book takes the work of these writers forward into the arena of community care.

Chaos and confusion exist in the minds of all of us, and even more so in the minds of those who suffer from mental illness. A chaotic mind muddles things up – thoughts, ideas, plans. In extreme cases, one's sense of identity gets lost. These internal difficulties (those that take place inside us) have a direct impact on our external relationships and on our lives. Misunderstandings arise, leading to feelings of anger and persecution and so to paranoia. Relationships become impoverished. In this manner, what started as inner chaos is likely to spread, 'contaminating' the people and systems around us – our families and friends, and our workplaces. There are, as we know to our cost, chaos and confusion in all our families and in all the teams and organizations in which we work. If we are honest, we acknowledge that our own 'mess', and that of our organizations, also adds to the chaos and confusion in any system of care.

Splitting, projection and projective identification

The basis of these concepts comes from the work of Melanie Klein. She suggests that in the earliest months of life, the infant splits his or her perception of 'mother' (using this term to designate primary caretakers) into good and bad. Positive experiences – feeling fed, warm and calm – are perceived as coming from a good mother whom he or she loves, while negative experiences – feeling hungry, cold or anxious – are perceived as coming from a bad mother whom he or she then hates and wants to destroy. Klein referred to this as the *paranoid–schizoid position*: paranoid because bad experience is attributed to others seen not only as depriving but as persecuting because the infant fears reprisal for these projections; and schizoid because the central intrapsychic process involves splitting. She chose the term 'position' rather than 'stage' because we are all prone to returning to this way of interpreting our experience throughout life, when anxiety becomes unmanageable.

With maturation, infants become aware that their mother is a single person who sometimes meets their needs and sometimes fails them, and for whom they feel both love and hate. This capacity for ambivalence – for recognizing that one has both loving and aggressive feelings towards the same person – is an essential developmental step. Klein called this more integrated relating to the world the *depressive position*, because it brings with it feelings of concern and remorse for the damage and pain that we have caused to those we love by our aggressive demands and attacks. From these feelings of guilt comes the drive to reparation – to atone, protect and repay the good care that one has received – which forms the basis of all creative, productive and caring activities we engage in from infancy onwards. However, if guilt is too strong, the anxiety about one's capacity to effect reparation can become overwhelming. In this case, reparative activity will be inhibited and the infant – or the adult in whom these early conflicts are revived – retreats to the earlier, more primitive mental activity of splitting their perception of others as all-good and all-bad, who can then be unambivalently and separately loved and hated (Klein, 1959).

People engage in caring work as part of the drive to reparation. However, this work inevitably involves some degree of failure: there are always clients whom we cannot help enough. In the depressive position, we retain some sense of balance between the pain of recognizing our shortcomings and our hope that our efforts are nonetheless worthwhile. If we become overwhelmed by a sense of inadequacy, we may start to feel persecuted by anxiety. We may then defend ourselves by going back to the paranoid–schizoid position, splitting off what we perceive as bad and locating it in others through a process of *projection* whereby these 'unwanted bits' of ourselves are experienced as coming from outside. Thus, workers may idealize themselves while blaming managers, or an agency may idealize its own work while denigrating the work of other agencies with their clients.

These processes in care systems are further complicated by the often massive projections from the client group into the staff who may – by a process called *projective identification* – unconsciously identify with the projections. Klein (1946) first used this term to describe an intrapsychic process whereby the infant fantasizes that he has split off aspects of himself and located them in another person. Bion (1967) extended the concept to refer to an interpersonal process whereby the other person comes to identify with the projections, which then profoundly affect their emotional state and behaviour. Thus, for example, adolescents may split off and project either authoritarian or rebellious aspects of themselves, and the staff of an adolescent unit may then begin to behave either like adolescents themselves, or alternatively become uncharacteristically harsh and punitive. When different staff members identify with different projections, this can produce serious discord within a team who then fight out what is actually an internal conflict within each adolescent client. Similarly, staff working with people with mental illness may experience a fragmenting of their own thought processes, or an emotional 'deadness' similar to that of some of their clients.

However, as Bion points out, projective identification is also an important form of unconscious communication. Pre-verbal infants, for example, can communicate their needs by projecting their experience into mother. If she can tolerate and use these projections to understand the infant's needs, she will respond appropriately and thereby *contain* his or her anxieties. If, however, she is not psychologically available to her child, or is made too anxious by the projections, she is likely to respond inappropriately, for example, stuffing a bottle into the baby's mouth when what is required is to hold and soothe the baby. In the first case, the mother transforms the infant's anxiety into something manageable; in the second case, the anxiety is returned to the infant unchanged, or even amplified into what Bion calls 'nameless dread'.

Similarly, if staff involved in caring work can make sense of the projective identification and 'hear' the unconscious communications of their clients, they are more likely to provide the containment needed. If they are filled up with their own preoccupations and fears, or feel overwhelmed by the projections, they will not experience these as communication but rather as a psychic assault to be warded off, for example by distancing themselves emotionally, or by acting them out as described above. When systems of care provide adequate containment for staff, then they in turn can contain their clients' anxieties and projections. Otherwise, they will resort to various defences, as described in the section 'Defensive care systems' on pages 4-5.

Containment and mental health work

People who have the misfortune to suffer from severe and enduring mental illness – and others in crisis – are acutely aware of their chaos (inner fragmentation) and of the feelings of anxiety that accompany it. They also have great difficulty in containing (integrating) this within themselves and are therefore even more likely than other people to use the unconscious processes of splitting and projection and projective identification in an attempt to rid themselves of what feels unmanageable. Unfortunately this only increases their feelings of disturbance as they come to feel, as a result of projecting so much of themselves, that something important is missing inside them. They then are likely to become less rather than more able to manage themselves.

These are the people most likely to be provided with care plans which identify those systems that will make up their individual 'package of care' in the community. These care plans are intended to contain their disturbance. But care plans are made by people. When the people and the agencies involved are themselves disturbed by the projective processes described above, then the plans and the 'packages of care' are unlikely to provide the intended integration and containment.

Hinshelwood (1989: 244–9) uses the verb 'containing' – rather than the noun 'containment' – thus emphasizing that this is a dynamic process in which there is a person or system that is containing those bits of another person or system, and that within this system the roles of the container and the contained are interchangeable. He quotes Bion:

> The clue lies in the observation of the fluctuations which make the analyst at one moment 'the container' and the analysand 'the contained', and at the next reverse the roles . . . . The more familiar the analyst becomes with the configuration 'container' and 'contained', and with events in the session that approximate to these two representations, the better.
>
> (Bion, 1970: 108)

Hinshelwood continues: 'Without a recognition of the reciprocity, the damaging aspects of the container–contained relationship are likely to crop up unheeded' (Hinshelwood, 1989: 249).

We have to recognize this reciprocity in order to preserve healthy systems of care. Our aim in creating systems of care is to provide a form of containment in which chaotic bits of an individual are, first, understood and managed by workers in the system. Subsequently – if possible – they are internalized by the individual, having been transformed into something that feels understandable and manageable. In this case, we can say that the individual has become able to act as the container to those parts of him- or herself that were previously contained by the system. However, as systems get bigger and ever more complex, there is much more scope for increasing chaos rather than increasing containment. We can all identify times when the 'caring' system appears to be more disturbing and more disturbed than the client; times when all people involved seem to be acting out the disturbance rather than thinking about and understanding it. Hence the emphasis that is placed on effective collaboration among providers of care in order that the system that is created is maintained as a containing one, rather than allowed to deteriorate into a chaotic and destructive one.

Defensive care systems

This book draws heavily on the psychoanalytically informed work of Isabel Menzies Lyth, Eric Miller and Geraldine Gwynne, and Tom Main who have all demonstrated ways in which – through processes of splitting and projection – systems of care can become unhealthy for both workers and clients. Their writings are referred to in subsequent chapters and in each case the theory is explained in everyday language. What follows is only intended as a brief introduction to their thinking.

Menzies Lyth identifies social systems within caring organizations that operate as defences against the anxiety generated by the pain of the task. Her first major work in this field was her study of nurses in a large teaching hospital (Menzies, 1959). She proposed that the life and death anxieties inherent in nursing work had brought about a complex system of locating responsibility and irresponsibility within the hierarchy. The strong emotions to which the work gave rise – love, fear, disgust, and so on – were defended against by splitting up the nursing job into routine tasks, so that nurses no longer related to their patients as whole persons. This did decrease anxiety, but also reduced the meaningfulness of the work, contributing to the high drop-out rate among student nurses which originally led to the study being undertaken. Later, she studied and wrote about many other kinds of caring institutions where similar processes had led to the development of defensive 'social systems' which ultimately worked against the interests of both clients and staff (Menzies Lyth 1988a, 1988b).

In other words, what is intended to make the work less painful results in its being less effective and less satisfying. Miller and Gwynne (1972) used these ideas in their study of institutions for chronically ill people where they identified two dominant organizational models of care: the 'warehousing' model which seeks to meet the dependency needs of clients, but ignores their needs and abilities to be independent in some areas of their lives; and the 'horticultural' model which focuses on enabling people to develop while overlooking their real and enduring dependency needs. To be effective, a model of care needs to be flexible enough to respond to clients as individuals with differing and changing degrees of need to be dependent and to be independent. This is a difficult task which requires constant thought and attention (see Chapter 3). Main (1989) notes how patients and staff in hospitals readily collude with each other to attribute and maintain all the sickness (dependence) in the patients and all the health (independence) in the staff, to the detriment of both groups.

In addressing and revisiting the work of these theorists, this book provides an introduction to some basic psychoanalytic theory as used with individuals, and on how it can be applied to understanding organizations and systems.

Theoretical approaches to mental illness

There are many different ways to think about mental illness and its treatments. These vary from a strictly medical view which locates illness firmly within the individual and takes a functionalist approach to treatment, to a moral view which sees treatment as re-training, and a sociopolitical view which implies a radical social approach to treatment. History of the treatment of those people deemed to be mentally ill (or deviant) provides us with evidence of these different views and of the different approaches to treatment and care that they have produced (see Ingleby, 1985). Most people currently involved in the provision of treatment and care for the mentally ill in society have some knowledge of all of these views, but professional training plays an important part in determining the opinions, values and biases of each of us. The inability of the medical profession to provide cures for mental illness, and the decarceration of the mentally ill, means that there are now even more people with differing views working in the field. While this provides a greater variety of skills and approaches, it can also lead to conflict and misunderstanding.

Some of this conflict and misunderstanding is about the nature and purpose of community care itself. Is it a way of saving money? Hospital care is expensive. Is it a response to the shortcomings of long-term hospital care and the effects of institutionalization? Is it a way of providing more humane treatment? Is it a recognition that care rather than treatment is what is required? Or is it a belief that through becoming reintegrated into their communities, those who suffer from mental illness will become more integrated within themselves and so become less disturbed? There are good arguments for all of these points. However, if the attitude of the community is at best one of liberal indifference, will those who are disturbed fare any better than they did in the large mental hospitals? Some people, including some ex-patients of these hospitals, would argue that life in the community is worse. We might take the view that the community (society) had a vested interest in 'warehousing' those people who were identified as being mad, bad or useless, if only in order that those of us who remained at large could safely project all our mad, bad and useless bits into them, disowning them in ourselves. To redress this requires courage and commitment.

New theoretical developments

This book applies psychoanalytic theories about individuals and systems to the arena of community care and, in doing so, proposes a triangular model for conceptualizing care in the community. This model was originally developed at the Tavistock Clinic by Angela Foster, Lorenzo Grespi and Julian Lousada (see Chapter 16). Within this model, the three corners of the triangle represent the client, the carer (professional or otherwise) and the community. It is argued (see Chapter 5) that all three aspects of this model need to be kept in mind. If we fail to do this, we are in danger of splitting off one of the aspects which then not only limits our perspective but also limits us to a linear model of thinking in which the reflective space required for processing the chaos of mental disturbance is lacking. The triangular model is extended elsewhere in the book to facilitate thinking about other triangles that emerge in systems of community care, for example the triangle of carer, client and professional worker (Chapter 9). The same model can also be used to think about the dynamics between issues arising from the client, issues arising from within a team, and issues arising from higher management and government policy; in this respect it is used by most of the contributors. Hughes and Pengelly (1997), in their book on supervision, also use a triangular model to identify the tensions for senior managers who are functioning within a triangular space bounded by political demands, professional demands and financial demands, and under pressure from the often conflicting needs, wants and rights of the electorate on the one hand and service users on the other hand (see also Chapter 8).

The triangular model is one that, by encompassing the tensions (rather than splitting them off), encourages depressive-position thinking in individuals, in teams, or among different agencies (see Chapters 6, 7 and 10).

Applying theory to practice

It hardly needs to be said that our services and the people working in them are under ever greater stress, with less control over which clients are taken on and having to work with more disturbed people, without a commensurate increase in resources. In theory, clients are supposed to make use of a service, internalize the gains, and move on. In reality, many are unable to internalize and hold on to good experiences – they cannot 'contain' these experiences – and are therefore emotionally unable to 'move on'. One way of obscuring this harsh reality at a time when resources for long-term care are scarce is to establish a work environment in which, for a variety of reasons, there is a throughput of workers in place of the desired throughput of clients. While it may be necessary or even desirable for workers to move on more rapidly than their clients, the degree of pain and stress that many of them suffer in the process of doing their work is – we believe – often greater than it needs to be.

We are also concerned that the emphasis on managerialism – on 'managing' both workers and clients – is encroaching on the space to think about the nature of the feelings that this work engenders, in a way that is both limiting and dangerous, and we believe that the constant emphasis on change at an organizational level, which itself puts workers under additional stress, can be viewed as a defence against the often unchanging nature of the client group.

Inevitably policy changes will continue to be made; some necessary and some perhaps unnecessary or inadvisable. These will fall into two areas, the first being the manner in which services are funded and the second being the way in which risk is managed. The former will lead to adjustments to the purchaser/provider split and the second to changes in service provision that exemplify the struggle to locate an appropriate distribution of services along the care and/or control continuum. But regardless of the changes, the fundamental nature of mental health work remains, as does the risk of excess pain and disturbance to those engaged in it. Essentially, this book seeks to attend to and understand the experience of the front-line worker, whose voice can so easily be muffled by the 'noise' of policy-makers, politicians, the media and even of service users.

References

Bion, W.R. (1967) *Second Thoughts*, London: Maresfield Library.

—— (1970) *Attention and Interpretation*, London: Tavistock.

Hinshelwood, R.D. (1989) *A Dictionary of Kleinian Thought*, London: Free Association Books.

Hughes, L. and Pengelly, P. (1997) *Staff Supervision in a Turbulent Environment: Managing Process and Task in Front Line Services*, London: Jessica Kingsley.

Ingleby, D. (1985) 'Mental health and social order', in S. Cohen and A. Skull (eds) *Social Control and the State*, London: Blackwell.

Klein, M. (1946) 'Notes on some schizoid mechanisms', *Int. J. Psycho-anal.* 27: 99–110.

—— (1959) 'Our adult world and its roots in infancy', *Human Relations* 12: 291–303.

Main, T. (1989) *The Ailment and Other Psychoanalytic Essays*, London: Free Association Books.

Menzies, I.E.P. (1959) 'The functioning of social systems as a defence against anxiety: a report on a study of the nursing service of a general hospital', *Human Relations* 13: 95–121.

Menzies Lyth, I.E.P. (1988a) *Containing Anxiety in Institutions: Selected Essays Vol. 1*, London: Free Association Books.

—— (1988b) *The Dynamics of the Social: Selected Essays Vol. 2*, London: Free Association Books.

Miller, E. and Gwynne, G. (1972) *A Life Apart*, London: Tavistock.

A note on the internal market and the purchaser/provider split in current funding arrangements for UK mental health services

This note is provided because the funding arrangements and the consequences of these for workers and services are often confusing for UK workers. It is also a way of providing an explanation for readers working outside the United Kingdom.

The main body within the NHS responsible for purchasing mental health services are the district health authorities. Each of these cover a certain geographical area and, therefore, a certain population. The Department of Health allocates funding to each health authority according to a formula which relates to the numbers and needs of that population. A commissioning team within the authority will be responsible for purchasing services for those residents within the locality with mental health needs.

In principle, the authority is free to purchase from any provider, anywhere in the country. In reality, the main provider from whom psychiatric services will be purchased will be health trusts. These are independent trusts which run the hospitals, in-patient and out-patient services, as well as other provision. Psychiatrists, mental health nurses, community psychiatric nurses, psychologists, occupational therapists, etc. will usually be employed by the trust. Whereas the 'internal market' was set up to introduce competition into the culture, people using psychiatric services want local provision and are unlikely to travel far from their existing support systems. Generally, therefore, the health authorities are limited in their choice of trusts from which to purchase, and have to spend the bulk of their resources on services provided by the local trust. The establishment of health authorities and health trusts has meant that the split between purchasers and providers within the health service has been fairly distinct and consistent throughout the country.

In mental health, a number of services besides those of the medical services are required. These can include day centres, work projects, residential homes, etc. These may be provided by private or voluntary sector agencies, by local authority social services, or by the local health trust. If the purchasing authority decides that there is a need for a specific service, then any or all of these providers may be invited to tender to run the service, and are required to compete with each other. The successful organization is likely to be given a contract for a fixed period – rarely more than three years.

The picture within social services is more variable and less clear-cut. Most local authorities have set up purchasing departments within the service which are responsible for purchasing on behalf of people in need living within that locality. However, both these departments and those providing services come within the same authority and are, therefore, accountable to

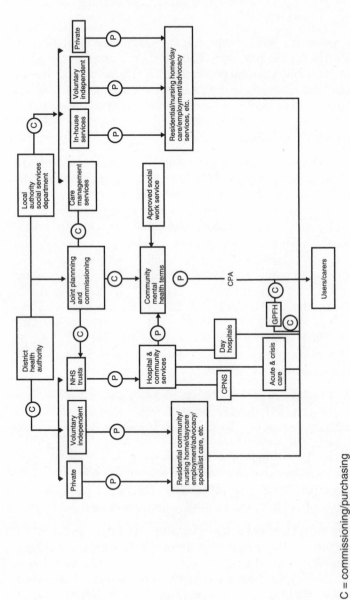

C = commissioning/purchasing
P = providing
NHS = National Health Service
CPN = community psychiatric nurse
CPA = care programme approach
GPFH = general practitioner fundholders

Figure 0.1 Commissioning and providing local mental health services

the same group. Local authorities are providing ever fewer services them-selves and are instead looking to buy them from providers in the voluntary and private sectors. The role of the local authority social worker in mental health has altered considerably. As care managers, their main task is the assessment of needs and, as approved social workers, their main task is to perform statutory duties under the Mental Health Act; these include mental health assessments and, where necessary, compulsory hospital admissions.

There has been considerable emphasis placed on cross-discipline provision in the form of community mental health teams. Many projects have multiple funding: from the purchasers in both health and social services, as well as charitable funding. Some funding may also come from joint commissioning by a combined body of health and social services.

The above is a brief description of the general structure for purchasing and providing mental health services at the time of publication (see Figure 0.1). While the change in government in May 1997 means that there will be a review of the details of funding and provision, it is predicted that the funda-mental ethos of the internal market introduced in the 1980s is unlikely to change substantially.

It is worth adding that the impetus for the purchaser/provider split, and some of its consequences, are similar to those of managed care in the United States. The impetus was a growing gap between demand and resources, and in both cases there was an introduction of a third party to identify and quantify need and agree a level of provision. The consequences of this are greater accountability, greater preoccupation with the 'bottom line', practi-tioners feeling that their priorities are over-ridden, and grief at having to withhold services from people who need them but who are not prioritized.

Helen Morgan

Part I

The move into the community

This part examines issues ranging from the political to the personal related to policies of community care.

Creatures of each other

Some historical considerations of responsibility and care, and some present undercurrents

R.D. Hinshelwood

In 1960, the then Minister of Health, Enoch Powell, declared that all large mental hospitals would close within ten years – by 1970.[1] In the event, this proved grossly over-optimistic, and the target has taken much longer to achieve.[2]

The optimism came from three sources. First was the belief that significant cost saving would come from dismantling the large institutions, many of which were sitting on prime real estate. The second factor was the development of the psychiatric 'wonder' drugs during the 1950s. They gave rise to a soaring hope that mental illness could now be curable like any other medical condition. Third, at that time there had been a long-standing revulsion at the conditions in the large mental hospitals – over-crowding, depersonalization and neglect. A 'dose' of incarceration was, until the 1940s, more or less the only treatment for mental illness (Scull, 1977). Following the Second World War, new ideas came from social science and from psychotherapy.[3] These questioned the usefulness of large institutions and pointed at their pathogenic properties (Main, 1946; Jones, 1952).

Added to this, in the 1950s there was the new self-confident NHS which believed itself the best in the world. That sudden optimism for care of the mentally ill in their families and communities has survived until very recently. Now, it is realized that things can go seriously wrong. Doubts and uncertainties about providing care in the community have risen sharply, as has the rhetoric demanding its improvement and success.

We have now reached little short of a crisis in British psychiatry. Increasing political commitment to community care has thrown increasing blame on the professionals for not providing it better (Eastman, 1997). Cost savings have begun to appear illusory even to politicians. The psychiatric services have been starved of the resources for 'retooling'. Better quality services might simply mean more financial resources, an argument familiar to politicians. It is partly true – but only in part. It is an argument – even an exhortation – that can conceal other problems and potentialities in community care.

There are three further areas of specific neglect. First, there is the lack of specific training for community care. There are many courses but they tend to be skills based, and in the mould of traditional medical and nursing practices. I shall argue that a different dimension – one of relationship – is essential.

Second, staff working in the community need very different specific support, one that blends professional with personal. Not only have long-standing patients in large numbers been set free to be cared for in hostels, community centres and day care and often to roam the streets, but institutionally trained staff, too, have been pushed out of the traditional tightly knit, or even rigid, teams in the old hospital wards. They are required to roam the streets too in search of their liberated patients. Too often both patients and staff become lost. Staff now have to confront seriously disturbed clients – and also their anxious, often pathogenic, families on the doorsteps in the alien environment of a domiciliary visit or the hostile neighbourhood. Staff are no longer on their home territory. They lack the immediate colleagueship of the old mental hospital teams, the regular procedures and comfort of their hallowed traditions. Very special forms of training and support are required for the lone worker in these anxiety-provoking encounters.

More often than not, the pain of the new role has been overlooked. The response to ordinary human experience has been rapidly professionalized (Craib, 1994). Something like a human needs industry has inserted itself in the place of ordinary human relationships. In the 'old days', when community care was only a gleam in the eye, it was hoped that mentally ill people could be inserted back into networks of ordinary (or genuine) human relationships which constitute the community. Instead, without training in the latter, ex-patients are inserted back into a network of professional care – with, moreover, a highly anxious network of professionals.

This leads into the third area of neglect from which community care has suffered. No attention was paid to what exactly went wrong with the large mental institutions that created the revulsion. We need urgently to consider the shortcomings of the large mental hospital – not just turn our backs in revulsion. If ultimately they failed their inmates, they did so for a reason. We have the opportunity, if we want, to learn from those failings when designing and running new agencies, services and institutions in the community. But we must also keep in mind that the specific pressures of treating very disturbed people will be the same now as before. We might then be better prepared when similar pernicious effects creep into our new community care organizations.

Institutions and institutionalization: containing madness

Too often we are driven by simplistic views about those large institutions, which then drive us forward blindly. For instance, it is sometimes implied that if large psychiatric hospitals have failed, then the answer would be to create small ones, or to be non-psychiatric (avoid labelling, etc.), or to have non-hospital-like treatment centres, and so on. Such simplistic reversals do not address many other important factors detrimental to our work. Important (and interesting) underlying factors need to be taken into account. We do know something about them. We now need to explore those factors that distort our institutions (whether a hospital or community care). And I shall attend to the roots in our relationships to the work and our patients/clients – rather than to the professionalized practice of our skills.

The patient arrives in the service, but more than this, his or her disturbance too enters the organization (Spillius, 1976, 1990; Conran, 1985). A psychiatric service exists to take disturbed people away from the community that can no longer cope with the degree of madness. This is no mean task. All mental health workers are immediately aware of its magnitude as soon as they go into the work. It is not surprising that something odd, and woeful, happened in those old psychiatric hospitals – institutionalization (Martin, 1955; Barton, 1959; Goffman, 1961). Though often in a campaigning style, these early writings indicate a quite sophisticated view:

> [T]he patient has ceased to rebel against, or to question the fitness of his position in a mental hospital; he has made a more or less total surrender to the institution's life . . . he is co-operative. Here 'co-operative' usually implies that the patient does as he is told with a minimum of questioning or opposition. This response on the part of the patient is very different from that true co-operation essential to the success of any treatment, in which the patient strives to understand, and work with, the doctor in his efforts to cure . . . [the] patient, resigned and co-operative . . . too passive to present any problem of management, has in the process of necessity lost much of his individuality and initiative.
>
> (Martin, 1955: 1188–90)

In this description, the distortion to the personalities of vulnerable people results from processes inherent in the institution itself. The power relations are clear, but the patients have lost much more than just power. They have lost significant aspects of themselves – individuality, initiative, enquiry and self-determination. They have lost their active selves. Not only their mental disorder, but now the institution takes a hand in them 'losing their minds'. A rather similar description was given by Main, in reviewing his experience which started in Northfield Hospital in the Second World War:

> [O]nly roles of health or illness are on offer; staff to be only healthy, knowledgeable, kind, powerful and active, and patients to be only ill, suffering, ignorant, passive, obedient and grateful. In most hospitals

staff are there because they seek to care for others less able than themselves, while the patients hope to find others *more* able than themselves. The helpful and the helpless meet and put pressures on each other to act not only in realistic, but also fantastic collusion ... [The] helpful will unconsciously *require* others to be helpless while the helpless will *require* others to be helpful. Staff and patients are thus inevitably to some extent creatures of each other.

(Main, 1975: 61)

Both staff and patients are implicated in a collusion, an inter-group exchange of personality characteristics: what patients lose of their healthy side accumulates in the staff; and what the staff get rid of in terms of their more negative attributes resurfaces within the patients. Personality characteristics are redistributed in the social field – and between two groups: the group of patients vulnerable to losing their personalities, and the group of staff who want to build themselves up in successful medical and curative careers. Care is, certainly, benignly intended but it can swerve off into malignant effects. These 'unintended' intentions are unconscious aspects of the people in the institution (or, loosely, the 'unconscious' *of* the institution). Therefore to understand these institutions, and their capacity to be malign – and therefore perhaps their potential to be curative – we need to direct our attention to these powerful, strange and unconscious relations between patients and their carers.

Because of their *unconscious* quality, these effects cannot be simply eradicated. We need to study these human processes and grasp that whatever goes wrong in psychiatric institutions involves the transfer of aspects of personality from one group into another, and vice versa. The work I have quoted targets in on the characteristic of helpfulness, and its matching partner, helplessness. These polarize between the groups.

Loosely, the distortion of attitudes, and ultimately of work practices, that comes from personal needs of the workers is called a 'social defence system' (Menzies, 1959; Miller and Gwynne, 1972). The *perception* of a helpful/helpless dimension and divide is part of a cultural set of attitudes that is sought, for defensive reasons, by all the members of the institution: for the staff in terms of their careers, and their sense of confidence in being care workers; for patients, the opportunity to regress in order to combat the frustration and conflicts of the real world. These are deep meanings transacted, usually unconsciously, between the two groups.

The psychotic experience

I claim therefore an important connection: the awful task of containing the intolerable psychotic experience directly influences the organization and enhances the problems of psychiatric institutions. Shared distress in the work arises from the nature of psychosis itself – or, perhaps we should say, from the nature of psychotic personalities themselves. Typically that distress is not formed or articulated in words; meaning itself gives way to an experience of meaninglessness. And this is contagious. It has a *direct* effect on others and, in fact, percolates through the whole system.[4] Psychotic patients are very effective at this non-verbal impact. Being a communication of meaninglessness, its communicative function is lost. It becomes merely an emotional impact, an unidentifiable experience. That impact is very unpleasant and by its nature very hard for staff to talk about in words.

Were we to treat a psychotic patient by psychoanalysis, we would be interested in these 'impacts' upon the *psychoanalyst* in the sessions. But when we deal with psychotic patients we are not working in this way. We do not specifically examine our feelings so closely. Nevertheless, all mental health workers – psychiatrists, nurses, psychologists and so on – do suffer from the strong emotional impact from their patients, and respond emotionally. Very often we simply react to our feelings by trying to stop them. I will describe what I mean.

A young woman came to my out-patient clinic when I was a young psychiatrist. She had previously been in hospital for a number of months and, typically, she had little affect or initiative. Each time I saw her I found myself trying to instil some hope and enthusiasm into her – to think of a job, to make friends, to attend a psychiatric club. Each time she agreed with me. And I felt better. And each time she came back to the next appointment she had done nothing; I would feel despondent and set about renewing my efforts to enthuse her.

That describes a repeated pattern with this patient. She made me feel despondent or despairing; and subsequently I managed to talk to the patient so that I could give back hope to myself. My efforts were useless in putting hope into her, but I was effective in removing the unpleasant despair in myself. At that time, in the early 1970s, we were familiar with the ironic instruction: you should give patients drugs if it makes *you* feel better. So the climate of opinion at the time helped me, with patients like the one just mentioned, to realize that I was operating as much for *my* benefit as for the patient's.

We must accept certain things about working with psychotic people: that they do affect their helpers; that the effects are unpleasant; and that our work may in turn be strongly affected by *our* internal state and our need to make it easier for ourselves, for example by giving drugs, or keeping an emotional distance (see Chapter 13). There are several general features to this impact and our anxious response to the way that psychotic patients rid themselves of the experience by making the staff feel it instead.

1   With my schizophrenic patient, one of the important features was the sense of despair and helplessness. She got through to me a feeling of

being hopeless about helping her.

2   This was not transmitted to me in words. A direct transmission of affect occurs by some other, non-verbal route.

3   There is often a connected feeling of fear. It is the fear of something going quickly out of control. This may be experienced as either madness or violence, a mind going out of control. This is frightening to us as mental health workers. It makes us afraid of our patients and we give it a meaning – that they may become violent and injure us.

4   There is another, less clear, fear. That is to do with a feeling that we will get madness inside us as well. We fear that *we* will become a mind out of control, and therefore mad.

5   There is a particular way in which we experience our patients. It is the sense of meaninglessness in the patient's experience and anxiety. It is connected to feeling overwhelmed by some*thing* out of control. It is a feeling that we are dealing with something that is without meaning, senseless.

6   And finally, the meaninglessness causes another reaction. We tend to pull away from our patients. We reach for a kind of emotional distance from them, as if they are not properly human; or not properly alive. And, sadly, patients very frequently become aware of such pulling away – and may, in the form of redoubled symptoms, express their concerns or protests about the staff's retreat from them.

Our work creates particular stresses and workers can often suffer burn-out. We feel that our personal resources are finished and we cannot go on. The implication is that a special attention needs to be given to the mental health staff, and to their specific need for support, since, in an important sense, the staff's experiences are a *cri de coeur* on the part of their patient.

Expectations and realities

In considering the 'mental health' of workers, the crucial factor of what makes people elect to go into the caring professions is important. Invariably we have high hopes of restoring people from dreadful states back into whole and happy persons. This task may have only limited chances of success, and perhaps this is especially so in working with psychotic people. Very small changes for staff may be a great achievement for a patient. But such small gains may seem insignificant to a member of staff seeking to create a completely healthy, new personality in the patient. Thus a major and painful gap opens between the achievement that members of staff demand of themselves and one that is realistically achievable. It leads to acute personal difficulties which often go quite unrecognized, and create an acutely lonely staff member in danger of burn-out, as the person strives for greater and greater evidence of success, against the realistic possibilities, and out of touch with their colleagues. It can equally be a burden for patients subjected to the insistence of a member of staff to 'change' or 'get better' for the sake of that staff member.

How do these phenomena, which make for stressed staff, affect the service itself?

Effects on the service

What has emerged in providing community care is that the distortions found in the old large institutions recur within the organizations of agencies in the community. Very little is specific to the large institutions. Some of these processes include the following:

- *Demoralization*: If many staff are subject to feeling despair, then the first danger to the team is that it will become collectively demoralized. People cannot give each other the support, encouragement and praise that is needed when they themselves feel that they are not doing a good job. Some simple indices of demoralization include: high rates of sick leave, absenteeism and turnover of team members. When such things happen, the team feels unstable and unsupportive, and the morale tends to get worse. A disastrous spiral, or vicious circle, takes place.

- *Stereotyped patients*: However, there are ways in which the team members can collectively help themselves. One is to deny the feelings of helplessness and despair. In this sense the collective attitudes support the individual psychological defences of the individuals in repudiating the experience. Then it is very common for them to agree that those feelings are located in their patients – only. A rigid perception of themselves and their patients grows up, as Main (1975) described in the extract above – 'only ill, suffering, ignorant, passive, obedient and grateful'.

- *Scapegoating*: The stereotyping process leads to a different outcome when one particular patient is elected into a position to carry all the hopelessness. He or she is the 'scapegoat', and usually gets worse clinically – thus confirming the way that the staff have decided to see him or her. Often this patient is then sent off to some other part of the service – the locked ward, the refractory behaviours unit, or wherever – upon which the team find another suitable patient to be 'elected' to the role. And that sequence may go through a number of cycles.

- *Routine*: The meaninglessness of the patient's experiences and anxiety is very corrosive of the staff's ability to continue with empathy and under-standing. The *distance* to which the staff retreat can then be institutionalized by a systematic process of turning the work into a set of routines – one could say mindless routines.

- *Blame*: Alternatively the staff team can change their direction of interest. Instead of feeling hopeless about their patients, a new attitude grows up. This is a view that the patients could be helped but there are not enough resources in the team. The problem is believed to be the authorities or managers who keep them so short of staff, training, money and so on. There may be some truth in the shortage of resources, but staff feel and behave as if they were under siege against their employers who do not understand them, or who are stupid, or who may be deliberately malign. The team can feel happy together, and maybe even happy with their patients, so long as they have an external enemy that they can fight.

- *Schisms in the service*: Alternatively, the team may become divided within itself. If each person has the feeling, absorbed from the patients, of being hopeless, then they can export that feeling by electing others *in* the team as the hopeless ones. This can lead to a lot of mutual denigration of each other, often not expressed. In this case nobody can really get a proper picture of who is doing good work and who is not. Realistic perceptions and mutual support are both lost. One common example of a mutual loss of respect is the one between psychiatrists promoting physical treatments, and psychotherapists and others emphasizing the human and relational aspects of their patients' distress.

- *Fragmented agencies*: The last process is similar, and one to which community care agencies are specifically prone. One agency can project the despair and hopelessness into another team within the community services. Different teams then get into the same mutual denigration of each other – the domiciliary team, the day hospital, the in-patient ward, etc. Then the service itself becomes fragmented.

These various processes operating within the organization or system itself reduce the quality of the work. Changes of staff, high levels of absence and temporary staff, scapegoating of patients or colleagues, and splits within and between teams all have a very negative effect. In turn, as people realize that they do not give the best chances to their patients, morale must fall, and it plays on the crucial gap between the high hopes that staff have of themselves and their apparently 'low' achievement. In addition, the processes in the organization bring out rather primitive processes in the individuals – splitting, denial and projection. Though unconscious, these processes reduce the individual to less mature levels of functioning, a sort of forced *im*maturity, and a hard-to-grasp experience of being de-skilled. Individuals are then more prey to the exaggerated expectations of themselves that come from immature unconscious levels. Thus in several ways the disastrous and 'meaningless' distress suffered by clients infiltrates the staff and ends up 'in' the organization, which becomes in reality a disturbed service.

Surviving in the market

Recently, the emotional pressures on the service have been redoubled due to reorganization of the NHS into the replica of a market (Hinshelwood, 1996). Although there are many features of the market that are hard to translate faithfully from the industrial business world into the NHS, there is one important feature that has passed across very well. This is the particular form of anxiety that is inherent in the business culture. Whereas in the NHS the fears are of death and madness, the related anxiety of the business world is survival of the enterprise. Specifically, insecurity and uncertainty about jobs and careers have been built into the system. It has introduced the anxiety that the contracts for work will not continue and that the enterprise, and all the personal involvements in it, will fail. My understanding is that the purpose of improving NHS efficiency is to employ a kind of threat – if you do not improve the efficiency of your work, then your unit will close and you will lose your job.[5] Therefore people will work harder. Such a view implies that people do not work as hard as they might, and that any reason for not working harder will be counteracted by the fear of losing one's job. It has not, I believe, been seriously questioned whether inefficiency in the mental health system exists, and if so how it might be eradicated. Specifically in the mental health field, we could argue seriously that people suffer, not from any cracks in their individual work ethic, but often from too *great* an expectation of themselves – and burn themselves out in trying. Thus there is a real possibility that this extra anxiety is not really a stimulus to better effort but a critical anxiety overload. It is important – and urgent – to address this. The future of efficient services and well-served clients depends upon it.

What to do?

Despite my rather negative assessment, most mental health services are extremely dedicated and well intentioned, and they do a great deal of good for their patients. The troublesome processes that I have described derive from the patients' distress and how it reverberates in damaging ways throughout the service, and many staff teams are able to 'metabolize' these effects well enough. Some do not, and all are affected by them. Things can go quickly wrong, and teams need a protection against these corrosive psychotic anxieties, but a protection that is not too rigid, defensive or damaging in the ways I have described. It is important to sustain an awareness of these processes consciously and systematically.

Reflective practice

Most of these practices entail the curious tightrope of *having* these feelings, and at the same time transcending them. Just to express feelings, overtly or covertly, and share them with each other is not enough: a focus is needed – a kind of *reflective space* (Hinshelwood, 1994) – specifically putting feelings in relation to reality. It is difficult and needs programming. The elements can be listed:

> (a) Professional supervision on a regular basis is necessary to keep in mind the normally expected standards and practices, and to address (b) the specific gap between personal expectations and realistic achievements, which in turn will allow (c) proper recognition of the successes and failures of the individuals and the team. Then (d) such unflinching assessments can be greatly helped by looking at the task and the outcomes from different professional points of view – nurses, doctors, psychologists, social workers, etc. – who provide a greatly widened perspective for each individual. In similar ways to a multidisciplinary team, (e) different agencies can usefully give new perceptions of each other's achievements. (f) The depersonalisation and distancing effects can be addressed by a continual questioning of the various practices and procedures which otherwise can become rituals.
>
> (Main, 1967)

The upshot of this reflective task is to give a new angle on the raw material. I have suggested that the raw material with which we work is the human experience of despair (among other things). The thrust of reflection is to change the focus from merely suffering (and reacting to) pessimism and despair about the job, towards doing a job *on* pessimism and despair.

Conclusions

I have said very little about the role of medication as it is not within the scope of this book. However, neither is this essay to be taken as an oppositional position. In fact, much of what I have said is to warn ourselves against getting into disputes from which we can easily emerge in a fragmented state with mutual lack of respect for each other; for example, between orthodox biological psychiatry and psychodynamic campaigning. The familiar fall into that temptation may be driven by a need to deal with despair through projecting helplessness and inadequacy onto others.

If we are truly to think about our institutions and how they might be constructed for more therapeutic effect, we need to take into account the circulatory system of emotions, especially of despair, as described in this chapter. Simple principles concerning the size of institutions, their location, the rhetoric of politicians over costs and markets, or the assigning of good or evil intention, are indeed relevant. But they only skate on the surface. They can be used as simplifying diversions, designed to find meaning where it is not.

What we do *not* need is a simple 'how to' manual, because the job of containing psychosis is performed by the whole of the personality of the worker – one's capacity to feel, empathize, worry, get a little mad oneself, reflect, and in the end do one's best to place oneself alongside the client (and, incidentally, colleagues). This constitutes *reflective practice*, and it goes beyond a simple skills-based practice. Quality work in mental health involves a human 'being with', rather than an operational 'doing to', our clients.[6] The key to good work is the quality of support for the staff and the protection of their capacity to go on thinking and reflecting. We need to understand the political economy of our emotions: despair and suffering, responsibility and guilt. To provide anything like adequate care in the community, we have to provide cared-for staff in the community. It might not be going too far to claim that attending to the mental health of the workers is as important as attending to the mental health of the patients – if not more so!

Notes

1 I restrict myself in this chapter to work with psychotic patients/clients, as psychiatric services are limited more and more to just this category of work.

2 In fact, certain experiments were under way from soon after the beginning of this century. Henry Maudsley, for instance, campaigned for hospitals within the community; Boyle (1905) started a day attendance service in Sussex. However, the political and professional will was not there until fifty years later.

3 During the 1940s in Britain, new methods of treatment were tried in military hospitals, notably Northfield in Birmingham (Bridger, 1985), and these derived in part from social psychology ideas developed in experimental settings (Asch, 1952; Sherif and Sherif, 1956; Lewin, 1950) which blended with the developing practice of psychotherapy. From this social dimension came social psychiatry, group therapy, the therapeutic community and community psychiatry.

4 We normally expect others to communicate with us through words, but in this case the primary communication is not explicit in words. Of course, ordinary relationships, too, are based on much more than words. In fact a certain kind of direct stimulus of another person's emotions is especially effective without words. We need only think of the cries of a baby which affect its mother very deeply without any clear semantic meaning or symbolic content to the noise.

5 Dave Bell has commented too on these changes but indicates a malignant intention (a negative narcissism) in them which is organized to oppose care, dependency and health (Bell, 1996).

6 This distinction between 'being with' and 'doing to' has been elegantly brought out by Heinz Wolf (1971), and is close to one of Fromm's central themes (Fromm, 1976).

References

Asch, S. (1952) *Social Psychology*, Englewood Cliffs, NJ: Prentice Hall.

Barton, R. (1959) *Institutional Neurosis*, Bristol: Wright.

Bell, D. (1996) 'Primitive mind of state', *Psychoanalytic Psychotherapy* 10: 45–58.

Boyle, H.A. (1905) 'Some points in the early treatment of nervous and mental cases', *Journal of Mental Science* 51: 676–81.

Bridger, H. (1985) 'Northfield revisited', in Malcolm Pines (ed.) *Bion and Group Psychotherapy*, London: Routledge and Kegan Paul.

Conran, M. (1985) 'The patient in hospital', *Psychoanalytic Psychotherapy* 1:31–43.

Craib, I. (1994) *The Importance of Disappointment*, London: Routledge.

Eastman, N. (1997) 'The Mental Health (Patients in the Community) Act 1995: a clinical analysis', *British Journal of Psychiatry* 170: 492–6.

Fromm, E. (1976) *To Have or To Be?*, New York: Harper and Row.

Goffman, E. (1961) *Asylums*, New York: Doubleday.

Hinshelwood, R.D. (1994) 'Attacks on the reflective space', in Vic Shermer and Malcolm Pines (eds) *Ring of Fire*, London: Routledge.

—— (1996) 'Psychiatry and psychotherapy', *Psycho-Analytic Psychotherapy* 1: 31–43.

Jones, M. (1952) *Social Psychiatry*, London: Tavistock.

Lewin, K. (1950) *Field Theory in Social Science*, New York: Harper Bros.

Main, T.H. (1946) 'The hospital as a therapeutic institution', *Bulletin of the Menninger Clinic* 10: 66–70.

—— (1967) 'Knowledge, learning and freedom from thought', *Australia and New Zealand Journal of Psychiatry* 5: 59–78.

—— (1975) 'Some psychodynamics of large groups', in Lionel Kreeger (ed.) *The Large Group*, London: Constable; reprinted in T.H. Main (1989) *The Ailment and Other Psychoanalytic Essays*, London: Free Association Books.

Martin, D. (1955) 'Institutionalisation', *Lancet* 1955/2: 1188–90.

Menzies, I. (1959) 'A case study in the functioning of social systems as a defence against anxiety: a report on a study of the nursing service of a general hospital', *Human Relations* 13: 95–121; reprinted in Isabel Menzies Lyth (ed.) (1988) *Containing Anxiety in Institutions*, London: Free Association Books.

Miller, E. and Gwynne, G. (1972) *A Life Apart*, London: Tavistock.

Scull, A. (1977) *Decarceration*, New York: Prentice Hall.

Sherif, M. and Sherif, C.W. (1956) *An Outline of Social Psychology*, New York: Harper.

Spillius, E. (1976) 'Hospital and society', *British Journal of Medical Psychology* 49: 97–140.

—— (1990) 'Asylum and society', in Eric Trist and Hugh Murray (eds) *The Social Engagement of Social Science*, London: Free Association Books, 586–612.

Wolf, H. (1971) 'The therapeutic and development functions of psychotherapy', *British Journal of Medical Psychology* 44: 117–30.

2

'Not in my backyard'

The psychosocial reality of
community care

Angela Foster and Vega Zagier Roberts

Introduction

Is the community simply the location for a form of care or can it be an effective container of mental disturbance? In other words, can a community offer
something that is caring – in a therapeutic sense – to those who live there?

Communities were not consulted about whether or not they wanted
community care and there is no shortage of evidence to suggest that many
communities are worried by the idea that others identified as being deviant
or mentally ill should live in their midst. Residents will argue that their
particular location is not suitable and – far from thinking in terms of
offering care in the form of containment – will be openly hostile, wishing to
ensure that the proposed new residents are kept out of the local community.
A national survey found that 'Over two thirds of all respondents (65% of
Local Mind Associations, all three voluntary organisations, 8 out of 9
(NHS) trusts, 6 out of seven housing associations) had encountered opposition to mental health facilities in the past five years' (Repper *et al.*, 1997: 4).
More often than not, what we see in such situations is evidence of communities whose members feel disturbed at the *prospect* of having mentally ill
neighbours – that is, community members who are disturbed by their own
fantasies of what this will be like – rather than by an experience of the
reality. It is, of course, a minority of mentally ill people who are a cause of
disturbance in their local communities.

This chapter brings together different pieces of work that examine the
processes that occur between people who live and work within defined
geographical boundaries, that is, within particular communities. It is in three
sections: the first examines the dynamics of NIMBY (not in my backyard)
and the nature of communities; the second examines the issue of homelessness, paying particular attention to mental illness and homelessness and to
the complicated psychodynamics that operate between the homeless and the
housed; and the third identifies and analyses two different responses to the
agitation of local residents who became concerned about the number of
hostels opening up in their area.

These three sections do not fit comfortably together, particularly the section on homelessness. They contain material that we thought important to include in this book, but which remained 'homeless' for a considerable time. It seemed to exist as bits and pieces that *should* have a place but that were difficult to accommodate in that there was no obvious place where they belonged. It is as if this chapter has come to represent a kind of 'reception centre' for these unintegrated bits, and is in itself an attempt to examine the difficulties of assimilation and integration that communities experience.

The main theoretical underpinning of this chapter is Bion's concept of containment – that is, that thoughts need a container in the form of a mind. He describes a model in which the container and the contained are in a dynamic relationship. 'The container can squeeze everything out of the contained; or the "pressure" may be exerted by the contained so that the container disintegrates' (Bion, 1970: 107; see also the Introduction to this book, pages 3–4). In the framework of this chapter, the community (including the houses and the minds within it) is the container, and mental disturbance is the contained. In focusing on the nature of the dynamic relationship between these two, we examine the ways in which communities squeeze out disturbance and the ways in which disturbance damages communities.

NIMBY and community

The NHS and Community Care Act of 1990 was produced, not in a society that was proud to accept and show compassion towards its weaker members, but in a society where the prime minister (Margaret Thatcher) claimed that there was no such thing as society; a society in which the Welfare State was under attack. Individualism was taking precedence over communalism, and local communities had largely ceased to provide care for their members. Bulmer (1987) writes:

> Community care policy is in a shambles in part because 'community' has become a vacuous term, meaning all things to all people. It is very difficult to give the term consistent and useful meaning, yet it goes on being used because of its powerful and evocative reference.
>
> (Bulmer, 1987: 214)

He makes this statement after having detailed the changes that have taken place in society affecting the nature of local communities: in particular, that it is now only the socially disadvantaged who are dependent upon local contacts for care and support, while all others, with cars, telephones and so on, make use of family and friends who are widely dispersed. Such is the nature of the communities in which the long-term mentally ill are housed.

In addition, people who suffer from mental illness often choose to restrict their involvement with others. Anyone who has been institutionalized, whether remaining seriously ill or not, is likely to be lacking in the social skills and self-confidence that are needed for the difficult task of establishing oneself in a new area.

As Tudor (1996) points out, the United Kingdom has a policy of de-hospitalization without a policy of de-institutionalization; that is, we set about re-housing the inmates of the old institutions without taking the more radical step of adequately preparing either the inmates or the communities for this move.

> The policy of community care, of placing people in the community – and not always their own – without de-institutionalisation, without addressing notions of 'madness', 'mental illness', or mental health let alone the financial, political and organisational issues which need to be addressed, may in itself be considered madness.
>
> (Tudor, 1996: 101–2)

As members of local communities – with all their insularity, their prejudices and their fears – react to the arrival of mentally ill people (who come with odd behaviour of their own), it is not difficult to see how some discharged patients come to experience life in the community – especially in the inner cities – as a sadistic attack, a form of torture filled with extreme loneliness and persecution. Given all these factors, it is hardly surprising that attempts to integrate people with enduring mental illness in local communities often fail.

Failure of integration, resulting in increased physical and emotional isolation from one's community, means that some people become more disturbed, resulting in frequent hospital admissions. Others largely disappear from view and remain isolated in their own homes, surrounded by four walls, watching 'life' through a television set. An extreme example of this was brought to a discussion group by a care worker. She described a woman who needed more help than the worker could provide because of her incontinence. However, in the course of discussion a fuller picture of this client's situation emerged. The client had vitrually no contact with the outside world; she did not see anyone else, nor did she wish to; she had no television and bought no newspapers. Her home was extremely sparse and she appeared to have no life in her. In fact she seemed to have given up any attempt to control her life or her body.

Here we have a sense of a container with nothing inside – not contained.

The homeless and the housed

The homeless present a different picture, one that we (the housed) see. We are forced to *see* the homeless as we go about our lives, and when we trip over them – if not literally, then metaphorically – homelessness has an impact on us. We feel disturbed by their plight, especially if they approach us wanting something from us. This impact is even stronger if the people we see in this state are mentally ill. They may communicate their disturbance to us by behaving oddly, talking incoherently or shouting aggressively as we pass in the street. Much as we might like to ignore them – and more often than not we pretend that we have not seen them – we are affected by them. They stir up our fear and anxiety.

Homelessness is a political issue, a social issue and – in terms of the dynamics between the homeless and the housed – a psychological issue. Very often these aspects of homelessness are divided or split between the players on the scene. The homeless client often takes on the role of wanting (or not wanting) concrete practical help. Workers often respond to this request at face value by providing practical help and accommodation or, when resources are not available, by taking on a political role, becoming indignant on the client's behalf about what should be available but is not.

Clearly the provision of adequate housing is important in any civilized society. Leff (1997) cites research indicating that there has been no rise in the proportion of mentally ill people among the homeless population, but rather

> the increased presence of the mentally ill on the streets must be a direct consequence of the increased number of homeless people. The mentally ill have few financial resources and so suffer the fate of others at the lowest socio-economic levels when low-rent accommodation becomes scarce.
>
> (Leff, 1997: 170–1)

He suggests that the mentally ill who are most likely to end up homeless are not those who have been carefully (and with extra financial resources) resettled in the community from the long-stay mental hospitals, but rather those who are discharged from admission wards in local hospitals without adequate after-care provision or, in the case of the young mentally ill, those running away from or thrown out of their family homes.

However, merely providing housing is not enough. All too often, homeless mentally ill people who are housed soon become homeless again. While it is important that we address the issue of resources, unless we are able to encompass the psychological element and to think symbolically about the meaning of the transactions that take place between the homeless and the housed, we are in danger of failing to achieve any common understanding and therefore failing to bring about any change even when resources are available. Research indicates that a high proportion of homeless people have histories of institutional care as a result of parental neglect or abuse, and concludes that 'These findings suggest that disruption of parent–child relationships has the long-lasting effect in some individuals of attenuating the formation of bonds and facilitating the drift into vagrancy' (Leff, 1997: 172).

For people with such histories, vagrancy may feel like a safer, better alternative to the homes that failed them. Such early experience also leads to a state of mind in which emotional containment in the form of relationships, and physical containment in the form of a home, are avoided.

A young homeless man responded well to the care that was offered to him on the streets so that workers were happy to be involved with him and keen to see him progress to a stage where he could move into his own flat which they helped him to furnish. But a few weeks later the flat was destroyed by its occupant, who then left it to return to the streets.

We can conceptualize this as the acting out of a mental state so destructive that it smashes everything inside the mind (the contained) and also smashes the mind (the container): a mental state that appears to be uncontainable. It is likely that what had made the move into a flat possible for this client was the relationships that he gradually built up with workers. Once he was housed, these were less available. The four walls of his flat could not replace the container that these relationships had provided, nor could his mind. Smashing the flat can be understood as an attack on the self – a self experienced as full of persecuted and persecuting 'bizarre objects' (Bion, 1956). We suggest that for these people, homelessness may be not only a physical reality but also a state of mind.

It is hard to conceptualize homelessness as a state of mind, yet we encounter examples of it when we feel disturbed or threatened by mad behaviour in public places. Whether or not we understand the content of what is being said to us, we feel that it is not directed at us personally. We just happen to be in what feels like the wrong place at the wrong time. Most of us, as we move around our local communities, carry with us a 'community in our minds' consisting of those from whom we get and to whom we give care and support. Our community is housed in our minds along with our sense of identity. Those for whom homelessness is a state of mind have none of these advantages. Sometimes our 'housed minds' are disturbed by what is inside us; if our ability to contain the disturbance is depleted, for example by stress, then we may 'act it out'. Sometimes our minds are disturbed by what is outside and we will manage to contain this or not – again depending on how adequate our mental container is at that time. Both these situations stir up our anxiety and we therefore react strongly to being confronted by others who clearly are failing to contain their own disturbance. These unfortunate individuals are then easily targeted as receptacles for mad, unwanted and feared aspects of ourselves which we wish to disown and locate in others. Having made use of others in this way, we then want to keep as far away from them as possible.

NIMBY might then be thought of as the community saying there is 'no room at the inn'. But in other ways, as illustrated above, the homeless might be saying that 'the inn, any inn, is unthinkable', that it is better to be out on the streets than enclosed somewhere with one's own bizarre mental contents. In addition, the homeless person who refuses to be housed, or to be housed in anything but the worst accommodation, might be saying that the inn is unsuitable, too 'posh' or too intrusive or too demanding. It is difficult enough to be confined with one's own madness, but many people fear that they will also become the receptacle of other people's madness. 'Care' in such circumstances is experienced as the intrusion of other people's bits, whether they are meant to be helpful – in the form of practical or emotional aid – or whether they are actually other people's projections (for example, when the client is expected to be pathetic, helpless and grateful when in fact he or she feels enraged).

Homeless people feel anxious that others will be intrusive with their curiosity, their looks, their questions and their knowledge. One homeless person, when asked why he and others were so reluctant to use the medical help on offer, said 'because we're afraid of what you might find' (El-Kabir and Ramsden, 1993: 163). As El-Kabir and Ramsden suggest, this fear is both concrete, for example fear of what physical illness might be found on examination, and psychological in terms of what might be 'seen' and 'interfered with' mentally. To overcome such resistence in clients requires patient and sensitive intervention by workers.

In an unpublished paper on work with young homeless people, Martin Roberts (1996) writes: 'I gradually worked with Mark to a point whereby I felt he was able to hear and understand that he was maybe in need of a supportive mental health project.' Roberts had been available to Mark over a number of years during which Mark would come and go, sometimes disappearing for long periods. During this time Roberts had been thinking and learning about how he and his project might provide the sort of containment that people like Mark could use. Roberts' struggle to find a way of holding Mark in mind, and Mark's recognition that in Roberts he had found someone prepared to engage in this struggle (rather than someone who sought a quick solution), meant that Mark was eventually able to consider the possibility of holding himself and his needs in his own mind.

To hold in mind that which the client finds impossible to hold in mind is no easy task. Roberts recognizes this and, in relation to another client, writes: 'Could I take the risk of caring for him?' When we seek quick solutions, we are avoiding taking this risk by organizing and controlling rather than connecting. We are afraid to connect: afraid that our minds will not be able to take the strain – not least because connection requires us to be in touch with our own homeless bits, those parts of our own minds that we do not wish to house. We are afraid that if we try to house them, our own mental homes/containers will collapse under the strain, leaving us too in a homeless state of mind. But this is the struggle in which we have to engage if clients with homeless minds are to find their own mental and physical accommodation. As Roberts realized, Mark needed the sort of accommodation that could hold him.

In a therapeutic community for ex-drug addicts, on good days the residents would play a song that went like this: 'Our house is a very, very, very fine house with two cats in the yard. Life used to be so hard. Now everything is eeasy 'cos of you.' The house was indeed 'nice' – luxury accommodation in comparison to what most residents and staff were used to. But the main point to this story is that it was a managed house and a communal house. Its disturbed and destructive residents were not left to their own devices, nor were the projections that flew around left unchecked. Chaotic clients need this, and if they are dealing with more than one agency, they also need these to be part of a well-integrated system of care that can hold rather than split further their fragmented bits. Thus, Roberts writes:

> [B]oth voluntary and statutory agencies ... are now linking together and integrating their work in order to provide strong enough and flexible enough care that is able to withstand and work with the unbearable feelings and the desperate situation that the young person is struggling to manage and is presenting the agencies with.

Is it conceivable that communities too might find ways of doing this?

Case studies

The two case studies below describe two different approaches to establishing mental health care agencies in ordinary neighbourhoods, and two different responses to the agitation of local residents. Both took place in similar places: prosperous enclaves in an inner-city area where property was already being used for mental health services, causing considerable alarm and opposition among local residents.

Scott's Green was an attractive triangle of enclosed garden surrounded by large Georgian houses. One side of the green belonged to the health authority, and houses previously used as nurses' residences were being turned, one by one, into mental health care agencies. On the second side of the triangle were elegant and expensive private properties, while the third side was a dual carriageway through-road. On one corner was a three-storey house which the local NHS Trust proposed now to convert into a twelve-bed residential unit for patients leaving long-stay hospital. They applied for planning permission, and in response to local protest they invited representatives from the local residents' association to a public meeting to discuss their concerns. Few turned up to this meeting, and those who did were so vehement in their objections that little dialogue was possible.

At this point, the Trust joined the Scott's Green Residents' Association as a local business, and two members of the Trust board began attending the association's regular meetings. Many of the residents who attended the meetings supported local provision of community care in principle, but were concerned about drugs, alcohol and violence on the streets, as well as about the number of mental health agencies that had recently opened around the Green, and about the implications of the arrival of twelve more acutely disturbed people into their neighbourhood. As the local residents became better acquainted with the Trust board representatives, they began to shift from global objections (fantasies) to voicing specific concerns (realities), for example that rubbish would accumulate, that their doorsteps would be fouled, that every time smoke alarms went off the area would be disturbed by fire engines – all these having been part of their experience of the Trust's acute psychiatric in-patient unit two streets away.

Promises were made. Residents were asked to telephone the Trust immediately that any such event occurred, or if they saw any of the Trust's clients behaving in a worrying way. Great care was taken to respond to these calls immediately, and initially there were numerous calls to test good faith. At the same time, the continuing meetings between the Trust representatives and the other members of the Residents' Association allowed for factual dispelling of assumptions about the links between mental illness and crime. Over a period of many months, mutual understanding grew, and eventually the Scott's Green Residents' Association voted unanimously to support the planning permission application which they had previously resisted so fiercely.

Meanwhile, in an adjacent area, an almost identical application had been made by another Trust. As in the early stages of the first example, local residents were invited to public meetings which very few attended, but in this case no representatives from the Trust went to the ordinary meetings which local people actually attended. The few residents who did turn up were predictably the most violently opposed, but the real community was not represented. Letters were sent to local businesses who expressed no strong views and were then widely quoted as 'supporting' the application, which in fact concerned them very little. Despite the continuing objection of the residents' association, astute lobbying of local politicians eventually led to a successful outcome for this application as well.

Both approaches were equally successful in the sense that both got permission for the desired use of a building. But only in the first case was there success in achieving the further objective of increasing the tolerance of difference and reducing the risk that users of the new facilities would be rejected by their new neighbours. One could argue that it is up to the staff of the agencies, once established, to build good links with the local community and, in so doing, to address this second objective. But as we see it, the former response to the concern of local residents speaks to a different concept in the mind of the relatedness of mental health service providers and 'the community', one where services are not only tolerated but are in harmony with the community. In contrast, the second Trust merely went through the motions of a consultative procedure. It is worth noting that under the heading 'Overcoming community opposition', MIND (Repper et al. 1997) identifies successful strategies as follows:

- taking neighbours concerns seriously
- providing information
- guaranteeing a response if problems do arise
- offering support/help to the local community
- working cooperatively with community leaders, police and local media.

The main difference between the two examples above is that *real* consultation – like real therapeutic work – is about *real* relationships. The representatives of the first Trust succeeded in providing a form of containment for the anxiety of local residents that enabled all concerned to appreciate the needs of different groups, and which had an impact on the thinking of those wanting to locate the hostel in the community as well as on the thinking of the local residents. In this example, the willingness of the Trust representatives to look for a way of establishing relationships with local residents and to become emotionally engaged in the struggle to find a way of working and living alongside each other parallels the work described above with the young homeless. As the representatives demonstrated that they were prepared to struggle to find a way of mentally and emotionally managing the initial extreme conflict of interest, so the anxiety of the residents lessened. The residents had found a container that was capable of processing their anxiety, recognizing the reasons for it, and responding appropriately. As one Trust representative put it, 'Community is not about a location but about a set of relationships. When the architects of a service build relationships, it paves the way for what happens when the service users move in.'

There is a cost to this approach beyond the time and trouble it takes. As another participant in this project said:

> Once you agree to want to know, to enter into dialogue, you cannot help but empathize with their objections. And once you empathize, you have to accept their concerns as valid. You can no longer use bureaucracy as a defence. We couldn't go ahead with two other projects we had in mind for the last two houses we owned on Scott's Green, even though they were really good projects. It just would not have been fair to ghettoize the area any further, so we have decided to sell the houses and look elsewhere.

Finding a way of entering into a relationship means engaging in a process of reciprocity between the container and the contained.

It is not just bureaucracy that can be 'faceless'. It can make life emotionally simpler for both service planners and service providers if they see themselves as having a 'faceless' community to deal with, a community that they can excoriate as 'uncaring', prejudiced and ignorant, so that they can rest comfortably in their identity as the ones who care.

Conclusion

If disturbed people are to live as part of the community, then we (whether workers, community residents or both) must have the courage to take back our projections and also the motivation to increase our ability to bear the projections of those who are not able to do this. In this process, we can become more whole people ourselves and free those who are easily identified as vulnerable from the additional burden of carrying what does not belong to them. Only then can we begin to think in terms of containing communities. D.C. Klein (1968) states:

> As we direct our thinking away from the more limited concept of mental health as a strictly intra-individual state of affairs, we inevitably become caught up in the quest for understanding of the community as the entity that gives rise both to the hazards of living and to the potential for coping successfully with them ... Rehabilitation of former mental patients, for instance, is not achieved by developing posthospitalization clinics and other follow up services. It will be successful in the final analysis when there is a community that accepts the person as valued, if not fully functioning.
>
> (Klein, 1968: 5–6)

Postscript

This chapter was presented at the 11th Annual Psychoanalysis and the Public Sphere Conference (January 1998). Much of the discussion that followed the presentation was concerned with the new government's apparent back-tracking on the move from hospital-based to community care, including recommending halting further hospital closures and suggesting the need for new rural asylums.

The impetus for this reversal appears to be a mixture of concern for the plight of severely mentally ill people and of societal anxiety. Whereas social values previously condemned the segregation and lack of liberty inherent in care in the old institutions, now there appears to be a push to return to segregation and control, whether by means of bricks and mortar or by the creation of systems of care intended to provide close monitoring and supervision of clients in the community. Is this an attempt to fine-tune existing policy by providing greater protection for the most vulnerable and secure care for the most dangerous? Is it a recognition that communities cannot provide this, as indeed they cannot? Or are we giving up on our efforts towards greater integration within our communities?

'Community' involves a matrix of relationships. For many of us, it refers to 'people like us' more than to a geographical location. When our sense of an 'us' is fragile, we are more than ever likely to reject (and project) 'otherness'. Perhaps increasing the number of institutions – besides providing accommodation for people regarded as dangerous to themselves or others – could be thought about as providing asylums for our projections.

References

Bion, W.R. (1956) 'Development of schizophrenic thought', *Int. J. Psycho-Analysis* 37: 344–6; reprinted (1967) in W.R. Bion, *Second Thoughts*, London: Heinemann.

—— (1970) *Attention and Interpretation*, London: Tavistock.

Bulmer, M. (1987) *The Social Basis of Community Care*, London: Allen and Unwin.

Department of Health (1990) *National Health Service and Community Care Act*, London: HMSO.

El-Kabir, D.J. and Ramsden, S.S. (1993) 'A pragmatic approach to the health care of the single homeless: its implications in terms of human resources', in M.P.I. Weller and M. Muijen (eds) *Dimensions of Community Mental Health Care*, London: W. B. Saunders.

Klein, D.C. (1968) *Community Dynamics and Mental Health*, New York: John Wiley.

Leff, J. (ed.) (1997) *Care in the Community: Illusion or Reality?*, Chichester: John Wiley.

Repper, J., Sayce, L., Strong, S., Wilmott, J. and Haines, M. (1997) *Respect: Time to End Discrimination on Mental Health Grounds*, London: MIND.

Roberts, M. (1996) 'In search of the depressive position', unpublished paper.

Tudor, K. (1996) *Mental Health Promotion: Paradigms and Practice*, London: Routledge.

3

When dreams become nightmares

Vega Zagier Roberts

Introduction

This chapter opens with a case study of an organization providing residential care for people with profound learning disabilities and also, in many cases, serious mental health problems. Efforts to develop services were repeatedly blocked by crises precipitated by real or alleged unprofessional conduct among staff and managers, crises that threatened the organization with scandal and even possible closure. The pattern suggested that staff were unconsciously behaving in a way that put them, their clients and the survival of the organization at risk because they were finding the work unbearable. It was, however, also unbearable for anyone to admit this, because the dream of providing community-based care for all, however disabled, was one that everyone was deeply committed to keeping alive.

The chapter goes on to consider how service providers, purchasers and policy-makers can all collude in maintaining impossible projects like the one described here, a collusion driven on the one hand by idealism and therapeutic zeal, and on the other by sociopolitical and economic imperatives. This collusive denial can get in the way of challenging or changing the design of such projects, and also with actively searching out ways to make them more manageable, for example by altering cherished working practices which endanger staff physically and emotionally.

Case study

Sarah first came for individual role consultancy shortly after taking up the directorship of Merryfields, a voluntary sector organization providing long-term intensively supported housing to people with severe mental handicap, behavioural and mental health problems, most of whom had previously been in long-stay hospitals for many years. She was very concerned by the state of the organization: there were no adequate policies and procedures, nor professional boundaries. Merryfields seemed to operate on a family or befriending model, staff bringing their children to work at weekends, inviting residents to their homes, staying on site late at night socializing, while making huge claims for overtime. Personal relationships cut across professional ones, gossip took the place of formal communication, and the trustees (to whom she was accountable) made decisions more often over drinks than in formal committee meetings. There was also a massive debt due to the excessive claims for overtime, cover for very high sickness rates, and unwarranted spending on fancy office furniture and lavish holiday outings with residents. In addition, Sarah also felt very vulnerable personally. Staff and managers were avoiding attending supervision, were unfriendly towards her in her presence and spread unpleasant rumours about her behind her back.

In the first phase of our work, the focus was on supporting her in getting basic systems in place and building a more cohesive management team to articulate a coherent philosophy and aims and policies. Gradually order settled. By the end of her first year, Sarah felt that she had built considerable personal credibility within Merryfields, and had good working relationships with all the house managers. Together she and they were reviewing and rewriting operational policies, attending to quality assurance, and getting spending under control. Bed occupancy was improving and the organization was almost out of debt. But there was no sense of achievement or pleasure in our sessions together. Instead, these were characterized by an enormous sense of fatigue on Sarah's part. The staff, previously so hostile, now seemed to be infinitely dependent on her. She felt that she had to carry the bleep all the time, and to come in often at weekends and in the evening, and she resented the lack of appreciation and support from the trustees who apparently still regretted the departure of her predecessor despite all the evidence of his unsatisfactory performance.

Over time, Sarah came to understand her experience as partly an unconscious communication from the staff about the burdensomeness of the work with the residents, its pain, its rare and small satisfactions, the ingratitude of the clients, and the weight of their extreme and often hostile dependency on the staff. As this understanding increasingly informed Sarah's work with the house managers, their dependency gradually lessened and they were able to take turns carrying the bleep. Sarah felt that at last she could free up some time for developmental work rather than putting all her time and energy into operational management, and began to feel enthusiastic about her job again.

But it seemed that this was not to be. There had always been periodic crises at Merryfields, but now these escalated in frequency and seriousness. Each was precipitated either by an employee's gross misconduct and dismissal, or by a public complaint by a member of staff about unfair treatment. There were several investigations by external bodies, each putting the organization's credibility and even its survival at risk. Each time, Sarah worked hard to understand the situation and to try to help the organization learn from it.

One of the most serious of these crises started with the allegation that Johann, the manager of Number 14, which housed Merryfields' most disturbed and disabled residents, had sexually abused one of them. The investigation was difficult – the tenant in question being virtually without speech – but Sarah carried it out carefully and methodically, despite her conviction from the outset of Johann's innocence. Eventually there was a hearing, the allegation was dismissed and Johann returned to work. Almost immediately afterwards came a new allegation: that Sarah and Johann were having an affair and that she had withheld evidence from the previous investigation. The allegation seemed absurd, and Sarah laughed in disbelief in telling it, but she was wounded and shocked. Mercifully, the investigation of her was relatively brief, proof being readily produced of the fullness of the earlier investigation. However, the whole chain of events threw up questions about what was going on in this organization that made this kind of event keep repeating itself so inexorably.

One way of understanding the pattern was as a way out of intolerable dilemmas for staff who seemed unable to leave Merryfields, yet also unable to bear the work – perhaps an unconscious attempt to get the place either sorted out or shut down by external authorities. But why the sudden return to attacking Sarah, after months of apparent mutual trust and understanding?

Inevitably, each of us comes to tell ourselves a story about the events in which we find ourselves involved. McCaughan and Palmer (1994) point out the usefulness of articulating our own story while also considering the alternative stories that others in the organization might tell about the same events. The story that had emerged in my mind over recent months with Sarah had cast her as a sort of knight of Camelot, a pure hero-saviour who had been fighting the good fight against the powers of evil, and who was now about to be vanquished. Perhaps Sarah and I had come to believe in this story as *the* story: that it was right and good to pull this organization towards professionalism, and therefore presumably wrong and bad of others to resist (although of course we would not have presumed to be so judgemental as to put it quite like that). Had we perhaps lost touch with the pain in the organization at giving up the satisfactions of the old ways?

And then Sarah fell seriously ill with heart trouble. On her return to work some months later, we focused on how she could set limits on her investment in Merryfields, lest it break her heart. We also explored how she could better mobilize her authority in other ways, to make clearer demands on the trustees for support and regular supervision. It was only after this that Sarah was able – with immense pain and reluctance – to voice her doubts as to whether projects like Number 14, with five such disabled and violent residents placed under one roof to live an as-if ordinary life, might not be ill conceived. She talked about a former resident who had been re-admitted to a long-stay hospital and was now much happier in a setting where she could wander safely in enclosed acres, rather than putting her life constantly in danger wandering in a highly agitated state of mind into the busy roads around Number 14.

Sarah's reluctance to entertain such thoughts at all, much less speak them aloud, until the risk to her own health and wellbeing pushed her to extremes, led us to wonder to what extent she and her staff might have become victims of a debate in society that is being stifled – more often acted out than thought through – about the limitations of care in the community. Their burning desire to succeed in providing good quality of life in ordinary neighbourhoods for everyone, regardless of how damaged or difficult they were, might be suppressing questions that needed to be asked. *If* Number 14 were indeed ill conceived, then no amount of consultancy or understanding could put it right, and I might even have been participating in obscuring issues that desperately needed to be confronted. It seems no coincidence that it was only after Sarah was able to talk about these doubts that she began to be able to think seriously about whether to stay at Merryfields or leave, and we began to explore what other career options she might have. It was as if we had both become more able to relinquish our mission to transform the organization against all odds, and to face the reality of our limitations without being overwhelmed by a sense of catastrophic failure.

The beginning of the dream

It has been argued that the anxieties inherent in the core task of an organization give rise to institutional defences in the form of structures and practices that serve primarily to defend staff from anxiety, rather than to promote task performance (Menzies, 1959). Based on their work with a number of institutions for people with incurable and often deteriorating conditions unlikely ever to improve enough to leave these institutions, Miller and Gwynne (1972) identified two prevalent models of care, each involving a different central defence. The first, the *medical* or *humanitarian defence*, is based on the principle that prolongation of life is a good thing. This tends to be accompanied by denial of the residents' unhappiness and lack of fulfilment. This defence produced what the researchers called the *warehousing model* of care, that is, keeping residents safe and as well and as comfortable as possible, encouraging dependence and depersonalizing inmate–staff relations and care. The second, the *anti-medical* or *liberal defence*, is based on the view that the residents are really normal, 'just like everyone else', and could have as full a life as their able-bodied peers if only they could develop all their potential. This defence produces what Miller and Gwynne called the *horticultural model* of care, defining the aims of the institution in terms of providing opportunities for the growth of abilities, while denying disabilities. There is often exaggerated praise for minor achievements, like the praise that adults give for a small child's first drawings, and denial of inmates' failure to achieve social status. Whereas in the first model, a 'good' inmate is one who is grateful and compliant, passively accepting the care provided, in the second it is one who is active and independent, happy and fulfilled.

That research was done in the late 1960s and 1970s, around the time of the 'Sans everything' report (Robb, 1967) with its damning portrayal of institutional life; nowadays, it is relatively rare to encounter either of these models in an absolutely pure form. Nonetheless, taken as two extremes on a spectrum, the first corresponds more recognizably to hospital-based care and the second to models of care in the community, particularly in the voluntary sector and the smaller social services units. It is easier to see the inadequacies of the warehousing model with its disregard for individuality, where the care is often provided by staff described by their critics as them-selves 'institutionalized'. The horticultural model, being more congruent with contemporary social values, appears inherently so superior that it is easy to overlook its shortcomings. For example, the demand to be indepen-dent may be distressing to some people, particularly to those whose infirmities are increasing or to those accustomed for a long time to the shel-tered and undemanding routine of a long-stay hospital. Others welcome the new choices and opportunities, or come to enjoy them after an initial transi-tion period. Yet others may require one sort of care at certain times, and another at other times, as their mental or physical state changes. This can be problematic. The two models involve significantly different working prac-tices, and also different attitudes in the carers. But when models of care are based on the defensive needs of the staff, such distinctions among different clients' needs may not be made, since they require thought and the facing of reality. Instead, one model is likely to be applied indiscriminately to all, on the basis of being the 'right' way to work, rather than as the most appro-priate for the needs of a given individual at a particular time.

Both models represent unconscious psychological defences against unbearable anxieties stirred up by the work, and by the very meaning of their charges being in the institution at all. These may include workers' guilt about residents' exclusion from the pleasures and opportunities of 'normal' life; sometimes even ambivalence about whether some of the most disabled might not be better off dead than alive; dislike or disgust or fear of certain aspects of the job; rage, frustration or despair when residents fail to take up the opportunities provided, or to be grateful for their care. Professionals are likely to gravitate towards organizations where the philosophy of care meets their own psychological needs, and where the particular defences operating defend against the anxieties with which they find it most difficult to cope. They may well then unconsciously collude with their like-minded colleagues, dealing with certain issues and feelings while projecting others onto other organizations which they then collectively condemn. In Chapter 1, Hinshelwood suggests that the splitting off of despair and locating it in the long-stay hospitals in order to preserve therapeutic optimism was crucial to the original design of community care policy.

The 'dream' of relocating mental health services into the community is one that most liberal members of our society share. The 'snake pit' of the traditional mental hospital is discordant with modern social values, while the notion that people with mental handicaps and mental illnesses can be supported to live more ordinary lives has considerable appeal (so long as they do not live in our immediate neighbourhood – see Chapter 2). Merryfields was part of this dream. Here, many people who had previously spent decades in hospital were living in ordinary terraced houses as 'tenants', choosing (in principle, at least) how to spend their time, what to eat and wear, how to use their own money. Staff and managers believed passionately in the dream, in the superiority of this way of life to the old one in the hospital.

But as the years went by, many of the residents made little progress towards greater independence and self-care. Some came to 'know their rights' only too well, so that the old compliance and gratitude which had made the lives of hospital staff relatively tolerable was gone, but without being replaced by the evidence of fulfilment that had been anticipated. Many staff were deeply disappointed and disillusioned, but seemingly could not bear to express or even acknowledge these feelings. Nor, apparently, could they leave. Staff turnover at Merryfields was extremely low, decreasing as morale sank rather than rising, as one would have expected. Instead of leaving, staff became more and more hostile towards management, complaining of unfair treatment, falsifying time-sheets and otherwise 'pilfering' from the organization, and not infrequently making public allegations which precipitated costly and embarrassing inquiries. At the same time, they gave more and more of themselves to the residents, exhausting themselves in the process.

Indeed, at the time that Sarah arrived at Merryfields, the one 'pocket' of high morale was paradoxically at Number 14, the house where the five most profoundly disabled and behaviourally disturbed tenants lived. Here there was an exuberant insistence that staff and tenants were happy and creative, always experimenting with new activities or going on exciting outings. Relations between staff and tenants were very warm and affectionate, the house was particularly homely both in appearance and atmosphere, and it was widely regarded both inside Merryfields and beyond as a model that others should imitate. It was extremely expensive, but was deemed to be doing what no one else could do, maintaining five people in the community for whom no other community place could be found, so threatening was their behaviour. Meanwhile, it was the staff of most of the other units, those with less disabled clients and with clearer boundaries between the providers and the recipients of care, who were the ones expressing anger and grievance.

Here we have two different responses to the dream. In most of Merryfields, rage and resentment were rife, as if the only way to cope with the disappointment in the tenants' lack of progress was to find someone to blame. In contrast, at Number 14 there was manic denial of the tenants' disabilities and of the limitations in the staff's ability to help them live 'normal' lives. It was as if the staff became more and more omnipotent until the strain cracked the system. At Number 14, there was (apparently) no resentment or despair or disgust or hate, only love and a passionate commitment to the work. The toppling of the charismatic Johann, who for years had been so idolized and later was so vilified, was one result, as the rage and hate which could not be felt for the work or the tenants was directed instead at the person who had led them into this impossible task.

Of course, it was not Johann alone who had done this. I believe that it required the collusion of many: the staff of Number 14, the rest of Merryfields' staff and managers, the purchasers of Merryfields' services, and the carers and campaigners in the field of mental health and mental handicap services. If we recall Sarah's pain in recounting the story of the tenant who 'failed' at Merryfields and who then found that she was happier in a locked rural setting, we can get some inkling of the pressure on staff in these kinds of idealistic organizations to continue to deny that the dream sometimes becomes an unbearable nightmare from which it seems impossible to wake up.

Denying the need for asylum

The dream for community care, which made possible the founding of organizations like Merryfields, was born from the wish to provide a more human-scale alternative to traditional psychiatric institutions. The passion behind the dream involved powerful splitting processes: the mental hospital was anathematized, while community care was idealized. As part of this splitting process, the need for asylum was denied.

Asylum is defined in the dictionary first as sanctuary or protection. There is also a second definition: 'institution offering shelter and support to distressed or destitute individuals, especially the mentally ill'. The term 'asylum' as referring to an institution has come to represent all that was repressive and cruelly depersonalizing (Goffman, 1961) so that society seems to have lost touch with the original meaning, or indeed with any recognition of mental hospitals as places providing shelter and care.

Perhaps we are fearful of facing our own need for asylum, for refuge; our own wish to feel safe and looked after, rather than always striving to progress. Today's psychiatric hospitals are under constant pressure to move patients on, their principal function having become to 'hold' and treat people until they can just manage (or be managed) outside their walls. Meanwhile, community-based 'homes' strive to make possible individual development and 'normality' while taking on the ever more disturbed people being discharged from the hospitals. Neither situation really provides a space for mentally ill people to just be, to be mad or disturbed without being pushed prematurely to move on or to blossom and fulfil their potential.[1]

There is evidence too of a parallel process affecting the staff working in this field. It can be difficult for care staff in modern institutions to admit to *not* having personal or therapeutic ambitions, to enjoying the safety and satisfactions of 'old-fashioned' working practices which some of their colleagues experience as obsolete and soul-destroying. Maybe in the past we projected our non-ambitious, non-achieving parts onto the old mental hospitals, and cannot bear to take them back now that the 'bins' are gone.

The denial of the need for asylum deepens the split between the ware-housing and the horticultural models discussed above, with the long-stay hospitals as the prime representatives of the former, and community care as the implementation of the latter. The ground is then laid for inter-institutional splitting, and the space for combining aspects of both models is eroded. Nowhere is this more problematic than in long-term residential care, where clients are most likely to need a combination of retreat from the stresses of independent living, and also support for making developmental changes. Not only will different clients benefit from more of one or the other, but any one individual may well need different kinds of support at different times.

This is not to minimize the efforts made by many residential care staff to offer a range of interventions sensitively attuned to individual needs. What I am suggesting is that in most agencies there is a dominant model 'in the mind' – either of therapeutic ambition, or of maintenance – which explicitly or implicitly shapes expectations (within the agency and externally, for example in purchasers) and defines what constitutes success or failure. And because the dominant model affects who is attracted to work in the agency, it is more likely to persist over time than to be challenged. Indeed, many community care agencies, particularly in the voluntary sector, are prone to self-idealization, with concomitant denigration of other organizations working to a different model, rather than identifying their own particular niche within a broad spectrum of other services.

This tendency towards idealization and denigration is not confined to inter-agency relations but can often be seen within a single organization. For example, at Merryfields, Number 14 was idealized for its innovative prac-tices, while another project, Number 8, was denigrated for its 'institutional' emphasis on order and cleanliness, and its low risk-taking. Similar splitting can indeed also be observed within a single team. Often one finds that there is a subgroup of young idealistic workers, often with psychology degrees or counselling training, who have considerable therapeutic ambitions for their clients but tend to move on fairly quickly to higher-status, better-paid work; and another subgroup, often older and with less formal education, with less ambition for themselves and their clients who provide the continuity and undemanding care which the clients equally need. This latter group often take on a greater proportion of the domestic work, and are often quietly resentful of their colleagues, while the former group is more likely to be vociferous in their complaints about managers and others who prevent their realizing their dreams, and to manifest symptoms of burnout. (See 'Bearing the brunt' in Millar and Roberts, 1986.) In many cases, this split occurs along lines of race and age, causing great and often unexpressed unease in 'politically correct' organizations.

It seems evident that one needs both sorts of workers in long-term residential work, and both sorts of organizations in community care. Ideally, both would work together with mutual respect. But what we see over and over again is fights over 'right' and 'wrong' approaches. And since neither model alone is successful, the space for continually teasing out the crucial contributions of each is too often taken over by therapeutic nihilism: that nothing works.

Miller and Gwynne (1972) encountered a similar splitting process in their study. They recommended that within each organization (or unit) there should be separate systems, one for meeting inmates' psychophysical dependency needs (for example, catering, cleaning and physical care) and another providing for their psychophysical independence needs (for example, work and leisure activities). However, they went on to point out that 'since these two systems are engaged in divergent tasks, they are to some degree in conflict', producing role conflict for both inmates and staff (1972: 159).

It is psychologically simpler when the two systems are physically separate, for example when a hospitalized patient has his or her dependency needs met on the ward and goes to a different location for occupational therapy, or moves from one residential unit to another depending on the current degree of disability, although even in this case each department or unit has to meet both dependence and independence needs to some extent. Where the two systems are separate, Miller and Gwynne identify the key leadership task as relating both systems to each other and to the whole.

In community-based residential care, the independence task system and the dependence task system are unlikely to be staffed and managed separately, especially in very small units. Even when an organization has a number of homes, as was the case at Merryfields, they are rarely able or willing to entertain the idea of organizing them in such a way that clients would move from one to another as their needs change. (One reason often given is that the residents are tenants who should be able to regard the house where they live as their home, for life if need be.)

Where the two systems are not formally separate, each organization or team has to determine its own balance in the emphasis put on each task. And even within any one team, different members are likely to weight the two differently. The leadership task in this situation is therefore particularly complex, since both the separation and the relating of the two tasks has to be done 'in the mind' rather than structurally. However, it is crucial that there is adequate provision for both kinds of needs, and sometimes what looks like unnecessary conflict might be construed as ensuring that this happens. Thus, 'resistant' or 'hidebound' staff could be regarded not merely as obstructive, but as holding on to the importance of meeting dependency needs (of staff as well as clients), so that the team or organization does not spin off into manic omnipotent denial of the clients' illness. Similarly, those pushing for innovation and risk-taking can be thought of as fighting against the danger of stagnation and despair on behalf of the group as a whole.

To return to Merryfields, it did not prove possible to take forward Sarah's doubts about the viability of residential units like Number 14, to consider whether these particular residents might be better off in a more hospital-like setting. Not only were the staff resistant to engaging with this question, but the trustees could not do so because there was too much money invested in the current model. Perhaps at the purchasing and policy-making levels there is still too much invested in the current determination to prove that community care is the answer for all. Already there are rumblings about the need for larger units set outside urban areas, providing space and safety for the most vulnerable and impaired, as well as for the most dangerous.

Meanwhile, we could argue that the staff of organizations like Merryfields are being exploited, seduced into working for an impossible dream, and left to bear the pain when it cannot be realized. However, the situation is not so simple. As I have written elsewhere (Roberts, 1994), people come to work in idealistic organizations for many reasons, not least to meet their own, often unconscious, psychological needs which this kind of work uniquely fulfils. As such, they make themselves (more or less willingly) available for exploitation, as they take on different 'self-assigned impossible tasks'. The system is maintained because there is collusion – witting and unwitting – among the participants at all levels: workers, managers, purchasers, policy-makers and society at large. The question that we need to address is how this collusion can be reduced, for the health of all concerned.

Keeping the dream alive

So far, the focus of this chapter has been on the cost of denial. The obvious remedy is a large dose of reality, for example to spell out clearly the limits of the possible, to contain excessive therapeutic optimism and ambition. But there is also a cost of too much reality, for what then makes the work worth doing at all? We need dreams, both as individuals and as a society. Without dreams, we would not embark on having children, or undertake demanding careers, or write books, or do much of what is most creative and satisfying in life. We must take care not to kill dreams, for once they are dead it may not be possible to revive them. Perhaps it is preferable to be a bit too omnipotent than to feel defeated before one even starts. Nor should we overlook that Merryfields achieved a great deal despite all the difficulties: the quality of life of most of the residents was indisputably better than what they had known before.

When defences are stripped away, the work can feel meaningless: at best flat, at worst unbearable. Without the enthusiasm of 'the bright young things', organizations like Merryfields could become merely dreary dumping-grounds for the unwanted, stinking of despair. It is a delicate balancing act, on the one hand keeping denial within bounds, supporting staff in acknowledging the limitations of what can be achieved; and on the other, fostering hope and enthusiasm.

In larger – usually statutory sector – agencies, workers may move away fairly quickly from front-line work into management and supervisory roles. In smaller organizations, there is less room for movement other than to leave altogether, and the pain of being disappointed by the results of the work is harder to escape. It can be very helpful to seek out alternative sources of work satisfaction apart from the visible improvement of clients. This can be achieved in a number of ways besides promotion 'upwards'. For example, workers may be seconded to another unit within the same organization, where they are exposed to different work practices and assumptions. They may take on special projects which allow them to experiment with their own ideas, or particular areas of responsibility which require new skills. Training and professional development opportunities may enable them to think about their work differently. All these can help to foster their capacity to maintain a questioning attitude and to challenge excessively rigid convictions about what constitutes the 'right' way to go about their work.

Note

1 The current debate about asylum in the community is discussed in depth in Tomlinson and Carrier (1996). See in particular ch. 9 by Wallcraft.

References

Goffman, E. (1961) *Asylums: Essays on the Social Situation of Mental Patients and Other Inmates*, New York: Doubleday Anchor Books.

McCaughan, N. and Palmer, B. (1994) *Systems Thinking for Harassed Managers*, London: Karnac Books.

Menzies, I.E.P. (1959) 'The functioning of social systems as a defence against anxiety', *Human Relations* 13: 95–121; reprinted in Isabel Menzies Lyth (1988) *Containing Anxiety in Institutions: Selected Essays*, London: Free Association Books.

Millar, D. and Roberts, V.Z. (1986) 'Elderly patients in "continuing care": a consultation concerning the quality of life', *Group Analysis* 19: 45–59.

Miller, E.J. and Gwynne, G. (1972) *A Life Apart*, London: Tavistock.

Robb, B. (1967) *Sans everything: a case to answer*, London: Nelson.

Roberts, V.Z. (1994) 'The self-assigned impossible task', in A. Obholzer and V.Z. Roberts (eds) *The Unconscious at Work: Individual and Organizational Stress in the Human Services*, London: Routledge.

Tomlinson, D. and Carrier, J. (eds) (1996) *Asylum in the Community*, London: Routledge.

4

Is authority a dirty word?

Changing attitudes to care and control

Vega Zagier Roberts

Organizations are part of the society in which they are found, and their members bring with them attitudes and aspirations shaped by their experiences of and in that society. Nowhere is this more evident than in organizations involved in providing care in the community. Whereas walled-off institutions with very long-term staff and clients might, by their very isolation, become quasi-separate – used by society as receptacles for projections of 'otherness' – community care organizations are in continuous direct interaction with the wider community. Indeed, their very existence emerged from changing social attitudes, and their relatively rapid turnover of staff and clients ensures that changing societal trends are continually 'imported' into the system.

This chapter will consider some of the difficulties that arise in relation to the exercise of authority, especially as these manifest in teams and organizations that set out to further particular ideals. These difficulties are related to widespread ambivalence in contemporary society about care and control, which affects our experience of managing and being managed, of leadership and followership.

Changing attitudes towards authority in everyday life

Some friends come to visit. Their 4-year-old daughter runs about, bangs on the piano and finally upsets a lamp. Each parent in turn asks her to stop, then uses a more peremptory tone, to no effect. Finally her father grips her shoulder roughly and says she will have to sit in the car if she cannot behave. The child wriggles free, hits her father and walks away. The adults return to their conversation, relieved but also embarrassed at having resorted to force, only half reassured by knowing that most of their friends have similar problems with their own children.

The director of a small voluntary organization complains of a particularly troublesome team: its members ignore directives and go their own
way. She is looking for a new manager for this team: it will need to be
someone really tough, she says, with a great deal of management experience, to whip them into shape.

A man relates with shy pleasure how members of his extended family
deferred to him immediately after the death of his father. When I
referred to his now being the head of the family, he protested in alarm,
'But I like to work *with* people, I don't want to be authoritarian.'

Similar evidence of changing attitudes to authority is all around us. The
very term 'the authorities' tends to be accompanied by derision or distaste,
rarely by respect. Traditionally, we have looked to parents, managers, the
police and other 'authority figures' to provide both care and control. Or,
perhaps more accurately, we have sanctioned their controlling function in
exchange for the care we expected from them, that is, to contain our anxieties by being dependable and 'in control'. When they fail to protect us from
danger, whether external or internal, we are likely to withdraw our sanction.
This shift in attitude to authority is, of course, two-sided. It is not only the
'recipients' of care and control whose expectations are changing in the face
of their experiences of their 'failed dependency' – that is, not having their
needs met in the same way as before (Miller, 1993). Parents no longer quite
believe that they can adequately protect their children or prepare them to
protect themselves; managers often doubt the value of the systems that they
are trying to manage; the state can no longer offer either dependable care or
control. As a result, there is waning conviction about the exercising of
authority, as well as greater resistance to sanctioning others to do so.

This has had enormous impact on the relatedness of individuals to the
groups to which they belong, and on attitudes to leadership and followership. The case studies below illustrate some of the difficulties to which this
gives rise in some organizations, especially in those endeavouring to offer an
alternative to traditional hierarchical or 'paternalistic' models of care, where
authority does indeed seem to have become a dirty word.

Case study I

I was asked to consult to the multidisciplinary team of Cannon Fields, a
new community mental health centre set up as part of a programme to close
down the local psychiatric hospital where most of the staff had previously

worked, and which they regarded as rigid, oppressive and suppressive of individuality. They were very committed to creating a service where both clients and staff would flourish and develop their full potential. To this end, clients were to come and go freely, choosing whether or not to attend formal treatment activities, and the door would be open to all, without the kind of repressive rules and rigid procedures typical of other settings. Similarly, staff could work as they chose, with individuals or groups, chronic or acute patients. Decisions were to be made by consensus.

At our first meeting, we could scarcely hear one another because two workmen were hammering at the window, yet everyone carried on as if this were not happening. When I wondered aloud whether I were the only person bothered by the noise, they explained that they had no authority over the workmen, who had been sent by 'central admin' at the hospital. At our third meeting, a new staff member lit a cigarette. No one said anything to her about the decision, made with great difficulty and taking up over half the previous session, that there would be no smoking in these meetings. She became visibly more and more uncomfortable and eventually put out her cigarette, as if absent-mindedly, to everyone's relief, although when I commented on what seemed to be happening, it appeared that only one other person besides me remembered that a decision had actually been made. The discussion then moved on to a problem client who had been arriving every morning drunk and abusive, intimidating other clients. Could they ask him to leave? Should they have a policy? But what about their policy of being open to all? It was only the risk to other clients that over-came their reluctance to have any rules curtailing any individual's freedom, and they agreed that no one would be allowed in the centre while under the influence of drugs or alcohol.

For over a year, this was the only formal rule, and the only decision they could all remember and tell to newcomers. However, there was a growing body of unstated ones, the most powerful being that everyone was equal and the same. They regarded interdisciplinary rivalry and abuses of power as the greatest threat to their objectives, and strove to obliterate all differences between individuals, disciplines, hierarchical level, and even level of expertise and competence. Although there was a designated team leader, she could not be allowed – or allow herself – to have any power or to exercise any authority.

Part of the difficulty here was the identification of the staff with their clients – distressed and disadvantaged people whom they saw as having been oppressed and victimized by the unequal distribution of power in society. Linked with this was profound ambivalence towards the 'parent' institution, the hospital on which they depended for referrals and resources, and where they located the power and authority that they disavowed. This ambivalence mirrored the unconscious conflicts of their most difficult chronic clients, who continually demanded help while refusing to engage with the team in any treatment programme, and kept getting re-admitted to the hospital that they both hated and needed. These dynamics were further complicated by their ideal to be as different as possible from settings using a medical model, so that to question their policies and practices became taboo. In the next example, similar issues led to extreme conflict within the team.

Case study 2

Longham Homes was a voluntary sector organization providing supported, semi-independent flats for people with learning difficulties and mental health problems. The aim was to help the tenants integrate into the community and the mission statement emphasized the tenants' rights to dignity, respect, privacy and safety. I was invited to design and facilitate a team development programme for this team because the staff were demoralized and in constant conflict, both internally and with their senior managers.

One heated argument that they were having was about communal meals. The tenants each had their own kitchen, but staff had become concerned about their physical health and nutrition, so they had recently started organizing communal evening meals three times a week. The idea was that, with help from staff, clients could develop independent living skills by sharing the shopping and cooking; in addition, the meals would serve as a social forum, as many of the tenants were terribly isolated and spent most of their time alone in their flats. However, things had not turned out as planned. The staff were doing all the work; some tenants would simply give their £1 contribution and take the meal up to their own flats. Should this be allowed, or should assisting in the preparation be a requirement for getting the meal? Were they turning into a mini-hospital by cooking for the tenants? But what about tenants' rights to making their own choices? Some staff argued that they should drop the idea altogether as it was not working. Others insisted that they had a responsibility to ensure that the tenants ate properly, and that without the communal suppers some were at risk of falling ill. Some team members refused to participate any further in the communal meals, which infuriated those who were left doing the washing-up late into the night. The team leader, Peter, who had initially supported those favouring continuing the meals out of a sense of responsibility for the safety and welfare of the tenants, now felt that he had a mutiny on his hands.

Clearly all three aims of the communal meals – socializing, training in independent living skills and ensuring adequate nutrition – were important, but until there was clarity about which had priority over the others, there was no basis on which to decide what to do. The first focus of the team development days therefore was to revisit the vision of Longham Homes and to articulate the *primary task*, that is, the core purpose for which it existed and which it had to achieve in order to survive (Rice, 1963). Authority in work systems derives from the primary task. In this case, this applied both to the authority of the staff in relation to the tenants, and to

Peter's authority as the manager of the team. In effect, Peter had been drawing on his own view of which aim had greatest priority in making his initial decision to continue with the communal suppers, but because this priority was not explicit, he had been seen as siding with some team members against others.

Underlying the bitter feelings was the team's rage at having their therapeutic efforts sabotaged, and they turned on Peter not least because he had not been able to spare them these very uncomfortable feelings. The fight within the team served to defend against despair. The despair got lodged in Peter, who was then unable to exercise his authority appropriately. If the communal meals had gone as planned, the team could have continued to feel that they were achieving all three aims. As it was, they had to prioritize them (for example, putting nutrition first), and thereby admit a degree of defeat in relation to the subsidiary aims (independent living and socialization).

Such experiences of hate and despair are part of all caring activities, from parenting (Winnicott, 1947) to care in the community, and the need of carers to suppress or deny negative feelings towards the recipients of their care is one of the most powerful forces mitigating against the appropriate exercise of authority.

Power, authority and leadership

The words 'power' and 'authority' tend to be used interchangeably. Both are charged with emotion and bring strong images – often negative ones – to many people's minds, especially in organizations providing care. I think it is very useful, however, to distinguish them along the lines proposed by Reed and Armstrong (Grubb Institute, 1991). They define power as an attribute of the person: *personal power* comes from one's knowledge, personality or skills; *instrumental power* from what one owns or controls, such as money or other resources, or a gun in one's hand; *projected power* from what is attributed to oneself by others and which can make one larger than life; and *official power* which attaches to the person by virtue of their title and what this leads others to expect.

Authority, on the other hand, they regard as a quality or attribute attached to a *role* within a system, whereby what one does and the powers that one has are related to furthering the aims of the system to which one has been appointed. Thus, authority is linked to responsibility for outcomes. While power can be, and often is, exercised without matching authority – and here lies its potential for abuse – authority cannot be exercised without having matching power, for example the competence to do the job, the necessary resources and reasonable confidence from others. Every person in a role in a system will need to exercise their own authority, whether to manage themselves or others, and therefore needs to be clear about the aims of the system, since their authority derives from these aims.

At Longham Homes, where this clarity was lacking, there was no basis on which to judge whether Peter's decisions came from his authority in role or from personal ambition and a need to control others. Redefining the aims of the project strengthened Peter's ability to exercise his authority, and also made it possible for team members to exercise their own authority, not only with clients but also in relation to Peter, since they could now be clearer about whether they agreed or disagreed with organizational priorities, and whether they wished to stay or to go.

Obholzer (1994) has identified three sources of authority in organizations. First, there is delegation of authority 'from above' – from the board of trustees, the executive committee, the government (which in turn derives its authority from the electorate).

Second, there is sanctioning of authority 'from below'. In principle, from the time that we sign an employment contract, we are recognizing the authority of our managers. However, this supposes a degree of freedom and choice to join or not to join; when employment opportunities decrease, more staff may sign contracts without truly joining. Furthermore, when the workforce feels let down by managers, or when the organization changes in ways with which the staff do not agree, they may withdraw their earlier sanction, leading to undermining and sabotage.

Finally, authority needs to be sanctioned 'from within', that is, we need to be in touch with our own authority and allow ourselves to exercise it. How much we are able to do this depends on our relationship with past authority figures, particularly parents, and the extent to which our past experiences have led us to regard authority as predominantly enabling or oppressive. Much of these relationships remain in our unconscious, and can lead either to an inflated picture of authority (and ourselves in authority) as omnipotent, or to paralysing self-doubt (the latter being much more common in helping organizations).

Case study 3

Crossroads was a voluntary sector organization set up to support women with serious mental health problems to live in the community after discharge from hospital. It comprised two teams, one staffing a residential unit and the other supporting women living in their own flats. In its fourth year, it began to receive referrals of increasingly disabled and chaotic clients, and also lost the input of a psychologist and a social worker, due to cuts in local health and social services. The outreach team found these changes particularly stressful. Sickness rates soared and the staff complained constantly about their clients. The director, Marian, proposed amalgamating the two teams, changing job descriptions so that all staff would do some of each kind of work. This was fiercely resisted, particularly by the outreach team who had previously done no shift work and saw themselves as having higher status than the residential team. The plan was then shelved.

Meanwhile, the behaviour of the outreach team became increasingly chaotic: money went missing, the state of their clients' flats deteriorated to the point of being unsanitary and unsafe, and team members avoided supervision. Alarmed, Marian instituted an organizational review of care practice. The previously warm and easy relationship between her and her staff became increasingly tense and hostile. They accused her of selling out, of having become 'a man in skirts', of being 'power-mad'.

Marian found all this unbearably painful, and eventually took early retirement. Her successor, Tricia, very quickly put in place firm standards of care practice, started two disciplinary procedures with uncooperative staff, and amalgamated the two teams along the lines proposed by Marian. She met with very little resistance from the staff who, instead of fighting her, became apathetic and cynical about their jobs and the organization.

It may be that if Marian had been able to bear for a while the rage directed at her, it might have become possible for her to bring about the necessary changes. Many things conspired to make this difficult. Marian had been instrumental in the setting up of Crossroads. Her own mother had died in a long-stay psychiatric hospital, and she was deeply committed to supporting women with mental health problems, as well as to the particular ideology of this organization. Many of the staff had been with her from the start, sharing her vision and looking to her to make their ideals a reality. For years they had confided their personal difficulties to her, trusting her to care for them, and they felt betrayed when she apparently changed, making decisions with which they did not agree, and seeming to be more preoccupied with the demands of purchasers than with the needs and wishes of her staff. While the staff saw her as becoming more and more powerful and authoritarian, her own experience was that she was powerless and had lost her authority.

For someone like Marian, with a strong drive to try to meet the dependency needs of her staff, their attacks on her for failing to meet their expectations were all the more unbearable because she was fundamentally at odds with the 'new managerialism' to which she was desperately trying to adapt. Her proposal to amalgamate the two teams was initially motivated by her concern for her staff. However, when nothing she did succeeded in making the new demands on the staff more tolerable, not only did they turn on her for failing them, but her sense of her own authority was sabotaged from within. Without inner conviction, she became somewhat authoritarian instead, as a defence against the pain that the whole situation was causing her. Tricia, on the other hand, was less identified with the founding ideology of Crossroads, and had different psychological needs. She saw herself as a manager with a job to do and authority to do it. Interestingly, the staff on the whole sanctioned her authority to make the decisions necessary for the survival of Crossroads in the new 'marketplace', although they withdrew their personal commitment from the organization.

Leadership, care and control

Turquet, in his classic paper on leadership (1974), refers to the leader's 'inalienable right to executive action', in line with his or her responsibility for the outcomes of the work of the system. At the same time, to be effective, leaders must – like the Roman god Janus – look always both inwards and outwards, staying in touch with the needs of members and also the needs and demands outside the group. To stay in touch with the internal state of the group, says Turquet, they have to act as a receptacle for the group's projections, neither distancing themselves too much nor joining in. Maintaining one's position at the boundary in this way is difficult and often painful and lonely, but the alternatives – to join the group or to cut off from it emotionally – entails abdicating authority. Then neither the leader nor the group can be effective.

In more stable times, organizations served as containers for negative projections. Now, as Stokes (1994) points out, constant restructuring and redeployment of staff is making our institutions too fragile to attack safely: the department that you loved to hate may not even be there next week, let alone next year. So hate stays nearer home, the titre of negative projections rises, and there are more personal attacks in place of the former, relatively impersonal ones. As institutions become less available as containers, managers need to become even more available and reliable ones, but this is often not the case. Indeed, particularly in idealistic care-providing organizations, managers are often experienced as too fragile to attack safely, too determinedly well-intentioned, and experiencing the same anxieties as their staff. With support from their own managers, or from an external consultant or supervisor, they need to develop their capacity to stay in touch with the emotional pain of front-line staff, and to bear being used as receptacles of negative projections. This means also bearing the necessary distance between themselves and their staff while not using it to cut off from them.

Miller (1990) writes about the splits so common in voluntary organizations when they outgrow their early days of being a small, face-to-face band of comrades engaged in a shared crusade: the distancing between what he calls the blue jeans (those who relate directly to the clients) and the grey suits (those who relate to the purchasers of services). In larger organizations, the changing requirements of the marketplace for accountability and professionalization are often accompanied by a lengthening of the hierarchy. Here the staff typically complain that managers are out of touch with the real work of the organization, while managers may well claim that the staff are out of touch with 'the real world'. The distance between hierarchical levels allows people to split off uncomfortable aspects of the conflict between financial considerations and the needs of clients (see Chapter 8).

In smaller organizations like Crossroads, where the distance between senior management and front-line staff is so small, the splitting can lead to violent and highly personalized conflict. It is therefore all the more crucial for the manager to maintain carefully her position 'at the boundary' between the staff and the external world, neither sucked in to join them nor losing touch with their emotional experience. It might have been helpful at an earlier stage if Marian and her staff could have worked at reducing this splitting by facing together the growing gap between available resources and the demands on those resources, working together on how to meet the new challenges facing the organization. Instead, Marian struggled to face these challenges on her own. When her efforts failed, she was unable to hold her boundary position, not least because the team's sense of having been betrayed by her resonated with and amplified her own sense of having let them down.

In my consultancy work with idealistic organizations, I see one aim as enabling people to face fundamental tensions between the ideals that give the work its meaning, and what is required for survival, so that neither is sacrificed. If idealism goes, libidinal investment in the work can be lost, at great cost to both workers and clients. If reality is ignored, the organization may die. The purchaser/provider split has brought these tensions to the fore. Furthermore, while contracting makes agencies sharpen their objectives, these objectives may well be ones with which the staff cannot identify, do not agree with, and distrust as being contrary to the primary task of social welfare (Biggs, 1994). Instead of supporting their ability to face difficult choices, these sharper objectives only serve to alienate them further, so that the task of trying to reconcile competing demands is rejected, left firmly on the doorstep of the managers. Thus at Crossroads, the problems evoked by the changing external environment were never owned by the team but remained firmly located with Marian – her problem, if not indeed her fault – and her attempts to solve them were experienced as attacks on all they held dear.

Part of the problem in these idealistic organizations is the managers' need to feel close to the blue jeans, to be loved by them and to be seen as their fellows in the good fight. The vision, after all, has often originally been theirs. Their own unresolved unconscious needs, which have played a large part in drawing them to this work, can make it particularly hard for them to bear negative projections from their staff. Yet the staff need a container for these negative projections: a manager who – to use Turquet's phrase about this essential quality of leadership – can 'bear being used' (Turquet, 1974: 73). Otherwise the negative projections go elsewhere: manager and staff may cling together and locate the blame with an external enemy – more senior managers, for example, or politicians; or the projections may go ricocheting around the organization, precipitating personalized conflicts among peers;

or the negativity may be re-internalized in all its rawness, so that workers can no longer find meaning or pleasure in their work.

A traditional view of leadership is that 'the leader should clearly know what he is doing, and how he is going to do it, while carrying his workers along with him in a way that makes them largely impervious to hardship and painful effort' (Adair, 1983). But what happens when the task is uncertain and constantly changing, and when there is no protection from hardship and pain? Many people in organizations – and indeed in society generally – cling to the notion that the current turbulence and chaos is temporary, and await a return to a steady state. A growing number of others, however, are recognizing that confusion and uncertainty are no longer the exception but have become endemic and are likely to remain so. In this transitional period between 'instability as the exception' and 'instability as the norm', there is an enormous sense of betrayal by leaders who can no longer protect us from pain and hardship. Both managers and subordinates often hold on desperately to the myth of management control which has traditionally been the basis for legitimizing authority (Gabriel, 1996: 9). Even when subordinates challenge this authority, they still wish to believe in the myth. When they oust a manger who has failed to control things, they feel frightened as well as guilty, as if they have created a runaway machine.

So what is the task now of the leader, if it is not to control the chaos and to protect us from anxiety? An alternative contemporary view is that leadership is about adaptive work, that is, enabling people to confront the gap between the values for which they stand and the reality that they face, 'to clarify what matters most, in what balance, with what trade-offs. . . . Neither providing a map for the future that disregards value conflicts nor providing an easy way out that neglects the facts will suffice for leadership' (Heifetz, 1994: 22–3). Heifetz goes on to say that, while leaders must meet the needs of followers (otherwise they cannot remain leaders), they must also elevate them – that is shift them beyond the need to be spared this painful adaptive work. The outdated model of taking organizational problems away to solve 'up there' not only no longer works, but diminishes the people involved; this diminishment is observable in all too many workplaces. But the delicate task of the leader is to prepare people to undertake the hard problems *at a rate they can stand*. This is the essence of containment. Too fast a pace becomes a form of dumping, pushing responsibility down the system in a way that increases anxiety beyond tolerable limits, in which case staff will almost certainly retreat to primitive, anxiety-driven modes of functioning. Too slow a pace or too paternalistic a style of management wastes the potential of staff to contribute to the complex tasks in hand, and ultimately alienates them.

Conclusion

All three organizations described in this chapter were set up partly as an alternative to existing services; their founding ideals were anti-authority and anti-management. The purchaser/provider split has made the pressures on managers in such organizations increasingly acute, indeed, life-threatening, since funding decisions can lead to closure. The 'rationality' of community care decision-taking can erode the space for consideration of the 'irrational', that is, of the psychological needs which give the work its meaning and provide the energy that the workers need to persist with their task.

This is further complicated by the societal processes described at the beginning of this chapter. Just as we are uncertain to what extent parents should control children's behaviour and to what extent their task is to enable (natural) maturation and development, so there is uncertainty in many community care organizations about whether their task is primarily about controlling behaviour or about fostering clients' self-realization. The supervision register, for instance, could be regarded as a tool for ensuring that clients receive adequate care and do not 'fall through the net', but the experience of many service providers is that they are now being expected to police their clients (while themselves being policed, and subject to severe sanctions if they fail in this duty). Furthermore, if there is validity in the concept that authority derives from the primary task, unresolved ambiguity about this task and ambivalence towards it will continue to make the appropriate exercise of authority extremely problematic.

Whether or not we are in designated management roles, we all have to manage ourselves, that is, to manage the boundary between our inner world and the external environment, between our individual self and the group, in order to be the author of our own actions. It is not only leadership that has become more difficult, but also authoritative followership: the exercise of our authority in relation to the task in hand so that we allow ourselves to be managed or led to the benefit of the system in which we have a role, to challenge others' decisions when necessary, but not their right to make them.

To the extent that we lack a good authority within ourselves – based on our earliest life experiences of care and control, and our later experiences at work – our capacity for authoritative leadership and also for authoritative followership will be impaired, to the cost both of ourselves as individuals and of our organizations. Without good enough authority, there can only be stronger and weaker, the exercise of power: the parents described in the opening pages of this chapter who resorted to force, the 'really tough manager' who was to whip the recalcitrant team into shape, the distant powers-that-be in the senior echelons of the health service that took Cannon Fields in hand. Inevitably, this is accompanied by loss of idealism and of the possibility of translating our ideals into action.

We need to work with our colleagues to define a shared sense of the core purpose of our work, and we need each to find our own authority to lead or to follow in relation to this vision. Otherwise we will be left with nothing but an exhausting struggle for (or against) 'efficiency', without creativity or energy or meaning.

References

Adair, J. (1983) *Effective Leadership*, London, Sydney and Auckland: Pan Books.

Biggs, S. (1994) 'Failed individualism in community care: an example from elder abuse', *J. Social Work Practice* 8(2): 137–50.

Gabriel, Y. (1996) 'The hubris of management', paper given at Syposium of The International Society for the Psychoanalytic Study of Organizations, New York.

Grubb Institute (1991) 'Professional management', notes prepared by the Grubb Institute on concepts relating to professional management.

Heifetz, R. (1994) *Leadership Without Easy Answers*, Cambridge, MA, and London: The Bellknap Press of the Harvard University Press.

Miller, E.J. (1990) 'Missionaries or mercenaries? Dilemmas and conflicts in voluntary organizations', *The Tavistock Institute of Human Relations 1990 Review*.

—— (1993) 'Power, authority, dependency and change', in *From Dependency to Autonomy: Studies in Organization and Change*, London: Free Association Books.

Obholzer, A. (1994) 'Authority, power and leadership: contributions from group relations training', in A. Obholzer and V.Z. Roberts (eds) *The Unconscious at Work: Individual and Organizational Stress in the Human Services*, London: Routledge.

Rice, A.K. (1963) *The Enterprise and its Environment*, London: Tavistock.

Stokes, J. (1994) 'Institutional chaos and personal stress', in A. Obholzer and V.Z. Roberts (eds) *The Unconscious at Work: Individual and Organizational Stress in the Human Services*, London: Routledge.

Turquet, P. (1974) 'Leadership: the individual and the group', in A.D. Colman and M.H. Geller (eds) *Group Relations Reader 2*, Washington, DC: A.K. Rice Institute Series.

Winnicott, D.W. (1947) 'Hate in the countertransference', in collected papers (1958) *Through Paediatrics to Psychoanalysis*, London: Hogarth Press and the Institute of Psychoanalysis.

5

Psychotic processes and community care

The difficulty in finding the third position

Angela Foster

Introduction

This chapter begins with a description of a woman who is both damaged and damaging. The mental disorder/disturbance felt by this woman generates levels of anxiety that she cannot contain and this is passed on to the others who constitute her community. It is argued that for community care to work, it must be possible within the community system to identify, think about and manage the anxieties that disturbance generates. A model for thinking about community care which encompasses mental illness, carers (including professional carers) *and* the community is described in which these three elements are seen as the corners of a triangular space which theoretically becomes the container of mentally disturbing anxieties. The purpose of this model is to enable workers to forsee some difficulties and to address others in a manner that will lead to greater containment and more effective management of mental illness in the community.

The language of community care, arising from the division between the purchasing and the provision of care, is contractual in nature. To quote Biggs (1991), 'This guiding principle is interesting from a psychodynamic point of view, largely because of the detail of interpersonal thought, feeling and action it leaves out' (1991: 73). It can encourage us to overlook the realities of mental illness, the pain associated with it and the conflicts that it stirs up. If not addressed, these generate more disturbance. Acute anxieties are felt by many workers which, if uncontained, lead to defensive anti-task strategies. When disturbance is projected and disowned, it is put out of mind and may then be passed between parts of the system. Even though it may no longer be possible, except as a short-term measure, to put the mentally ill out of sight in mental hospitals, the mental disturbance and those in whom it is located are all too often marginalized. This has serious implications for the safety of the mentally ill themselves and of their carers. This view is often borne out by advertisements for mental health workers that list as priorities the ability to develop advocacy services and establish centres for information, advice and support. While it is not my intention to devalue such services, I would argue that, on their own, they are inadequate as a means of addressing the needs of users and carers as they effectively overlook the nature of the core task: the very complex and difficult one of dealing with mental disorder and the chaos that it creates.

Chaos surrounding the user in the system

As external consultant to a residential mental health unit, I had the task of facilitating a weekly staff support group. It was in this setting that I heard about Kate, whom I do not know personally although I have known others like her. She grew up in Northern Ireland in a poor Catholic family which was harassed by the RUC. Later she moved to England where both she and her family were again persecuted by the police. She has fits of rage, apparently without any warning. The element of surprise in these attacks and the force accompanying them would appear to leave her unaffected, although the effect on the recipients is devastating. Kate takes the view that the system is unfair and often conspires against her, and that she does not have a mental health problem.

I was struck by a comment made in one group session that her behaviour was typical of people from her social background, and I found myself thinking about her while watching a film about young joyriders in Belfast who epitomized the desire to 'get it out of their system' – 'it' being the hatred and violence that has been the experience of their families for generations. It is important to recognize that people who, like Kate, are the victims of institutionalized oppression, are disproportionately represented in the mental hospital population and that by this measure we, the community, have in the past attempted to get the Kates (this disturbance) out of our system.

Now we are required to care for such people within the community. However, there is little evidence to suggest that the community wants this or is able to think about its implications, let alone what preventative measures we might take. The danger is that what we get is not community care but more stigmatization and marginalization which this time isolates the disturbed victims of these processes in the community rather than outside it, and that for many this amounts to yet greater neglect. The experience of being marginalized, of growing up within a group that is rejected or persecuted by the wider society, leaves its mark. This, depending upon the quality of primary care given to the infant and how this is internalized, can find many different forms of expression including mental and physical ill health. People like Kate, who may be diagnosed as borderline or with a personality disorder, are difficult to manage because they use psychotic mechanisms to rid themselves of intolerable anxieties. O'Shaughnessy (1992) writes: 'In that part of the personality which is psychotic (which to a greater or lesser extent is in everybody) the mind is neither thinking nor perceiving' (1992: 92). Reflection becomes impossible as thoughts have to be got rid of and mental processes are used to this end rather than to further the processes of assimilation and integration. O'Shaughnessy describes her experience with a screaming boy thus: 'I felt shattered by his screams, ruined in the eyes and ears of the household or neighbours, wrong in my approach to him, and if right momentarily, soon wiped out' (1992: 95).

The feelings described here by O'Shaughnessy are similar to those felt by the staff members in the group to whom I was consulting. They certainly felt (unlike Kate) that they had a mental health problem to deal with. That which Kate found intolerable and uncontainable was violently expelled, leaving individual members of staff feeling abused, helpless, inadequate and damaged. But surely, these are also the feelings that Kate would have had if she were able to bear them; as she cannot, she expels them and they become lodged in the staff members. This process, whereby a person rids themselves of intolerable anxieties, is referred to in psychoanalytic literature as projective identification.

It is an occupational hazard that workers in the mental health field working with severely damaged people are on the receiving end of violent projective identification and there is an expectation, often implicit rather than explicit, that they function as effective containers for this. Segal (1986) describes the process in this way:

> When an infant has an intolerable anxiety, he deals with it by projecting it into the mother. The mother's response is to acknowledge this anxiety and do whatever is necessary to relieve the infant's distress. The infant's perception is that he has projected something intolerable into his object, but the object was capable of containing it and dealing with it. He can then reintroject not only his original anxiety but an anxiety modified by having been contained. He also introjects an object capable of containing and dealing with anxiety. The containment of the anxiety by an internal object capable of understanding is a beginning of mental stability.
>
> (Segal, 1986: 134–5)

In the case of psychoanalysis it is the professional rigour of the analyst and the reliability of the setting (the physical and emotional space of the consulting room) which create an environment providing the patient with an opportunity to reintegrate and contain feelings that were previously felt to be unmanageable. In community care, the counterpart of the psychoanalytic setting is the community and the network of care that we establish within it.

Chaos within and between workers in the system

For Kate and those like her, it may well be that internal reality and external reality have both been equally persecuting, and this complicates matters.

However, even those users for whom this is not the case will project their internal reality onto the community/carers and where that internal reality is felt to be unbearable, the process used will be that of violent projective identification as described above. As Menzies' (1959) valuable work on nurse training so clearly and usefully points out, unless anxieties can be identified, addressed and contained within the system, it is likely that the system itself will produce defences that actively hinder rather than help any therapeutic (whole person) intervention. In mental health work, this means that we often stigmatize, marginalize, institutionalize, and dehumanize others (and ourselves) even though we would not wish to do this.

The problem experienced by Kate's carers specifically illustrates this point. As facilitator to the staff group, I did not hear about Kate for some time; what I heard about was how abused, damaged and immobilized some of the staff were feeling. They felt inadequate, rubbished, and were afraid that they would be viewed in this way by their colleagues. This made it very difficult for them to share their experience in the group. Gradually I realized that one particular client, namely Kate, was at the centre of this. I had to struggle with the desire in myself, and I suspect also in the group, to avoid this and to leave well alone, before I could begin to grasp the pieces and seek to put them together in a coherent fashion. Those staff members who had been on the receiving end of one of Kate's outbursts certainly wanted to leave Kate well alone, although this left them feeling inadequate as workers, just as the desire in me to leave well alone left me feeling inadequate as a consultant. 'Leaving well alone' in the group would have meant leaving people with their feelings of fear and inadequacy, i.e. leaving ill alone. However, even this felt preferable to the feared alternative which was that they would seek the help and support of the group but end up with more of the same persecuting treatment, this time at the hands of their colleagues.

Presumably they also feared persecuting treatment from me, and part of my struggle was to find a way to address the issues without being persecuting. I spoke about these fears, suggesting that they were feelings with which everyone in the group could identify and I suggested that to engage in a process of sharing one's work with one's colleagues felt very risky indeed. The risk was that if anyone began to share their disturbed feelings, the disturbance would be passed on from one person to another until someone was identified as the person in whom it could be located and where it could be left. This person would then be identified as the disturbed and vulnerable member of the group. This may be a particularly difficult dynamic for people in the helping professions to bear because of our desire to view ourselves as the well rescuers of the sick and underprivileged. It is our desire to locate our disorder in others that fuels the process.

None of us wants to be the one who is left with the destructive feelings and there is always a temptation to leave them where they have become lodged, identifying them in a personal way with this week's victim. Through this process the disorder that cannot be tolerated by clients is marginalized by them and located in someone else, often a carer, a relative or a professional, who then fears being marginalized by their colleagues and often behaves in such a way that the fear of marginalization becomes a self-fulfilling prophecy. It is easy to see how these processes obstruct cooperation and collaboration.

When we work with severely damaged clients, it can often feel as if there are only two roles on offer, those of the abused and the abuser, or of the damaged and the damager. These same roles are shared among the people constituting the system of care and we fluctuate between the two, sometimes identifying with the abused and sometimes feeling like the abuser. Once one feels locked within such a system there is no space for reflection. The question therefore is: how can the workers in an agency contain the terrifying anxieties that users stir up in and project into individual workers, thus avoiding destructive consequences for both workers and users? One way of attempting to do this is through external consultancy to the staff groups within mental health agencies.

The consultant in the system

The presence of a third party – the consultant – alters the shape of the system from a two-person (client/worker) bi-polar system to a three-person (client/worker/consultant) triangular system. This triangular structure can be thought of as creating a reflective space within which it becomes possible for the projections – in this case the feelings of being abused or abusing, helpless, inadequate and damaged – to be acknowledged, owned and processed. We all have our damaged bits, and the aim of the reflective process is precisely to sort out what belongs to whom so that all concerned might get something of what they need. Users like Kate, who cannot do it for themselves, benefit from being better understood and therefore better contained by the staff group; and workers benefit in that they no longer feel so de-skilled or de-motivated and are therefore able to be of more use to Kate and others like her.

Britton (1989) stresses the importance of finding this third position which 'provides us with a capacity for seeing ourselves in interaction with others and for entertaining another point of view whilst retaining our own, for reflecting on ourselves whilst being ourselves'. He goes on to recognize that there are times when one cannot do this:

> Anyone, however, who has treated a psychotic patient or been involved in a psychotic transference will know what I mean when I refer to times when this seems impossible, and it is at those times that one realizes what it means to lack that third position.

> (Britton, 1989: 87)

Thus, he highlights the difficulty of maintaining the capacity to observe when one feels caught up in a two-person, two-role scenario. Through their weekly meeting with me, the team working with Kate were able to talk about themselves and Kate, to reflect upon the impact she had on them and on how they might manage this. Through this work they were able to think sensitively about Kate without fear of annihilation. This was in contrast to earlier discussions when, in response to the distress of a number of staff members, the manager had felt that the only way to protect the staff from the abuse they were experiencing was to discharge Kate prematurely.

Premature discharge is always an option available to professional carers (if not to the relatives). There are times in residential and day care, for example, when others are at risk, that it may be necessary to implement such a sanction. Once discharged the client might, if plans are made, be picked up by a more appropriate network. However, when the aim of the workers is primarily to rid themselves of an unbearable experience and of responsibility for a difficult person, the client may well fall through the net. In short, the disorder is passed around, pushed out of the localized network of care, instead of being confronted and managed within it (see Chapter 7).

Managing versus managing away: the wider system

In fieldwork, this process is easily reproduced. Kate has relations and she needs help with housing, and one can guess that her social relationships – like her professional ones – are chaotic. She may have a large professional network and a care manager whose job it is to coordinate this. It is not difficult to imagine the extent of the splitting and projection that is likely to be going on within this wider system, with the accompanying risks that the disturbance will not be contained.

Take for example a client who leaves his flat when he is feeling most vulnerable, and incidentally is being most difficult. It is possible for workers from any number of different professions to claim that, as he is now out of their area, he is no longer their responsibility. While this might be legitimate, it is surely not in the spirit of community care. It is an indication that the system has become contaminated by defensive professional practices whereby professionals attempt to distance themselves from anxiety and anger generated by the client's behaviour.

It is not only what clients inject into the system of care that affects workers. The constant change and upheaval in community care legislation and practice also injects anxiety, so that both workers and managers can at times experience their institutions as persecuting rather than supportive. The emphasis on management as monitoring the behaviour of workers, to the detriment of management as processing the feelings and facilitating thinking, devalues the therapeutic skills that are central to the task and leaves staff at all levels in organizations involved in community care feeling anxious. This renders the task of looking after the clients more difficult and can lead to an emphasis on activity and 'doing' to the detriment of reflection and the ability to stay with the client. In essence it feels as if what the client is doing to the worker is duplicated by their own institutions, and the possibility of locating a containing space for third-position thought and reflection appears to be very slim. When this reflective space is missing, then – as we saw in the work with Kate – what is not contained is split off and projected elsewhere.

A theoretical model for thinking about community care

The theory of a triangular model of community care – developed at the Tavistock Clinic by Foster, Grespi and Lousada (see Introduction) – is to enable workers to retain the third position in their thinking about the work. In this theoretical triangle the corners represent mental illness, the carers (both paid and unpaid) and the community. All three elements need to be kept in mind if care in the community is to become a reality. Only when this is done is it possible to find the third position, that is the position from which it is possible to think about the system as a whole and the different relationships within it in order to avoid getting stuck in the dyadic (him/her and me, or us and them mode). If any one of these three aspects is excluded – split off or overlooked – the possibility of finding the third position in our thinking is lost and the system becomes dysfunctional. Through examining the nature of these actual and potential splits, it is possible to identify and even predict the different kinds of difficulties that arise in systems of community care (see Figure 5.1).

(a) Splitting off illness

This occurs when the network of carers and the community collude in splitting off and projecting all the disturbance in a system of care into an identified individual, client or worker. Such a process leads to the *marginalization* of these individuals, as illustrated in the example of Kate and her carers. When a safe reflective space cannot be located within the system of care, the situation continues unchecked and those who become marginalized are blamed for their own fate. Marginalized professional workers and dedicated relatives become burnt out and cease to function while marginalized clients are left without adequate alternative forms of care. Should these clients then become a public nuisance, identified professionals (approved social workers, police and doctors) act on behalf of the community in order to remove the disturbance from public view.

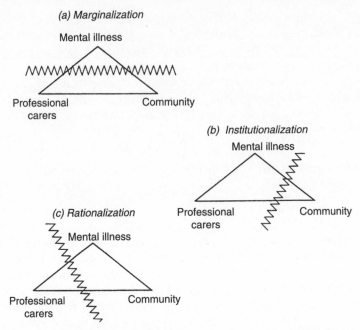

Figure 5.1   A theoretical framework representing the potential difficulties between the three elements involved in community care

(b) Splitting off the community

When the disturbance is removed from public view, as described above, another version of the dysfunctional triangle occurs whereby the community is split off from the mental illness and the carers. This feeds dependence and produces *institutionalization*, which we are used to thinking of as a process that takes place within institutions but which can also occur within the community if the mentally ill and their carers are isolated. We know that many users and carers in such situations are at risk of abuse (see Chapter 9) and that it is precisely these dangers that community care seeks to avoid.

That this situation is also unhealthy for the community is less well appreciated, yet when we (the general public) turn away from disturbed individuals, we are more likely to turn away from our own disturbance and that of those closest to us, with the result that we are slow to recognize when help might be needed.

(c) Splitting off the carers

The third way in which this model can operate dysfunctionally is when we, the community, behave as if we believed it were possible to accommodate the mentally ill in our midst without the need for skilled and experienced carers. Adverts such as the one referred to earlier are indicative of a view that disturbance will disappear provided we give practical support and information to those who suffer. This is a *rationalization* of mental illness: a contradiction in terms. It occurs when we split off the experience of carers who are aware of the complex range of skills that are required in order to care effectively for severely damaged people. This range of skills encompasses skills in forming and maintaining relationships which are therapeutic (and this includes management where appropriate) and in which it is possible to offer a range of services including those of providing practical support and information.

If we ignore the experience of mental health professionals and appoint too many untrained staff to key positions in community care, we are in danger of neglecting the users through creating systems of care that are unable to address their dependency needs. However, the main point about rationalization of mental illness is that it marginalizes the expertise of carers (paid and unpaid) and in this manner fails to support them. As a member of the staff group working with Kate commented, 'We know people do work with psychotic people but they have a system behind them that supports them. How can we do it otherwise?'

Conclusions

These three dysfunctional models exist to a greater or lesser extent at different times in any system of care. They are not mutually exclusive, nor are they the only ways in which community care becomes distorted, but they are an aid to thinking about the nature of the distortions. The triangular model – with mental illness, carers and the community located at the corners – provides us with a basic framework for thinking about what needs to be kept in mind and for reminding us of what we are splitting off or overlooking at any given moment. This is necessary if we are to attempt to deal more effectively and more humanely with those suffering from mental illness in our communities. To keep all three elements in mind is difficult because to do so is uncomfortable (see Chapter 16). However, what matters is that we are intellectually and emotionally able to identify with all the different positions within the trianglar system, albeit not necessarily always simultaneously. This offers the possibility of being engaged in different dyadic relationships, and of standing back to observe and reflect on the nature of the different relationships and on one's own position to them within the total system of care.

Essentially what workers have to do is to place disorder clearly within systems of care and keep the community and themselves in touch both with it and with each other. This is not to assume that all disturbance can or should be contained within the community. Clearly this is not possible. But a team that can locate within it a space in which disturbance can be owned,

tolerated and confronted, and where a range of management and therapeutic skills are valued, becomes a team that is able to think reflectively and
care appropriately. This is what is needed if we are to create anything new
and of value in community care.

References

An earlier version of this chapter appeared under the same title in *J. Social
Work Practice* 7(2), 1993.

Biggs, S. (1991) 'Community care, case management and the psychodynamic
perspective', *J. Social Work Practice* 5(1).

Britton, R. (1989) 'The missing link: parental sexuality in the Oedipus complex', in
R. Britton, M. Feldman and E. O'Shaughnessy *The Oedipus Complex Today*, ed.
John Steiner, London: Karnac Books.

Menzies, I. (1959) 'A case study in the functioning of social systems as a defence
against anxiety: a report on a study of the nursing service of a general hospital',
Human Relations 13: 95–121; reprinted in Isabel Menzies Lyth (1988) *Containing
Anxiety in Institutions*, London: Free Association Books.

O'Shaughnessy, E. (1992) 'Psychosis: not thinking in a bizarre world', in Robin
Anderson (ed.) *Clinical Lectures on Klein and Bion*, London: Tavistock/Routledge.

Segal, H. (1986) *The Work of Hanna Segal: A Kleinian Approach to Clinical Practice*,
London: Free Association Books.

Part II

Managing anxiety in the system

This part looks at some of the structures and systemic defences used to manage the anxieties in mental health work (both inherent task anxieties and 'external' anxieties such as those about resources). How is anxiety passed around? Are current systems managing anxiety or avoiding it?

6

The psychic organization of community care

Jack Nathan

Introduction

This chapter describes psychoanalytic concepts developed by Melanie Klein and demonstrates their use in enhancing our understanding of developments in community care. Although no attempt is made to arrive at preconceived 'answers', a way of thinking is demonstrated that will hopefully illuminate current debates. I will begin by giving a short summary of the Kleinian concepts, and then look at the insights that these can offer at three different levels of practice:

1 the organizational/management level (policy)
2 the level of manager–worker interaction (supervision)
3 the level of worker–client interaction (practice).

Klein's developmental model

If there is a developmental model in Klein's ground-breaking work, then it revolves around her formulations of what she calls the *paranoid–schizoid* and *depressive positions* (Klein, 1946). The 'if' refers to the fact that this model is not ultimately developmental in a chronological sense. Rather, it refers to an essentially existential experience with which every human subject is constantly struggling. There is no once-and-for-all maturing from the paranoid-schizoid to the depressive state.

For Klein a struggle begins at birth with the human infant's attempts to deal with the enormous anxieties stirred by the innate conflict between life and death instincts, and is compounded by the impact of external reality, whether anxiety-producing like the trauma of birth, or the absence of the care-giver when feeling hungry; or life-giving like the love and the food received from the mother or care-giver (Segal, 1964). The infant deals with these conflictual experiences by resorting to paranoid–schizoid defences which produce a *splitting of the object* into 'good' and 'bad' by *projecting* (through projective identification) its hate into the 'bad' object and its love into the 'good' object.

The consequence of this is that the infant feels confronted by a threat to its very existence and is assailed by *persecutory anxiety* (hence the paranoid element) as fear of the death instinct that originates *within* is converted into fear of annihilation from *without*. Aggression then becomes justified as an act of defence, i.e. as a *response* to an external threat. The life-enhancing force (the life instinct), which also originates within the infant, is likewise projected into the object which then is experienced as 'good'. This state of mind is reinforced by positive experiences of being held and fed. Such an object becomes the fount of all that is 'good' and is, almost inevitably, idealized. Almost from birth, then, the infant is seen as having two relationships: one with a terrifying, persecuting object, and another with a benign, all-giving one.

This form of experience is called, in Kleinian terminology, 'part-object relating' since mother is *not* recognized by the infant as the receiver of both the 'good' and 'bad' projections until about the age of 4–6 months when the depressive position begins to be negotiated. In the sense that a chronological dating is given to the onset of the depressive position, Klein's theory has a developmental foundation. However, and probably more importantly, she did not call these experiences 'phases' because the point that she wanted to emphasize is that throughout our lives human beings are oscillating between these two positions, struggling to get beyond a paranoid view of the world to a concern for others where we take more responsibility for the complexity of our feelings and for the consequences of our actions. This struggle corresponds to the depressive position, as the infant comes to the painful realization that the object that he or she hates, and which is seen as the source of all that the infant experiences as a living hell, is the same object that he or she loves, and has experienced as celestial.

The process of recognizing essentially ambivalent feelings towards the same object is a never-ending, arduous one. It begins in infancy and involves what Klein called *depressive anxiety* as the difficult process of integration of formerly fragmented perceptions of the mother takes place. Good and bad part-object relationships are brought together to form a 'whole-object' relationship and the infant pines for the loss of the idealized object and thus experiences the earliest form of mourning. Hinshelwood (1989) explains that depressive anxiety is the core of mature relationships as efforts to mobilize the loving aspect of natural ambivalence are brought into play. Fundamental to the Kleinian paradigm is the view that for the infant, and subsequently the adult, existence takes place in the context of *anxiety*. In the paranoid–schizoid position it is of a persecutory nature, where the object is perceived as being 'out to get you'. In the depressive position it is of a *depressive* kind, as the individual struggles to repair the damage that is wreaked on the (m)other. Essential to a psychoanalytic understanding of maturity, then, is the capacity to acknowledge and thereby contain both loving and hating feelings towards the same object.

I will now turn to look at the way in which these concepts can help us understand some of the dynamics of community care.

Level 1: Policy issues

It hardly needs stating that the purpose of community care is to enhance the quality of the service delivered to the client. The current defects are legion. There are inadequacies in the amount, range and quality of provision of services. There is poor coordination and the size of organizations ensures difficult access to the consumer. The first task, so the argument goes, is to move away from service-led to needs-led provision. The services need to be community based, adopting a comprehensive approach.

These interesting observations do not come from the most recent tranche of policy documents, but from the 1968 Seebohm Report (DHSS, 1968)! That 'community care' are buzz words that have been part of the welfare vocabulary for nearly thirty years does, I think, signal that policy has been formulated and then again reformulated in an attempt to deal with a problem that troubles the 'societal psyche'. It is part of a collective 'repetition compulsion', a term used by Freud (1920) to describe the recurrent resurfacing of unresolved conflict. 'A thing which has not been understood inevitably reappears' (Freud, 1909). In Freudian terminology, resolution comes only as a result of 'remembering' – otherwise repetition is inevitable, a re-staging over and over again.

For Melanie Klein, a final resolution is perhaps never possible. If it were to be possible so far as policy is concerned, then it would be dependent on a maturation in policy beyond the paranoid–schizoid to the depressive position. I hope to show that, for depressive-position functioning, Freud's notion of 'remembering' entails what I call the *principle of consequences*. I will return to this point later.

As with the compulsion to repeat, policy – like history – never repeats itself in exactly the same way as before. One important development in the 1990 NHS and Community Care Act is the introduction of a long-term strategy to change the structure of service delivery, with social service departments being ultimately cast in the role of service purchaser.

At the heart of current community care legislation, then, is the belief that to create a more efficient, appropriate system of provision and to increase user choice, a mixed economy of care has to be developed (HMSO, 1989). This will result in a burgeoning market of providers, flexibly responding to the needs of clients. Social workers are now meant to facilitate this process by undertaking a needs-led assessment of their clients and ensuring that the appropriate service is provided. At the level of policy, a core principle of community care was articulated by the SSI's Chief Inspector in his 1993 annual report (DoH, 1993) when he stated that 'there must be an *unflinching* focus on the needs and preferences of the people who use services and on the best ways of using resources in meeting them'. He went on to say:

'it is also important that agencies do not over-reach themselves or commit resources *beyond what is necessary*'

(emphasis in original).

There is, of course, a profound conflict inherent in these statements since whatever the client requires has to be set against budgetary constraints. This tension has in some authorities resulted in a legal conundrum, in that a statutory duty to provide a service has come up against a lack of resources to carry out this requirement. Thus a community care policy document for the elderly issued by a local authority had to set 'eligibility criteria' stringently drawn in order to ensure 'that the number of people for whom a service must be provided does not exceed the number of people for whom it is financially possible to provide a service'.

It is not part of my argument to suggest that these contradictions can be eliminated. Rather – in psychoanalytic terms – we consciously have to tolerate living with 'the square peg and the round hole'. The fact that they do not always fit makes recognition of their existence all the more imperative. Indeed, I want to claim that these contradictions are an inherent aspect of the depressive position. Like the infant having to hold its ambivalence, policy-makers have to come to terms with their own ambivalent contradictions and therefore face that painful reality. Perhaps resolution is never possible but an awareness of tension is. Acknowledgement of these contradictions does not figure in public policy pronouncements for (I suggest) important, institutionally defended reasons.

Menzies Lyth (1988) has written for many years about social institutions and the kind of defences that they erect. She draws on Klein's view of the way in which we all struggle with anxieties that are either persecutory or depressive and guilt-inducing, and she suggests that within all institutions, individuals have to deal with those deep anxieties specifically related to the conscious intention to improve services for the client. In other words, they have to manage anxieties that relate not only to the external pressures, such as shortage of staff, lack of resources, etc., but also to an internally generated dynamic that causes anxiety. In order to get on with 'the work' in hand, human beings have to deal with what is experienced as the intrusion of persecutory and depressive narratives; or more precisely – because of their often unconscious nature – phantasies. These phantasies take a conscious form when we find ourselves ruminating over questions such as, 'why is my boss not talking to me?' (persecutory anxiety) or 'why didn't I help my client more before she overdosed?' (depressive anxiety).

As I am trying to indicate, in the persecutory state the worker is feeling attacked, i.e. the problem is located in the external environment. In the state of depressive anxiety, the worker is having to deal with feelings of guilt that he or she has damaged the client by not having done more to help. Menzies Lyth goes on to suggest that, as a way of dealing with these extremely difficult feelings, a defensive system is collusively set up which:

1   fragments the 'core problem' so that it can no longer be consciously recognized in its original form,
2   scatters (projects) these fragments into bits of 'the ambience of the job situation' and,
3   then consciously and honestly, but mistakenly, experiences these bits as the problem that something needs to be done about, perhaps invariably by *someone else*.
4   The defensive 'task' is now completed as responsibility is now fragmented and projected into different bits of the environment 'often into unknown others'.

(Menzies Lyth, 1988: 287; my emphasis)

The importance of Menzies Lyth's work is that it purposefully draws our attention to the way in which a collusive system operates, since all parties – practitioners as well as policy-makers – are having to struggle with these anxieties and set up defences against those experiences. Neither are able to contain the inevitable conflicts over need (even where legally defined) and resources.

What is denied and split off, by all parties, is any overt recognition of the *principle of consequences*. This is crucial for an understanding of what constitutes a depressive concern – maturity, in the terms of this paper. Namely, that any behaviour or action has to be instituted with as fully conscious a recognition of the consequences as possible. This ultimately requires having to acknowledge and thereby contain the contradiction of that which, in public policy terms, is *not* being provided. Instead what we get is an essentially paranoid reaction which is most commonly manifested as blame.

In this state of mind, the infant that continues to operate in us all deals with conflictual experiences by a paranoid response; namely, by blaming the (m)other. This tendency is elevated to the sociopolitical level, where policy feeds into a growing culture of blame. Although it is a complex concept, what I want to stress is the way in which parts of our own less palatable self can be disowned and located in other people. Aggression, hatred or our own contradictory ambivalence are key examples. Our experience in this paranoid–schizoid state of mind is that 'someone is out to get me' and this person must be blamed.

Thus to continue our example about public institutions, they are often seen as wasteful of resources, for example by employing staff that are not really needed. It might be possible to identify organizations in this position. The suspicion is all the greater because these public institutions are thought to be outside the marketplace and are funded by the 'beleaguered' tax-payer.

This view of profligate public workers is vital since it helps government, and specifically policy-makers, to shift the burden of responsibility onto managers and practitioners. In its crudest and most often articulated form, 'the problem' then becomes a matter of 'getting rid of the fat', 'becoming more efficient', etc.

For policy-makers to articulate the issues in terms of wasteful local authorities absolves them from having to face their part in not providing the resources and therefore the depressive pain resulting from their (in)actions. Yet financial shortfalls are already having a number of deleterious effects. First, as the Health Committee report (HMSO,1993) suggests, in future community care is increasingly going to be targeted only on those in 'desperate need'. Preventative work, surely a touchstone of any care in the community worth the name, might maintain a user at home and be cheaper in the long run. Yet this has already given way to crisis management. Second, even the government's own wish to see a mixed economy of care provision (HMSO, 1989) is undermined as social service departments are using in-house service providers as they are cheaper (through bulk contracting) than the more individually tailored contracts.

And what of the practitioners? How are they implicated in what Menzies Lyth sees as institutionally structured defences which involve collusion by *all* engaged in the enterprise? In other words, how do practitioners manage their own anxieties? I would suggest that, as a group, they defend themselves against the pain of what they see every day in their practice by blaming the policy-makers. This does not take away their pain. It does, however, help the practitioner to feel absolved of responsibility. After all, it is not their fault that the client cannot cope, but rather the fault of those in positions of authority who are failing to provide the requisite resources. There can be no doubt that what gives this perspective its potency is the sense that, as I have tried to show above, there is some truth in the argument. Hinshelwood (1986) talks of 'hooks' that those projecting can find in the environment to bolster their argument. And yet I think that, within each individual, what is being defended against is a full recognition that they themselves have a responsibility for the client's situation. Such recognition would confront the worker with their own failures toward the client.

What I am wanting to stress is that maturity, associated with depressive anxiety, requires taking account of consequences. For the practitioner this means having to abandon the idealized mother, who is seen as being able to provide for every need. In ordinary parlance, this means recognizing that there are finite resources and that difficult choices have to be made. It is therefore simply not good enough to say that 'more money is needed' without recognizing the consequences – that this involves a cost of some kind to all of us, the client as well as society.

In an imaginative and interesting twist to the argument relating to the dire financial straits that social service departments are in, Croft and

Beresford (1993) suggest that it becomes even more important that people are encouraged to become more directly involved in negotiating the services they want. In terms of this paper, they are putting forward a case that recognizes the constraints, without resort to blaming others, and are attempting to find ways of working that generate positive ideas rather than encouraging inertia.

The DoH's summary of practice guidance states that 'the rationale for this (community care) reorganisation is the empowerment of users and carers' (DoH,1991). Whatever scepticism there might be about the boldness of this statement, it is, as Parsloe and Stevenson (1993) point out, important to recognize that central government is setting an objective by which they and the local authorities can be judged. By making their expectations explicit, they have put themselves in a position in which policy intention and policy outcome can be open to public scrutiny. Clients and practitioners need to rise to this challenge.

Level 2: The supervisory relationship

Relatively little attention has been paid to what effects the changes brought about by community care have on the supervisory relationship.[1] In *Caring for People* (HMSO, 1989) there is an account of the 'roles and responsibilities of Social Service Authorities' with an emphasis on the role of the 'case manager', but nothing on their right to supervision. It is an especially curious omission as, in the arena of child abuse, inquiry reports have found that poor practice may have arisen from inadequate supervision. Indeed, a DHSS review of eighteen reports into the death of children concluded: 'Effective supervision is crucial to supporting and monitoring staff, ensuring the regular and objective review of cases, and securing the best deployment of available resources and staff' (DHSS, 1982: 69–70). This quote summarizes succinctly the two fundamental elements of supervision. These are what I call the 'inquisitorial' function and the 'empathic-containing' function (Rushton and Nathan, 1996). It seems that in child protection work there is at least a theoretical recognition that both have to be attended to. Whatever searching questions the supervisor has to ask (inquisitorial function), he or she has also to address the emotional impact on the worker (empathic-containing function) and which can be ignored only at the cost of poor practice. In the area of work with adult clients, this empathic-containing function seems to be missing.

Yet similar dynamic processes will be taking place in both fields. In a paper that draws attention to the increasing bureaucratization of social work, Howe (1992) argues that there has been a fundamental shift in child abuse work: a 'translation' of the problem away from therapeutically orientated practice towards discourse advanced in terms of judicial and bureaucratic procedures – the checklist approach. In the area of community care for people with mental health problems, there has been a comparable shift towards 'paper work'. The social workers' contribution to community care is now couched in the language of 'assessors' of need, with the clear implication that the task of the social worker is to carry out locally prescribed guidelines which detail what areas have to be considered by the worker, and thereby codify the client's needs.

In such circumstances the team manager/supervisor's task is one of ensuring that the social worker has correctly carried out the guidelines and ensuring that the work done is correctly codified. The manager/supervisor's primary – some might say only – task has become one of designing systems of surveillance and codification. In terms of the supervisory role, there is a growing emphasis on the manager's inquisitorial function, with very little room left for their empathic-containing one.

A number of writers have described this as 'masculinization' of the work, with a move away from the equally important 'feminine' virtues associated with caring (Hearn, 1982; Hugman, 1991). In the terms used in this paper, one possible outcome is that supervision will eventually be separated out so that the line manager will undertake the inquisitorial aspect and the empathic-containing aspect will be seen as part of professional development and may become encapsulated in an external consultant or supervisor.

A Kleinian perspective would suggest that this would be a detrimental move in supervision as it would encourage splitting between what Hinshelwood has called 'the "mother" and "father" parts of the analyst's [supervisor's] mind' (1989: 64). An important, often unconscious, aspect of supervision includes the social worker's need to have an experience of how the supervisor manages the contradictions inherent in the work of being able to be both challenging and concerned. For this is surely what the workers themselves have to do when dealing with clients. This constitutes the modelling aspect of supervision.

Further, and perhaps even more important, the structuring of supervision into separate entities where the inquisitorial, line management work is kept apart from the empathic-containing, 'caring' consultation work, will perhaps inevitably lead to another kind of splitting. Thus the consultant may be experienced as sympathetic and may even be idealized, while all the negative feelings are associated with the line manager.

For the supervisee, this could result in supporting a paranoid kind of relating in which others are seen as unambiguously either good or bad. There will have been little help for the worker to deal with a more painful, complex reality. As part of this process, the social worker is likely to become less able to help the client come to terms with their own depressive anxieties and feelings about the reality of their lives.

Level 3: Practice implications in social work

Changes in the operationalization of community care are having a massive impact on the very nature of social work practice. Most starkly for the practitioner, there is emerging a career choice to be made between resource management and therapeutic work. This too seems to be a false dichotomy, as once more it implies a separation between the 'masculine', information-collating aspect and the 'feminine', caring aspect of the work.

The task of the care manager is to ensure that the individual's needs are assessed and an appropriate package of care designed to fit those needs, the guiding principle being that the clients are at the centre of the service they receive. In a preface to a CCETSW document (Biggs and Weinstein, 1991) this perspective is seen as a 'radical shift' away from a service-led provision: 'The new approach should ensure that users will only receive therapy as part of their care package ... *if they agree to it being provided'* (Biggs and Weinstein, 1991: 5; emphasis in original). Once more we can hear the importance that is being placed on listening to the client – the oldest of case-work principles, or – in the language of today – 'client empowerment'.

However, Biggs (1991) has taken issue with such a simplistic view of client and worker together 'finding an agreeable solution to a mutually agreed definition of need' (1991: 73). He argues that the relationship cannot be assumed to be an equal one since the worker has access to resources that the client needs. The rationalist, checklist world assumes no conflict of interest between the two parties and therefore a package of care is there to be objectively and jointly arrived at. But such a perspective takes no account of assessment work as a process taking place in the context of a relationship that requires time to build up, has to deal with the differences of power, conflicts of interest, and has to take unconscious motivation into account.

We can see that a client may experience difficulties, for example, not wanting to discuss the loss of a particular function and therefore denying a need for a relevant home aid. But the worker also brings their own unconscious agenda. Perhaps the one that will be most familiar to us all is the need to be 'helpful'. In this situation, the client might be forced to accept help – even to be case-worked – when what the worker might have difficulty in confronting in themselves is their own sense of not being able to help, i.e. impotence or simply rejection by the client. This again highlights the importance of a properly conducted supervision. Where the client is denying some kind of loss, we are confronted with a professional and even ethical dilemma which the recitation of the mantra of client empowerment does not address.

In their book *Community Care and Empowerment*, Parsloe and Stevenson (1993) make plain the ethical dilemmas that can arise between the client's right to autonomy on the one hand and their need for protection on the other. They are reminding us that, however long overdue is the need to take seriously the voice of the client as fundamental to any process of assessment, the practitioner also has a moral responsibility to weigh up that which the client may refuse to consider – denial of painful realities that could endanger the client, their family or any member of the public. The 'reflective practitioner' (Schon,1987) cannot avoid having to take responsibility for weighing up the ethical issues as part of the assessment process. Indeed, to do otherwise would constitute an abdication of the client's (and the agency's) right to a professional service based on the practitioner's knowledge and expertise. In the language of Klein, depressive anxiety functioning requires that the worker live with their own doubt and yet sometimes carry out actions to which the client is opposed. Ultimately, this means having to deal with being wrong. In the area of a paranoid kind of relating, the 'service user' is idealized and a collusion is constructed that denies any difficulties in the worker–client relationship. Any problems can then be projected into known or unknown others, such as senior management.

Conclusion

If social work is to remain an activity that takes a holistic account of the client's needs for practical assistance, as well as a process where the practitioner can reflect on the underlying dynamics (in themselves and the user), this requires analysis, debate and action.

In what seemed a timely and considered report on the care and treatment of Christopher Clunis (a man with a schizophrenic illness well known to the mental health services who killed an innocent bystander in a public place), interesting conclusions were reached in the light of the issues discussed in this chapter (Ritchie, 1994). It makes clear that what is required for care in the community of the mentally ill is both a 'considerable injection of funds' to meet the deficiencies identified *and* better practice among professionals. It is hoped that the latter problem will be addressed through the development of community mental health teams (see Chapter 11).

There are choices to be made but they do not *have* to be made, in the sense that there is no prima-facie obligation to enhance care in the community. However, in the context of this chapter, mature functioning requires that – whether as policy-maker or practitioner – we take responsibility for our decisions or lack of them.

Note

1 A recent exception to this is Hughes and Pengelly (1997).

References

Biggs, S. (1991) 'Community care, case management and the psychodynamic perspective', *J. Social Work Practice* 5: 71–81.

Biggs, S. and Weinstein, J. (1991) *Assessment, Care Management and Inspection in Community Care*, London: CCETSW.

Croft, S. and Beresford, P. (1993) 'Practice: user involvement', *Community Care* 11 March.

DHSS (1968) *Report of the Committee on Local Authorities and Allied Personal Social Services*, London, HMSO.

—— (1982) *Child Abuse: A Study of Inquiry Reports 1973–1981*, London: HMSO.

DoH (1991) *Care Management and Assessment: Summary of Practice Guidance*, London: HMSO.

—— (1993) *The Chief Inspector's Annual Report 1992–1993*, London: HMSO.

Freud, S. (1909) 'Analysis of a phobia in a five-year-old boy', *Standard Edition* 10: 3–149.

—— (1920) 'Beyond the pleasure principle', *Standard Edition* 18: 3–64.

Hearn, J. (1982) 'Notes on patriarchy, professionalization and the semi-professions', *Sociology* 16: 184–202.

Hinshelwood, R.D. (1986) 'A dual materialism', *Free Associations* 4: 36–50.

—— (1989) *A Dictionary of Kleinian Thought*, London: Free Association Books.

HMSO (1989) *Caring for People*, HMSO: London.

—— (1993) *Health Committee Report on Community Care: The Way Forward*, vol.1, London: HMSO.

Howe, D. (1992) 'Child abuse and the bureaucratisation of social work', *Sociological Review* 38: 491–508.

Hughes, L. and Pengelly, P. (1997) *Staff Supervision in a Turbulent Environment: Managing Process and Task in Front-line Services*, London: Jessica Kingsley.

Hugman, R. (1991) 'Organisation and professionalism: the social work agenda in the 1990s', *British J. Social Work* 21:199–216.

Klein, M. (1946) 'Notes on some schizoid mechanisms', in *The Writings of Melanie Klein*, vol. 3: 1–24.

Menzies Lyth, I. (1988) 'A psychoanalytic perspective on social institutions', in E. Bott Spillius (ed.) *Melanie Klein Today, Vol. 2: Mainly Practice*, London: Routledge.

Parsloe, P. and Stevenson, O. (1993) *Community Care and Empowerment*, London: Joseph Rowntree Foundation.

Ritchie, J.H. (Chair) (1994) *Report of Inquiry into the Care and Treatment of Christopher Clunis*, London: HMSO.

Rushton, A. and Nathan, J. (1996) 'The supervision of child protection work', *British J. Social Work* 26: 357–73.

Schon, D.A. (1987) *Educating the Reflective Practitioner*, San Francisco, CA: Jossey Bass.

Segal, H. (1964) *Introduction to the Work of Melanie Klein*, New York: Basic Books.

7

Thinking about risk

Angela Foster

Introduction

What do we understand by risk in the mental health business? Like any other member of the community, we think about risks to the general public; as professionals, we think of the danger that we face in the course of our work, and of the risk to the mentally ill themselves which we are in danger of overlooking at times when 'moral panic' takes hold of attitudes to mental illness in the community. Part of the overall task of caring for the mentally ill in the community is to hold, to assess, to monitor and to manage risk, and on the basis of this work to make informed decisions regarding the lives of our clients.

As Davis (1996) points out, there is an element of risk assessment in most aspects of the work, from decisions that affect an individual's liberty and the amount of support they receive, to policy decisions about the provision of resources. We can only make these assessments if we are able to acknowledge the reality of risk and to consider our responses to it. Davis (1996) identifies two such responses as those of risk minimization and risk-taking, and argues that 'Risk-taking is ... an essential element of working with mental health service users to ensure autonomy, choice and social participation. It is a means of challenging the paternalism and over protectiveness of mental health services' (1996: 114). Paternalism and over-protectiveness are characteristics of the risk minimization position evident in policies of care programming (CPA), care management, follow-up on discharge from hospital (S117 Mental Health Act 1983) and supervision registers (DoH, 1994) which, if we are not careful, may lead to unnecessary restrictions being placed on the liberty of those identified as being a risk to others and to themselves. This in turn limits the possibility of integrating the mentally ill in their communities. We have to find a middle road between being over-cautious by unnecessarily limiting our own and our clients' experiences, and being cavalier by putting ourselves and others in too much danger.

This chapter is a difficult one to write. The difficulty is not due to a shortage of thoughts on the subject but to a difficulty in structuring these thoughts. I want to pass on my thoughts in a way that is logical rather than chaotic, and I do not want to achieve this by leaving out those bits that do not easily fit, i.e. I do not want to have a logical plan at the expense of half the truth. I suggest that this is a difficulty that one might anticipate when the subject on our minds is *risk* of violence, mental breakdown, medical abuse (for example, over-use of drugs and other physical treatments), suicide or public condemnation, because these issues make us anxious and it becomes hard to keep the full picture in mind. When we feel anxious, we are tempted to rush into action (for example, to write without a plan), or to rid ourselves of those thoughts that 'do not fit' by a process of rationalization in order that our equilibrium may be restored.

Mental disturbance in any of us makes us emotionally and behaviourally unpredictable. There is no formula or government policy that is going to eliminate either risk or mental disorder, although some debates would suggest that this might be possible if only we could devise a way of more effectively monitoring the behaviour of the mentally ill and of the professionals who care for them. Such a view is an example of how we are tempted both to rush into action and to forget (or leave out) those things that we know, when knowing them is uncomfortable or inconvenient, or both. As such it is an example of mental disturbance within our society.

There are risks to workers, to clients and to the general public in the liberal and relatively unbounded and unstructured setting of the community, and my focus is on how anxiety about risk is handled. While we aim to avoid the extreme caution exercised in keeping the identified mentally ill hidden away in 'out of town' psychiatric hospitals, are we in fact finding other ways of putting disorder out of mind?

It is my contention that an unspoken but powerful expectation is placed on professionals whose job it is to care for the mentally ill in the community: that they will make mental illness disappear, either by curing the clients or by making them invisible. I propose that the real task of professionals in mental health work is to do what highly anxious and disturbed people, communities or systems cannot do: that is, to think while keeping in mind the disturbing and conflicting aspects of the situation. In order to illustrate what I mean by this, I will take examples from a range of practice settings (see also Chapters 5, 13 and 16). These examples are mainly ones where those who suffer from mental illness are seen as putting others at risk and although, in reality, those most at risk are the mentally ill themselves, I have chosen these examples because they are the sort of examples that make news and which therefore attract the most attention and ultimately inform policy.

Residential care

Many workers in community care want to provide their clients with something more humane than long-stay hospital care could provide. They also hope that they can make much of the illness disappear. Their commitment to their clients is impressive, yet there is a danger that the clients become idealized and that their destructiveness, and therefore the risks, are not taken into account. Workers hope that their clients will blossom and flourish in the community, and indeed some do. But if one subscribes to this 'horticultural' model of care (Miller and Gwynne, 1972; see also Chapter 3) without paying adequate attention to the limitations of the clients, the situation can become dangerous. While some clients flourish, others behave abominably.

One such client in a small residential unit in the community started a fire. Fortunately no one was hurt, but it had been a very near miss and many lives had been at stake. Staff brought this situation for discussion in a clinical meeting. They began by talking about whether or not it was possible to continue working with this woman. They experienced great conflict between their fear and rage towards her for abusing them, which made them want to get rid of her, and their hope that they could find a way of keeping her in their care, as they had promised her on her admission to the unit when she was told that this was a home for life.

This particular unit aimed to empower residents by offering them considerable freedom to live as they wished, and although the woman in question was very demanding and staff often felt annoyed with her, they had mixed feelings about restricting her. As a result, she constantly tested the limits by increasing her demands. Clients who have long histories of psychotic illness with an accompanying personality disorder can be the most difficult to manage, precisely because they are so demanding. They are so anxious to get rid of unwanted bits of themselves through projection that they end up feeling empty and desperately hungry; but their hunger, which feels insatiable, is not for our therapeutic work in the form of our talking to them about their behaviour, which they find persecuting, but for practical evidence of our continuing ability to care for them despite their difficult behaviour. Although they do not request that we curb their activities, they are also desperate in their need to feel 'held' in a manner that enables them to feel safe from their own destructive impulses. How are staff to do this within a liberal regime based on ideas of empowerment?

I invited the staff to talk about this client and how she had behaved prior to this arson attack. On hearing about her increasingly demanding, disrespectful and ungrateful behaviour, I wondered aloud if they ever felt like 'killing her'. 'Oh yes,' was the reply from the manager of the residential unit, as if it was a great relief to have permission to acknowledge this; and her response, of course, gave permission to others to express their own anger. Once the murderous feelings (which the client could not consciously own, but which she engendered in her workers even prior to this event) could be owned and acknowledged by her carers, the group could begin to think about their client and to piece together what they knew of her history.

This same client had a male friend who lived in another residential project. Much of her difficult behaviour had been around ever-increasing demands that she should have the financial and practical freedom to visit him and stay with him, and for him to stay with her, in spite of clear indications that too much contact between these two people led to violence in their relationship. In other words, for their own safety, these two people needed to limit their intimacy, yet the female partner could not do this for herself. As the discussion went on, it emerged that her friend had seriously threatened the life of his ex-wife. Clearly there was more risk in this situation than the workers had at first been willing or able to acknowledge. For the first time in the course of this discussion, the full horror of what might have happened could be thought about. The staff were able to feel relief that this time no one had been hurt, while realizing the enormity of the task that confronted them if they were to provide ongoing care for this woman and indirectly for her male friend.

Clearly staff needed to think carefully about their policies in order to put timely and effective limits on the destructive behaviour of clients who were unable to do this for themselves. This necessitated finding a balance between policies of permissiveness and of social control, taking the view that individual freedom needs to be accompanied by an individual sense of responsibility; where this is lacking, freedom may need to be curbed for the safety of all concerned.

Part of the difficulty for residential staff is that they are not always provided with the information about a client's history that they would need in order to make a full risk assessment prior to the client's admission. Often, particularly in the case of people who have been hospitalized for many years, this information is not readily available; but it is also the case that, at times, information is withheld from residential staff in the belief that if it were made available admission would be refused. Residential staff are under considerable pressure to take people who are known to be very difficult, and become concerned about whether a social service department will cease to purchase their care should they appear to become 'too fussy' about who they will take or 'too fussy' about insisting that they can only admit 'difficult' people at times when their current residents are relatively settled. While we need to concern ourselves about defensive practice – only taking the 'easy' clients – we should also applaud good risk assessment that takes into account not only the history of the client but also the capacity of the environment to cope with disturbance and the level of anxiety generated by it. A further concern arises if a residential unit refuses admission to someone when apparently there is no better equipped alternative resource available. Bed and breakfast accommodation, which may be the only remaining option, is clearly inadequate in such a situation.

Day care

A female user of a therapeutic day care unit was discharged because she had broken the rules by threatening violence. This is an example of the way that agencies put limits on individual freedom in order to protect the safety of the setting. The provision of a safe setting, and our willingness to ensure that it remains safe, provides the basis for our therapeutic work. Without this, our efforts will be in vain.

In the following few months the day centre was broken into several times. Each time the break-in was more violent in its nature and more destructive in its consequences. Staff and users of the centre felt that 'someone was out to get them' – to intrude into their space and violate it. The cost of the damage, in financial terms, put severe strains on an already stringent budget.

In supervision sessions with the staff I heard about these events, about the enormous degree of distress felt by both staff and clients and about how the situation was being managed week by week. I wanted to suggest that the suspended woman might have something to do with the break-ins but I was given very clear messages by the staff group that, as there was no evidence against her, it was not possible to pursue this line of inquiry. Instead, discussion focused on how to continue the service to clients in the face of such monstrous attacks.

However, I persisted, not least because it is unhealthy if people feel that they are not free to voice what is in their minds and I was fairly confident that, while I was made to feel as if I was the only 'unreasonable' person prepared to suspect (and, by inference, condemn) the suspended client, others, including other clients, had similar thoughts which they dared not express. In fact it may well have been a more difficult situation for some clients (who had friendships with, who identified with and who empathized with the woman who was suspended) than it was for me. It was also important to note the extreme lengths that someone had gone to in order to 'get inside the centre' and thereby to ensure that they would be talked about.

I was reminded of a situation that occurred in a therapeutic community where I worked many years ago (see Hinshelwood and Grunberg 1979). On three separate occasions, someone started a fire in the occupational therapy department during the time when all staff were in their weekly support group and therefore unavailable to supervise clients' activities. Apparently no one had any idea who was responsible for the fires and, whilst we were not afraid to speculate in the staff group or to raise it for discussion in community meetings, we still had no clear indication as to who the perpetrator might be. We therefore took the view that this behaviour was split off from the consciousness of the person concerned and from the consciousness of the community as a whole. This suggested to us that the community had become fragmented and that we needed to do something to foster greater integration. We set aside time for a community psychodrama in which we recreated the scene where the fires were started. We then invited everyone present to imagine that they were the person starting the fire and to tell the others why they would want to burn the place down. Not surprisingly, we could all think of reasons that we hated the place and the psychodrama progressed to the point when the perpetrator was able to get in touch with that aspect of herself that had previously been put out of her mind; she became distressed and confessed to what she had done.

The theory behind this is the assumption that it is only by owning the split-off bits of ourselves that we are able to be in touch with our destructiveness and to enable others to be in touch with theirs. Prior to the psychodrama, we all had a vested interest in locating our destructive feelings towards the community in one unknown person who was starting the fires. People with a psychotic illness are prone to split off awareness of things that feel uncomfortable; they then become available receptacles for the projections of others. This unconscious dynamic of splitting off and projecting feelings of rage and murderousness increases the disturbance of those who are already unstable, and increases the likelihood that those who are prone to violence will act violently.

In thinking about this situation in relation to the predicament of the day centre I saw my task, as their supervisor, to enable staff to become *less reasonable*. They needed space to be angry about the attacks on the centre and on their therapeutic work, and also to acknowledge their own anger at the centre itself for whatever injustices they individually felt had been done to them. Over time, it was possible for the staff to own their suspicions (not least because, as the attacks continued, it became increasingly difficult not to). Once this happened they could talk more openly with their clients and piece together bits of evidence. The task then was to think about how to manage and contain the suspended woman. Unless a way could be found of curbing her behaviour, she was at risk of going to prison, others were at risk of being attacked, and the day centre was at risk of closing its service. The manager averted these dangers through negotiation with senior managers who then took legal action which prevented any more acting out, thereby protecting both the perpetrator and the victims of the violent behaviour, and through this means it was possible for the staff of the day centre to return to their therapeutic work. However, with reference to the dynamics of the situation it is important to note that initially the senior managers (like the staff) had been reluctant to intervene. I will return later in this chapter to the role of the organization in managing risk.

Primary health care

A general practitioner (GP) had a female patient who would frequently take to her bed. Whenever she did so, her husband would request that the GP make a home visit. However, when the GP responded to these requests she was unable to find any signs of illness that made it necessary for the patient to be in bed or indeed for her to be doing a home visit. She felt angry at having been called out because, as far as she could see, there was nothing seriously wrong with her patient. In spite of this, she always left this home with very uneasy feelings, feeling that there was more to this situation than met the eye, but also feeling helpless.

All the medical evidence suggested that there was little wrong with her patient; it was *only* her feelings that suggested otherwise. She might have concluded that, while there might be nothing seriously wrong with her patient, there seemed to be something seriously wrong in her home; but she did not. Instead she put the uneasy feelings to the back of her mind. Steiner (1985) refers to this state of mind as one of 'turning a blind eye'.

On a subsequent home visit, the patient's husband said that he could take no more of this and gestured that he would kill himself if the situation did not change. The GP felt even more helpless and useless. Soon after, the husband killed himself. After his death, his widow spoke for the first time about their unbearable sado-masochistic marriage.

Not all unrecognized mental illness results in such dramatic consequences but nevertheless it does mean that people's lives are impoverished. Goldberg and Huxley (1980: 85–6), referring to research on 'hidden psychiatric morbidity', note that 'for every two patients recognised by the family doctor (Dr Blackwell), a third psychiatric patient could be identified by a research psychiatrist (Dr Goldberg)'. They also note that:

> In a more experimental study, Johnstone and Goldberg (1976) showed that if a family doctor was made aware of these hidden illnesses, then the patients were more likely to get better quickly, and would have fewer symptoms when seen at follow up a year after their initial consultation.
> (Goldberg and Huxley, 1980: 85–6)

They make the point that GPs are most likely to miss 'psychiatric morbidity' in patients who themselves hide it, that is patients who only talk to their doctor about physical symptoms unless specifically requested to do otherwise. In a poignant example they quote a female patient saying 'Why should I tell the doctor such things – how can he treat a profound sense of loneliness and isolation?' (ibid.: 86). In a six-month follow-up from her psychiatric treatment, she talked about her life having completely changed. Remarkably, even her breast abscess had healed for the first time in fifteen years.

I want to suggest that both these examples – one of mental illness that remained undetected until a death occurred and the other that was detected through a research project – illustrate how patients can be a cause of great concern to their GPs and other primary health professionals yet at the same time seek to hide their emotional distress from them. It is not uncommon for people to feel ashamed of their feelings and desires. This shame, which cannot be put into words because that would be to expose it, is nevertheless communicated but the communication is unconscious. The professional worker then responds unconsciously with an unspoken agreement that the distress felt by both parties will not be the subject of open enquiry. In fact, the underlying feeling is that it *must not* be spoken about. It is as if such patients believe that the disaster of living with the situation is easier to bear than the disaster that they are afraid will occur if their distress is made known – 'better the devil you know'.

When we find ourselves in such situations, in which we *feel* uncomfortable but, because we have no clear evidence, we *think* that there is nothing we can do, we may choose to 'turn a blind eye', adopting an attitude of 'out of sight, out of mind'. We support this defence by busying ourselves with other things: things that enable us to feel more in control, more competent and more useful. It is also the case that if something is out of our minds, it is likely to be out of our sight. In other words, if we are not thinking about the possible dangers in a situation, then we may well not see the danger signs.

Fieldwork

The GPs referred to in the previous section knew their patients well. Risk assessment is made even more difficult when one is meeting someone for the first time – as many mental health professionals do – either in their own agencies or in clients' homes. Even if the client is not 'new', the worker may be. It is unfortunate that junior doctors (and, to a lesser extent, other trainees) who provide treatment for people with long-term illnesses are only able to offer this over a short period of time because their training requires them to change their place of work at frequent intervals.

Davis (1996: 117) states that 'Aids to risk work such as risk minimization checklists are only adjuncts to lengthier more detailed and time consuming work which is focused on getting to know an individual and building trust and confidence over time.' Landau and Wallbank (see Chapter 14) argue the benefits of care managers retaining provider functions in order that they can develop close relationships with their clients. They also point out the advantages of working with clients suffering from severe and/or enduring mental illness in mixed groups where they benefit from this in that they are less likely to feel 'ghettoized' with other seriously ill people and over-identified with their illnesses.

It is likely that workers also benefit from mixed caseloads. A major difficulty in having a caseload consisting largely of people with psychotic illnesses is that one is so often on the receiving end of a particular form of transference described here by the psychoanalyst Hanna Segal:

> The psychotic tries to project into the analyst his terror, his badness, his confusion, his fragmentation and, having done this projection, he perceives the analyst as a terrifying figure from whom he may want to cut himself off immediately; hence the brittleness of the transference situation.
>
> (Segal, 1986: 134)

We can see from this how difficult it is to remain in contact with and emotionally open to such clients, and workers will find a number of ways of defending themselves. To limit one's involvement because one's post is short-term is one way. To engage in defensive practice, ensuring that all the procedures are carried out while suspecting that one is avoiding client contact, is another.

The people who cannot know in advance what they will face are those who are called out to deal with particularly threatening situations, for example workers from community mental health teams (approved social workers, psychiatrists, community psychiatric nurses), police and outreach workers. Clients who have a dual diagnosis of psychotic illness and substance misuse are particularly volatile and unpredictable. Workers in these situations run the risk that they become too familiar with high-risk situations and the danger is that they deal with the continual high level of anxiety this generates by becoming omnipotent, shrugging off the danger and adopting what some workers have identified as a 'macho' defence.

Discussion

We can all identify situations in our own lives in which we choose to 'turn a blind eye' to those aspects that do not seem to fit, that do not make sense, and which make us feel uneasy. In a horrific killing, Christopher Clunis, a man suffering from paranoid schizophrenia, attacked a stranger, stabbing him in the eye. We could not find a more powerful example of how persecuting it is for someone as disturbed as Clunis was to be *seen* and yet how important it is that those of us in the caring professions should not 'turn a blind eye' to their increasing levels of distress. The Ritchie Report (Ritchie, 1994) provides detailed accounts of professional involvement with Clunis, indicating how easy it is to lose touch with clients like this and therefore how important it is that workers create effective systems of care by communicating their concerns with each other, rather than putting them to the back of their minds.

When we fail to do this, we are gambling with fate in the hope that we will win. We opt to take a chance that the situation will either resolve itself or in some other way indicate to us that our worries were unfounded. In many instances we are lucky and we breathe a sigh of relief, but nothing has been learned. We can also note that often those times when we prefer *not* to think are the times when we are wanting to avoid the feelings that would accompany the thinking. At such times we resort to defensive strategies to deal with our anxiety. The situations described above all teach us something about the defensive strategies that we sometimes employ in order to feel better in frightening situations. The problem is that when we employ these defences, instead of reducing the risk to others and to ourselves, we increase it:

• We may *idealize the client, and 'play rescuer'*.
• We may *deny what we suspect, locating the destructiveness elsewhere*.

- We may *turn a blind eye.*
- We may *become omnipotent and 'play macho'.*
- We may *adhere strictly to the rules and 'play bureaucrat'.*

It is evident that these formulations are not clearly distinct, nor are they mutually exclusive, but they are pointers to some of the traps into which we can fall. A consequence of these defences is that important information remains locked away, either in people's minds or in files. Either way, it is unavailable when it is most needed, and even when information is available we may still defend ourselves from the anxiety it stirs up by resorting to a manic defence. I presented an earlier version of this paper as the last speaker at a conference on risk and noted that, as the day wore on, the mood of the conference changed from being fairly calm to being full of laughter. The impact of this was such that I began my presentation by making reference to the manic mood in the room and linking this with the anxiety generated by a day in which we had all been asked to *think in detail* about risk.

Structural and organizational support

As workers with people with mental illness, we need to keep in sight and in mind as much as we can. We need to be consciously aware of the signals coming from others and from ourselves, and to be prepared to struggle with the apparent inconsistencies. We need to be alerted by the voice inside us saying 'don't be silly' or 'be silly' at times when we are feeling anxious, so that instead of responding by turning away, we attend to our feelings with greater respect. In other words, we need to find a mental space inside ourselves and a physical space outside ourselves where it is possible to see and to consider what is going on inside us and around us.

We can all identify circumstances in which it feels impossible to do this: when we are very busy, rushing from one thing to another, when the office is so chaotic that it becomes impossible to think and when we feel surrounded by so much disturbance that it feels quite impossible to consider anything. These are the times when we are most at risk. Policies and procedures can be useful structures for thinking, provided that they are used to this end. Supervision that encourages reflection is vital to effective risk work, but this too can be hard to find (see Chapter 6) . It is important to own personal authority in the work, yet policies that appear to be constantly checking up on the worker undermine this. At times we may even feel tempted to act against our own better judgement in order to say 'I told you so' when a crisis arises.

Front-line workers often complain about lack of adequate support from their organizations. Ryan (1996: 103–4) describes this conflict in the following statement: 'The philosophy of empowering service users which is present in most health and social care arenas is often incongruous with the nature of larger organisations. Since a significant proportion of mental health services are provided by statutory organisations with risk-averse cultures this can create ambivalence for practitioners.' He concludes that 'Support for practitioners through clear risk management policies and a commitment to system analysis rather than scapegoating is (also) a key component of effective risk management'.

Carson (1994) identifies four tasks of managers, which are to provide front-line workers with training, information, monitoring and 'a framework for making their decisions which promises to support those who follow their policies, even if harm results'.

When the external environment is able to provide us with opportunities for developing good relationships with managers and colleagues, long-term relationships with clients, and effective inter-agency collaboration, then we are able to *think about risk* and to take decisions that are responsive to the changing needs of individual clients. While not seeking to eliminate risk, we can seek to reduce it, at the same time taking calculated risks that provide our clients with greater freedom and therefore more opportunity for integration in their local communities.

References

Carson, D. (1994) 'Dangerous people: through a broader conception of "risk" and "danger" to better decisions', *Expert Evidence* 3(2): 51–69; quoted in 'Risking legal repercussions', in H. Kemshall and J. Pritchard (eds) (1996) *Good Practice in Risk Assessment and Risk Management 1*, London: Jessica Kingsley.

Davis, A. (1996) 'Risk work and mental health', in H. Kemshall and J. Pritchard (eds) *Good Practice in Risk Assessment and Risk Management 1*, London: Jessica Kingsley.

DoH (1994) *Introduction of Supervision Registers for Mentally Ill People from 1 April 1994*, Health Service Guidelines (HSG (94) 5), London: HMSO.

Goldberg, D. and Huxley, P. (1980) *Mental Illness in the Community: The Pathway to Psychiatric Care*, London: Tavistock.

Hinshelwood, R.D. and Grunberg, S. (1979) 'The large group Syndrome', in R.D. Hinshelwood and N. Manning (eds) *Therapeutic Communities: Reflections and Progress*, London: Routledge and Kegan Paul.

Mental Health Act (1983) London: HMSO; see also M. Mandelstam and B. Schwehr (1995) *Community Care Practice and the Law*, London: Jessica Kingsley.

Miller, E.J. and Gwynne, G.V. (1972) *A Life Apart: A Pilot Study of Residential Institutions for the Physically Handicapped and the Young Chronic Sick*, London: Tavistock.

Ritchie, J.H. (Chair) (1994) *Report of the Inquiry into the Care and Treatment of Christopher Clunis*, London: HMSO.

Ryan, T. (1996) 'Risk management and people with mental health problems', in H. Kempshall and J. Pritchard (eds) *Good Practice in Risk Assessment 1*, London: Jessica Kingsley.

Segal, H. (1986) *The Work of Hanna Segal*, London: Free Association Books.

Steiner, J. (1985) 'Turning a blind eye: the cover up for Oedipus', *Int. J. Psycho-anal.* 12: 161–72.

8

The pain of managing

The dynamics of the purchaser/provider split

Tony McCaffrey

The NHS and Community Care Act has had an enormous impact on the health service, social services and voluntary organizations through the creation of a purchaser/provider split and the need for contracting arrangements. To quote Simon Biggs:

> As one would expect from a method rooted in the free enterprise culture of the US and the project to turn the British Welfare State into a mixed economy, case management assumes a marketplace model of interpersonal relationships – that is to say a meeting of two equal individuals coming together to agree a bargain on the exchange of goods and services. This guiding principle is interesting from a psychodynamic point of view, largely because of the detail of interpersonal thought feeling and action it leaves out. It proposes a vision of single persons rationally in possession of relevant information and a cool grasp of their own motivation, finding an agreeable solution to a mutually agreed definition of need.
>
> (Biggs, 1991: 73; see also Chapter 6)

So what are the consequences in terms of the services of the public sector? And in particular, how are the managers in the various organizations coping with and making sense of this new culture? My sense of some of the issues emerging for public sector managers can be illustrated by reference to an example drawn from some consultancy work that I undertook with a large NHS Trust.

Case study

I was commissioned by the directors of a large health trust to carry out a series of workshops with service managers, that tier of managers responsible for the service units that deliver the medical and mental health services of the trust. They were worried that the service managers as a group seemed to be unable to meet the budgetary targets that each had been set, a failure that threatened the success of the purchasing/providing system that comprised the framework within which the trust operated. In essence the trust seemed to be faced with bankruptcy. It was agreed that the work would be undertaken by myself as an external consultant, with an internal consultant as a partner.

The broad aim of the initial workshops was diagnostic. They were designed to try to understand what made the job of the service manager so stressful and difficult, in order that their development needs could then be addressed. But we also had in mind the question of 'Why the service managers?' What did their dissatisfaction and 'failure' mean in the context of the wider system?

Two groups of service managers each attended two afternoon workshops. In the first of the two afternoons, the focus was on exploring the managers' experience of their task and identifying the issues that got in the way of effective working. In the second afternoon, the focus was on identifying the issues around the roles and responsibilities of the service managers. Attendance at these workshops was not compulsory.

Some of the themes that emerged were as follows.

Stress

The service managers exhibited a high degree of stress. They linked this to the ambiguity of their tasks and roles, and the organizational structure in which they found themselves. They were not sure what to do, or how to do it in an organization that seemed to be constantly changing. They felt themselves constantly running just to stay in place. Crucially, they feared that they could lose their jobs at any moment. This made it difficult for them to commit themselves fully to the task of the workshops, and it manifested itself in a collective touchiness about what was felt to be the self-exposure demanded by the workshop task. They gave a sense of being at the end of their tethers. In other words, the workshops themselves added to the stress.

Mistrust

They exhibited a high degree of mistrust of and cynicism about managerial superiors. For example, there was considerable scepticism about the workshops themselves, and anger about what was perceived as a 'three-line whip' to ensure their attendance. Although attendance was ostensibly voluntary, in effect they felt coerced. There was hostility towards and suspicion of both consultants. We were seen as lackeys of the persecutory higher management. The in-coming new chief executive appeared to recognize that the service managers had been labouring in a culture of blame in which mistakes were punished, and in which the greatest sin was to be seen to be not coping. This climate produced herculean but unfocused efforts by the service managers, and involved them exhausting themselves by working an inordinate number of hours to try to keep their sinking ships afloat. A statement by the chief executive that was intended to be wholly positive, and to recognize the struggle that the service managers had had to deal with – 'I now want to see you *managing, not just coping!*' – was routinely given a negative connotation by the service managers: 'He thinks we're *just not coping!*'

Hopelessness

They described as a sense of *powerlessness*, of being nakedly exposed, under a spotlight, in the service manager role, to the critical and hostile scrutiny of both their superiors and their subordinates as if they were the meat in a hostile persecutory sandwich. They also experienced a sense of *hopelessness and defeat*. This had two components. First, they described how they found it difficult to make sense of the bewildering *present*, there being too many variables to integrate in doing a task that seemed to them undo-able. But this was exacerbated by the second factor, the expectation of continual change, the sense that the next change in the *future* might render inapplicable all the work being done here and now.

Isolation

Perhaps most significantly, and the theme on which I propose to focus particularly in this chapter, the service managers exhibited a significant degree of disconnectedness, an almost purposeful isolation – from each other, from senior management, from their subordinates and from the patients. Some of this seemed structural: there were no peer group meetings in the normal working week, for example. But they also noted, with some chagrin, that there seemed to be few social or friendship ties among themselves either. Friendship was feared; it was felt that if you did not get together with your mates, then you would not be reminded of and would not have to think about and acknowledge the painful experience of the job. Thus social and structural isolation was identified as one way of defending themselves against the feeling of being overwhelmed by the surrounding turbulence.

Sources of anxiety

As a way of making sense of these feelings, the service managers were invited to consider, as an analogy, the electromagnetic spectrum. In the trust, the service managers could readily agree that there were 'visible' issues that could be identified by rational analysis in their situation. However, it was also possible to detect and to examine with them an 'invisible' set of forces, the 'irrational' or 'unconscious' forces that illuminated the whole picture. These were identified and linked to the extremes of feeling experienced by the service managers and were thought about as in Figure 8.1.

Figure 8.1 The spectrum of rational and irrational forces

Infrared	Visible light	Ultraviolet
The 'non-rational' difficulties	The 'rational' difficulties	The 'non-rational' difficulties

What became clear was that the service managers were having to cope, consciously and unconsciously, on a daily basis, with an inordinate amount of anxiety that constantly threatened to engulf them. Anxiety is probably the most important unpleasant feeling that human beings experience. It is, in essence, a response to perceived danger. Human beings, like all higher animals, have developed two major responses to external danger – fight or flight. Evolutionary survival depended on a judicious admixture of these. The physical effects of anxiety can be seen as triggers, or warning signs, heralding danger. These effects are commonly experienced in similar ways by everyone. For example, we sweat, we feel a tightening of the muscles and a rapid beating of the heart. But the causes of anxiety are intensely subjective and depend on the way that each individual perceives and interprets a situation.

The sources of anxiety can be thought about in two ways. As well as the *external* dangers and threats discussed, anxiety can also have an *internal* origin in the individual mind. This happens when the current situation resonates with old, often forgotten losses and dangers. These feelings and memories can stir up intolerable anxieties which may seem out of proportion to the current event that has triggered it. However, whether anxiety is 'objective' (from without) or 'neurotic' (from within), it is experienced as the same painful emotional state, and in essence is dealt with in the same way – by fight or flight. The internal equivalents of fight and flight are the psychological defence mechanisms, the ways in which we protect ourselves by the evasion of difficult feelings. Of key importance here are the defences of denial, splitting and projection, identified by Melanie Klein (Klein, 1946; see also Chapter 6).

Defending against anxiety

I suggest that the inability of these managers to cope was due to the impact of overwhelming anxiety in their organization, an anxiety that disabled them and caused them to defend themselves with what Menzies has called a 'social defence system' (Menzies, 1959).

In her classic study of stress in the nursing profession, Menzies showed how anxiety from both internal and external sources, working in tandem, can overwhelm the capacity to carry out professional tasks. She argued that, when faced with a sense of impending annihilation, nurses defend themselves by fight and flight mechanisms. The nature of the anxiety is as follows. In common with many jobs in the medical field, the jobs that the nurse has to perform are frequently frightening and disgusting. Human pain and suffering are omnipresent. Yet intimate contact with patients may also stir up libidinal desires. Death can be a constant companion. Then, too, the response of patients and their relatives can be difficult to deal with due to the strong ambivalence that they feel towards the nurse. Gratitude for her care and attention jostles with hostility at the dependency that they feel towards her, and envy of her health and vitality. According to Menzies, this confused and highly emotional situation confronting the nurse 'bears a striking resemblance to the phantasy situations that exist in every individual in the deepest and most primitive levels of the mind'. This results in a confusion arising between internal and external dangers.

As adults, we are all susceptible to a stirring up of infantile anxiety. It can often be coped with by projecting it onto our work situation. Work can be used as a symbolic representation of the inner phantasy situation. By achieving and succeeding in our work task, the phantasy situation is conquered, leading to internal reassurance and a lessening of anxiety. However, when the inner phantasy and the outer reality are very similar, a confusion occurs. The deep resonance between the inner terrors and the outer horrors actually cranks up the experience of anxiety, and can be literally overwhelming. This is what happens with the nurse. It leads to the amplification of unconscious defences on an individual level, and to a 'social defence system' at the level of the group or organization, in which individual nurses collude with each other as they attempt to operate their own psychic defence mechanisms.

Menzies identifies a number of different defensive structures shared by the nurses. Of particular interest for our case is the way that they dealt with the anxieties surrounding the taking of responsibility. Each nurse experienced a powerful internal conflict between the responsibility demanded by her work, and her wishes to avoid this heavy and continuous burden by acting irresponsibly. This conflict was partially avoided by the processes of denial, splitting and projection, which converted this intra-personal struggle into an inter-personal conflict, each nurse tending to split off aspects of herself from her conscious personality and to project them into other nurses. The irresponsible impulses were projected *down* the hierarchy into subordinates, who were then treated with the severity which that part of the split-off self 'deserved'. The stern and harsh aspects of herself were split off and projected *up* the hierarchy into her superiors, so that she expected (and often received) harsh disciplinary treatment from them.

Let us now consider the relevance of Menzies' work to this case study. There are two strands that may be teased out:

1   What was most strikingly missing from the discourse of these service managers, as compared with Menzies' nursing staff, was any sense of what might be called the 'clinical' task, the treatment function of their

respective services. Instead, all their experiences seemed to be mediated solely through the lens of the 'business' perspective.

2   What was also striking was the ambivalence of the managers towards the consultants and the workshops, shown by good attendance and yet suspicion and hostility towards the consultants.

These factors seem to be particularly important, and I would like to explore each of them in some detail. But first I would like to describe an example that catches the flavour of both of these particular points.

The start of the second workshop was punctuated by the following vignette. It ensued from the late arrival of the manager of the accident and emergency service of the trust. The group had spent much of their first workshop exploring the burden of 'balancing the books', and the dilemma of trying to run a service when there is no money left. This particular manager, in explaining her latecoming, described a crisis that had occurred for her team. There had been a terrible road accident. The helicopter service, always a high-profile operation, had responded, and picked up a critically injured patient. In full public gaze, it transported the patient back to the Intensive Care Unit of the Accident and Emergency Department. 'Luckily,' she announced, *with no trace of irony*, 'the patient was dead on arrival!' 'Nice one!' murmured the other managers in response, *again without a trace of irony*.

What seemed to be to the fore in the managers' minds was the realization that the Intensive Care Unit had run out of funds. But the simple human consideration (linked, after all, to the primary task of a hospital) of a human death was simply split off, as if it were not available for consideration. When this was pointed out to the group, it produced major discomfort and caused this particular group to refuse to participate in the rest of the workshop.

Splitting clinical and business anxiety

How might this be understood? Put rather simplistically, before the purchaser/provider split, the anxiety in the system could be seen as being associated with the clinical task. This *clinical task anxiety* was generated by the 'hands on' work of dealing with death, pain and suffering of patients, and the associated distress of relatives, as described above. It was coped with by being dispersed throughout the structure, with different tiers of the hierarchy 'containing' different bits of the anxiety (Bion, 1959).

It is worth teasing out this theoretical idea of containment a little further. Bion argues that in order for anything to develop, there must be an appropriate apparatus or container to hold or contain the development. Bion described thought, which he considered 'trial action', in such a way. He argued that there must be an appropriate 'container' for thought to develop, which in the early stages of development is provided by the mother. Failure to provide such a container leads to a state of 'nameless dread' in the infant. These ideas are useful, for example, in conceptualizing the role of the consultant to an organization as trying to create a setting (container) in which difficult emotions can be safely explored or, as Bion might put it, where thought can emerge and develop. Containment in an organization is provided by effective management. It is embodied in clearly defined tasks and clearly defined roles, and in the systematic provision of spaces in which reflection can occur and difficulties can be struggled with.

The advent of purchasing/providing can be thought of as introducing a radically *new* quantity and quality of anxiety into the system. This *business anxiety* is about balancing the books: business planning, 'downsizing', redundancies, cuts in services and trying to meet the increasing demands of the public with decreasing resources.

Furthermore, as Hinshelwood has argued:

[T]here is also another significant addition to the level of anxiety and this is deliberately introduced as policy. The rationale for the market system in the NHS is to create a stimulating sense of competitive insecurity – we should be energised by the anxiety that if we do not do well we will lose business and we shall be closed down. This is intended to keep people on their toes and thus to improve performance and productivity, etc. However the medical and nursing professions are beset by particularly high levels of anxiety already, just from the nature of the work. What happens if they bear extra anxiety? It is possible that, instead of increasing performance, it will increase the intensity and scope of defensive measures and collective phantasy-based attitudes.

(Hinshelwood, 1994: 287)

Thus, trusts have had to cope with a doubling up of anxiety, but without an increase in capacity to contain it. As the saying goes, you cannot fit a quart into a pint pot! This can be shown as follows in Figure 8.2.

For the purchasing/providing system to work, it would seem to be necessary for the two functions, the professional task and the business task, to be held in mind at once. That is, after all, the mission of a modern trust. But the double dose of anxiety associated with the two functions is so great that one or other gets lopped off, pushed out of mind as if it did not exist. Hence the focus of the service managers on 'business', and the absence in their discussions of the 'clinical' task. The service managers were seemingly being asked to carry the anxiety associated with 'business' on behalf of the whole trust, because it is they who had to operationalize the business framework and make it work. Thus, they were caught between the proverbial rock and a hard place.

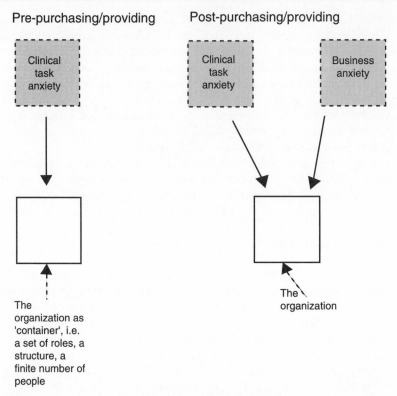

Figure 8.2 The increase of anxiety with the advent of purchasing and providing

Some consequences of splitting the task

Hinshelwood shows that clinicians in a purchasing/providing regime 'experi-ence (managers) as extremely intruding and blindly jeopardising the clinical service' (Hinshelwood, 1994: 292). In reality, there is some truth in this perception. The business anxiety corresponds to the 'visible' part of the spectrum shown above in Figure 8.1. Managers *do* have the responsibility to ration scarce resources. They are responsible for increasingly intrusive deci-sions that affect clinical output, but also for balancing the budget, which can mean cutbacks and often redundancies of subordinate staff. They have to do this against the backdrop of the competition in which they themselves are involved – the competition for their own jobs. This also stirs up primitive or unconscious anxieties (the 'ultraviolet' part of the spectrum). I suggest that they deal with the pain of this responsibility in ways similar to those identi-fied by Menzies-Lyth for the nurses. They split off that part of themselves that rations, that seems to be destructively intrusive, and project it up the hierarchy into the senior managers. Senior managers then are imbued with these negative characteristics, and the service managers can feel more guilt-free. Hence their inability to perceive their chief executive's comments about their workload as being benign, and their conversion of the potential 'good' of the workshops into something experienced as persecutory. In similar fashion, the consultants were perceived as representing the board, and were identified as 'Big Brother' – the spies and representatives of senior management. They were experienced as particularly persecutory when they pointed out these processes, because it challenged the managers to re-own the projected parts.

It is interesting to speculate who then carries the 'clinical' anxiety? My consultancy work across a number of different organizations has shown that this gets squeezed in two directions. First, it gets pushed down the hierarchy to lower levels. This increases the anxiety and stress of first-line managers and nursing staff, who are left 'holding the baby' of clinical care while their superiors, the service managers, are locked into their anxiety over rationing. Second, it gets pushed sideways into the medical consultants of the trust, who are picking up even more of the anxiety associated with this clinical task than before.

It is my contention that this is a key emerging dynamic across the public sector. In many of the organizations to which I have consulted there seems to be a fault line that cuts across the hierarchy, *a horizontal split*. Above the line, the focus is on the anxiety around *rationing*, the business task. This tends to be carried at the 'service manager' level and above. The anxiety around the *clinical task* gets pushed down below the line, and is held by the subordinates. Thus nursing managers, junior doctors and, due to their collateral but peripheral position in the hierarchy, psychotherapists and psychologists carry it in hospitals. First-line supervisors in social work carry it, as do first-line managers in the mental health services. All of these are situated just below the fault line and carry this anxiety on behalf of the entire organization.

It is not clear how this situation might be ameliorated. In 1994, Hinshelwood mused on the possibility that, in time, different professions might be able to each contain a part of the anxiety while leaving the rest to someone else. Thus, the medical profession might carry the clinical anxiety, while managers would carry the business anxiety (Hinshelwood, 1994: 291). I feel less optimistic about that. My experience is that when an organizational split is explicitly built into an organization whose task involves a lot of anxiety, the split will inevitably be hi-jacked by others as part of their unconscious defence systems.

The squeeze on middle managers

Difficult as it seems, the only way forward for the health service may be to attempt to heal the unconscious splits. This would mean that the rationing task *and* the clinical task must be held in mind at the same time. This is where the role of the service managers is so vital. They are located at that interface in the organization between the clinical task and the business task. The challenge to senior managers therefore is to create for the service managers the organizational climate in which both kinds of anxiety can be thought about together and understood in their interrelationship. Only in this way can the service managers do their jobs effectively. This would inevitably mean a new or renewed effort to bring managers together in supportive task-centred groupings. There are a number of foci for such groups that might be helpful. I would like to focus briefly on two of these.

Service managers need to cope with a chaotic *present*. But they also need to work with the constant threat of change that the *future* represents. These two aspects could be dealt with by formally building into the structure two different kinds of group meetings, run in tandem. The first, focused on the present, would be a peer group meeting, *a work discussion group* in which members would take it in turns to present aspects of their tasks which would be discussed by the other members of the group. This format provides support, a space for reflection, mutual learning, containment of anxiety and the opportunity to bring together the clinical and business anxieties. This group would be facilitated by a consultant – either internal or external – who is not part of the line management, and who would focus not just on the *content* of the discussion, but also on the *process*, in helping the group to do its work. It is through consideration of the process that the group might begin to get to grips with the infrared/ultraviolet aspects of the work. A crucial added ingredient would be the agreed occasional attendance of a senior manager, for example a board member, to receive feedback from the group based on the learning of the members. Thus the difficult, problematic issues identified in the group, which are of vital importance to the whole trust, are not split off and lost inside the boundaries of the group.

A second kind of group, focused on the future, and comprising of a cross-section of people from across the organization, including different tiers of managerial responsibility, might be called a *'What If?'* group. This would be, in a sense, a play space, but for a very serious kind of playing (see Chapter 17). Its aim would be to speculate constantly on what the shape of the service may look like in the future, and attempt to chart the paths that would have to be taken to get there. The advantages would be similar to the work discussion group, but with the added focus of reflecting on the moving film rather than the snapshot, and – by helping people from different levels to work together – would decrease the possibility of unconscious splitting. Again, this kind of group would be facilitated by a consultant. Both activities would decrease the sense of persecutory isolation.

Whether an organization uses these methods or others, it must find some way to contain anxiety enough so that the two tasks can be simultaneously held in mind. Ideally, one might argue (some do argue) that everyone – from junior nurse to chief executive – should hold both in mind. In practice, this is difficult. Splits are to some extent inevitable and, up to a point, can be helpful in allowing different groups or disciplines to carry bearable amounts of anxiety. Service managers need special attention, as they are on the 'fault line'. Ways need to be found and built in to keep the various levels of the organization in touch with each other's preoccupations and concerns, and also their ideas.

References

Biggs, S. (1991) 'Community care, case management and the psychodynamic perspective', *J. Social Work Practice* 5(1): 71–82.

Bion, W. (1959) 'Attacks on linking', *Int. J. Psycho-anal.* 40: 308–15; reprinted in W.R. Bion (1967) *Second Thoughts*, London: Heinemann, 93–109.

Hinshelwood, R.D. (1994) 'The relevance of psychotherapy', *Psychoanalytic Psychotherapy* 8(3): 283–94.

Klein, M. (1946) 'Notes on some schizoid mechanisms', *Int. J. Psycho-anal.* 27: 99–110.

Menzies, I.E.P. (1959) 'A case study in the functioning of social systems as a defence against anxiety: a report on a study of the nursing service of a general hospital', *Human Relations* 13: 95–121; reprinted in Isabel Menzies Lyth (1988) *Containing Anxiety in Institutions: Selected Essays*, London: Free Association Books.

9

Carers, clients and workers

On the relationship between policy and collusion

Simon Biggs

Introduction

The observations in this chapter have arisen from group work, with social work and health service practitioners, and an examination of the impact of social policy on caring relationships. The two areas were closely related. In support groups and workshops with practitioners, it became difficult to make sense of their experiences – the way that certain aspects of a problem became the focus of attention while other parts were relatively ignored – without understanding the corresponding policy environment. In a similar way, it was possible to observe characteristic patterns occurring in the group work process which led to a critical analysis of formal policy, particularly in terms of what was emphasized and what had become eclipsed in the arena of community care.

The relationship between societal phenomena and interpersonal dynamics has been recognized by writers such as Lawrence (1979) and Khaleelee and Miller (1985). Lawrence observed that activities within and between groups can be subtly influenced by social climate. Khaleelee and Miller have developed this argument, suggesting that small group meetings within larger social systems or contexts can be used to interpret what these wider influences might be. That is, the dynamics of smaller groups are influenced by societal forces which can unconsciously shape the behaviour within them, and under certain conditions participants can become aware of these shaping processes.

The question thus arose for me of how far the processes and positions adopted by participants in workshops and training groups could inform a deeper understanding of the influence of policy climate on caring relations. This was especially important when the situations discussed were imbued with issues of power that were not always made explicit. It also begged the possibility of developing a framework that could be used by practitioners and others to move beyond the traps and omissions that any one climate might provoke.

In this chapter, it is intended to examine power relations between carers, clients and workers and to construct a model based on insights gained through small group work. The argument that follows is based on two premises: first, that it is difficult to understand the form that interpersonal relationships take in health and social services without placing them in their social policy context; second, any discussion of the relationship between the principal users of services, their informal carers and paid, professional workers would need to take into account the changing balances of power that can exist between them.

Power and collusion

Key to this understanding is the concept of collusion, which, as will be outlined below, can take binary and triangular forms. In other words, collusion can occur between two people as a sort of 'folie-à-deux' or among three people in which two maintain a pretence at the expense of the third party. Both forms are based on the recognition that meaning is created and sustained between people rather than individually. In its binary form, collusion exists between two people as a sort of shared phantasy in which both parties unconsciously agree to uphold a mutually important understanding of their situation and chosen identities. They might, for example, create a phantasy and act as if both were the most loved and loving people around, or that they were both independent people, or that one was always sick and the other always caring, or one always dominant and the other always submissive. Of course, this does not mean that these identities are necessarily true. Laing (1961) defined collusion as

A 'game' played by two or more people whereby they deceive themselves. The game is the game of mutual deception ... each plays the other's game, though he may not necessarily be fully aware of doing so. An essential feature of the game is not admitting that it is a game.

(Laing, 1961: 108)

Once the game of collusion is in play, the ground is set for prolonged evasion of uncomfortable aspects of external reality.

Collusion becomes triangular with the involvement of a third party, who is placed in the role of outsider (or the 'ex-colluded') by those in the binary relationship. Over time, the continued viability of the phantasy shared between the colluding pair comes in some way to depend upon keeping the other in a certain fixed position. In some cases this may involve the projection of unwanted or unacknowledged qualities onto the ex-colluded party (see Figure 9.1). For example, two people might maintain their phantasy of independence by depositing feelings of neediness and dependency into a third person. This third participant is thereby held by others in what, from her or his own perspective, is a false position. Goffman (1971), in his chapter entitled 'Insanity of place', points out that triangular collusion often takes place under circumstances of control. He cites the example of a physician and family member colluding about the organic origins of mental illness, in an attempt to secretly manage a patient's conduct and reinforce their own authority.

The form that collusion takes, who is allied to whom and who becomes the 'ex-colluded', may be expected to vary depending upon external circumstances. For example, in Britain in the 1970s, when Laing's classic studies of collusive alliance were at their most popular, a certain view of family relations dominated professional thinking on the relationship between clients and their carers.

The nominated clients (those thought of as mad) were often seen as being trapped like flies in the family web. Other family members were, more often than not, perceived as part of the problem, insofar as they sustained psycho-noxious environments that kept people mad. A guiding principle for intervention by helping professionals was to rescue clients heroically from their families. This involved a considerable exercise of power by the profes-sionals involved and often resulted in the client's illness being denied so that they received only rudimentary social and life-skill support. Here the collu-sive alliance between professional worker and client resulted in a limited view of the problem in which illness and the needs of the client were overlooked and 'badness' was located in the family. This form of alliance can be seen as a reaction against historically earlier forms of collusion which were marked by paternalistic attitudes. During that period the dominant collusive alliances were usually between families and professional workers – the authority figures – to the detriment of the nominated client. It is, of course, to that period that much of the writings of Laing (1961) and Goffman (1971) were critically addressed. However, little attempt was made by Laing or Goffman to examine how collusion changed its form in differing social environments.

To further understand how certain forms of collusion occur under different conditions, one must examine the dominant forms of discourse of which they are part. In other words, who is empowered to speak 'seriously' and what are the social processes whereby this is decided and supported?

Each of the situations described earlier could be seen as characteristic of successive phases of thinking about mental health, families and professional activity. They can be represented as collusive triangles in which two parties

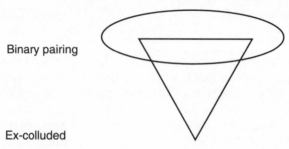

Binary pairing

Ex-colluded

Figure 9.1 Collusive alliance

form an alliance against a third. However, the intellectual tradition of criti-cally examining power and collusion has fallen from favour during the individualist 1980s and 1990s, and is currently in need of re-examination to accommodate new circumstances. The question thus arises of 'what counts as serious?' in contemporary discourse on community care. Are there certain forms of collusion that might be thought of as 'typical' of our times, and thus certain key issues that are thereby avoided? If so, can anything be done about this? Perhaps by articulating the prevailing assumptions and the particular forms of collusion to which they tend to give rise, we can mitigate against some of the more unfortunate consequences. To this end, arrange-ments that have followed the British 1990 NHS and Community Care Act will be used as a case example.

Markets, symbolic systems and community care

Contemporary notions of community care, as encapsulated in the 1990 Act, have been shaped by a particular view of interpersonal relationships, reflecting the demands of a market economy of welfare. This arrangement tacitly endorsed an individualized conception of citizenship and has signifi-cantly affected how responses are made to issues such as dependence, independence and interdependence. Elsewhere (Biggs, 1994) I have argued that one of the consequences of the above has been to locate unacceptable attributes within 'failed individuals' who find it difficult to participate in a market model. The priorities of the market model include moves toward indi-vidualism, a marked distinction between public and private activity, and an underplaying of inequalities. These conditions will shape patterns of collu-sion that are not simply a consequence of the personal histories of people involved in health and welfare services, but a product of certain arrangements that make one form of collusion more likely to occur than others.

It has been argued by Nathan (see Chapter 6) that the marketization of welfare has led to the dominance of paranoid–schizoid psychological processes, including splitting and denial of contradictory or unpalatable aspects of the caring task. Part and parcel of this change has been a polar-ization of what counted as acceptable behaviour between the public and private spheres; between the 'clear-cut', rational world of the marketplace and the 'messy', emotional world of family life. Bauman (1995) has suggested that a rigid distinction between values associated with conduct in the public world of the marketplace and the private world of the family, is key to the way that a market economy works. A split between the two protects the free flow of market forces from contamination by vested inter-ests and familial obligations. There is thus a binary division at the heart of contemporary community care policy, which is almost certainly driven by concern for the operation of the market rather than the complexity of human relationships.

This binary division is, on closer examination, part of a wider system which has given rise to a collection of symbolic pairings. Within these pairings, interactions were envisaged primarily as a series of binary relationships between autonomous individuals. Thus, throughout the early 1990s, community care workers were encouraged to see the world as consisting of relationships organized as pairs: between 'purchasers and providers', 'customers and service providers', 'carers and service users'. In the public sphere, relations were dominated by purchaser/provider relationships (as, by a quirk of policy, those who purchased services were in fact other professionals, rather than the end users of services themselves), while the private sphere contained informal carers and those whom they 'cared for'. In moral terms, the public sphere came to contain an uneasy mix of market hedonism and coercion, while the private sphere was – at least in policy terms – the domain of obligated duty.

This emphasis on binary structures can lead to a number of problems within the caring system. First, by allowing only limited expression to the personalities of those involved, it can result in a heightened psychological need for a place or person, outside the pair, onto which personally or socially unacceptable attributes can be projected.

A second problem with such binary arrangements is the difficulty that they present to seeing the system as a whole. At any one time, only certain relations would come into conceptual focus, leading to a very partial understanding of a complex web of relationships. In terms of collusion, it predisposes the caring system toward pairings whose shared rationale excluded the voice and perspective of the third party. An example of this process will be considered in the next section.

Collusion and community care

Once the symbolic system described above is placed in the context of actual conditions of care, the increasingly contradictory nature of contemporary community care becomes apparent. This is largely because, while the dominant system is binary, the basic 'unit of care' is actually triangular in form, as it includes carers, clients and professional workers. Workers, in other words, are expected to support carers in maintaining clients in the community. Each participant can be regarded as occupying one point of a triangle (see Figure 9.2). Each will have their own life tasks and their own expectations of available services. They will thus have their own priorities with regard to how alliances with other participants in the caring triangle develop over time. At the same time, this system will need to absorb the tensions created between the bias toward binary thinking implicit in market models of welfare and the triangular relationships that community support actually requires.

A policy of partnership between clients, carers and professional workers

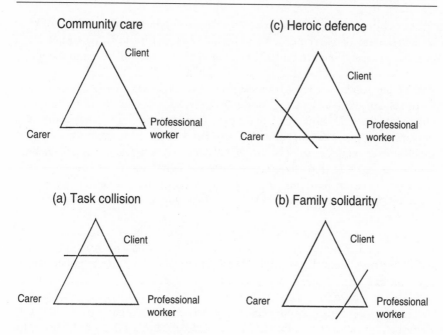

Figure 9.2 Community care triangles

allows three possibilities for collusive alliance in domestic settings, each bringing about particular problems. These possibilities are outlined below.

Task-based collusion

This form of collusion centres around mutual identification, often concerning a shared task such as the care of a third party (see Figure 9.2(a)). It is a form prefigured by contemporary arrangements for community support and one to which it is especially prone. The carer and professional worker form an alliance that ex-colludes the person regarded as being 'cared for' and places them in a dependent or 'crazy' role. The following example displays many characteristics of task-based collusion.

A female care manager, as part of a routine 'monitoring' visit to a client (E) living in the community, became aware of a number of needs that the client's daughter (D) was unable to express without help. D was a middle-aged woman looking after her mother, E, as well as her husband and children. E had a history of manic episodes which she was able to control through the self-administration of medication. She lived in a self-contained flat, a short walk away from D's home. D worked part-time and was becoming increasingly stressed due to the multiple demands being made upon her. She was concerned because she had lapses of memory and that her mother might also forget things including her medication. The worker encouraged D to explore the possibility of supervised accommodation for her mother, while making an assessment of carer need. She also felt stressed herself due to her large number of cases. She attempted to engage D in a counselling relationship.

The worker reported that she found the counselling sessions a rewarding part of her work, not least because they made her aware of her own resentment towards her own ageing mother's demands and of ways that she might cope with these. D, however, was finding that she could not sleep easily, was beginning to feel anxious about leaving her house in the morning and had taken up smoking again. The worker attempted, as part of her counselling role, to reassure D that she was not suffering from abnormal stress and that her long-standing fear that she might also be prone to mental illness was unfounded. She gave D the address of a local yoga class that she herself had found beneficial.

We do not know that E would forget her medication or that she needed to move out of her home. Neither do we know that D had no reason to worry about her own mental state, and we might consider here the extent to which the worker's identification with the carer hindered her from offering a more balanced response to D's distress.

Despite the complex nuances contained in situations such as the one described above, it is possible to discern a determining policy influence. The considerable weight placed upon informal care as the first line of support to vulnerable adults in the community would mean that the immediate concerns of carers and professional workers come to contain similar priorities, which differ from those of the identified client. In the example above, the worker and carer increasingly share concern over the caring task and the effect it is having on them, while the needs of the original client are eclipsed.

The distancing of the professional worker from direct care may also contribute to situations in which the carer is 'pulled' over the boundary from the private into the public sphere. It has been argued, for example, that informal care should become a para-professional skill, complementary to that of the social work manager (Bond, 1992). In this process, the carer is defended from her own dependency needs and enabled to keep the whole community care show on the road. In such circumstances, the question of 'who cares for the carers?' remains unaddressed as they increasingly become the vehicle for wider policy objectives.

In workshops for professionals on abuse in adult caring, workers' responses to the carer–worker relationship often reflect a need to see the carer as essentially 'normal'. In other words, carers are seen as having similar attitudes to themselves, with a clear distinction being made between their own needs and those of the client being abused. While these perceptions often change as workers examine the situation in greater depth, it is open to question whether this initial guiding principle is so easily dislodged when space for reflection is less readily available.

In these and similar ways, alliances between workers and carers may come

to marginalize the voices of the identified recipients of care who find themselves at the ex-colluded edge of the triangle. A collusive alliance between
carer and worker sustains their 'independence' through the evacuation of
dependency/irrationality into the client, who is then held in that depen-
dent/'crazy' position. This distinguishes the help extended to the carer in
their role as one who looks after a dependent person from support that is
directed at their personal needs for dependency. Ultimately, this position
rests on denial by the worker of triangularity and on collusion against the
nominated client.

Family solidarity

This form of collusion occurs when the carer and cared-for exclude the
professional worker (see Figure 9.2(b)).

Whilst helper–carer collusion may be primary in the current policy
climate, it is by no means the only alliance that can occur. It is equally
possible for the worker to step outside the triangle and look at the
carer/cared-for relationship as if it were essentially binary. Workers may
accept exclusion in an attempt to maintain existing family bonds, or may opt
for a monitoring/surveillance role from the outside. Indeed these two
options might reinforce each other if contact with welfare services brings
with it the risk of criminalization or intrusive surveillance, in which case
family members may well try to protect each other from formal inquiry.

Such a collusive relationship involves the distancing of the worker while
maintaining the carer/cared-for relationship as it stands. Protection of the
existing family dynamic may reduce the possibility of the worker suggesting
alternative ways of meeting each party's needs; the worker is then relegated
to a voyeuristic role. A sign that collusion with family solidarity is occurring
might be when decisions are made simply to monitor the situation even
when evidence of therapeutic need is present.

Heroic defence

This form of collusion occurs when the professional worker and cared-for
combine to exclude the carer (see Figure 9.2(c)).

It arises when the worker forms a strong bond with the nominated client,
at the carer's expense. In these circumstances, the worker 'heroically defends'
the client and the carer becomes excluded. Contact stirs up powerful needs
to protect the nominated victim from a potentially damaging domestic environment, and workers come to believe that only they can heroically
intervene to protect and that their relationship with the client contains an
exclusive specialness. Under these conditions, legislation may be used to
rescue the client and blame the carer.

Even if the carer is indeed abusive, there are dynamics in such a system that remain neither examined nor understood and the risk is that the so-called rescuing system ends up abusing both the carer and the identified client. This is likely to happen if the collusive need to perform the 'heroic rescue' overrides the need to examine the part played by the identified client and their disturbance – in other words, if the system in mind is maintained as a binary one. When this occurs, the carer's position is inadequately appreciated and the needs of the client remain unaddressed. In such cases it is likely that the client, once removed from the care of the family member, will simply re-experience similar relationships and that this process of 'failed rescues' will continue until someone is able to take account of the essential triangularity of the system.

Discussion

A more satisfactory situation occurs when clients, informal carers and workers can acknowledge the potential contribution of each participant. This requires an ability to see also the different priorities and limitations that each brings, and an ability to tolerate dependency, insanity or irrationality both in oneself and in others, and thereby contain the complexity tacit in three-person collaboration. Genuine participation would require that each party negotiate a working process, checking and balancing their conduct if it impedes resolution. Solutions based on the needs and resources of all participants would then be more likely to have positive and lasting consequences. However, under the symbolic constraints of the market, there will always be a tendency to break triangular relations down into relationships between different pairs of people.

If the momentum toward particular forms of power alliance varies with policy climate, then it is reasonable to assume that practice will be drawn toward certain conclusions and actions rather than toward others. While such sources of bias are present in any period, the move toward marketized welfare has increased the rigidity of boundaries and promoted the collaboration of informal carers with professionals. This trend may make task-based collusion a relatively common form of contemporary community care for adults, while rescue and solidarity may be more likely in other policy contexts. It should not be overlooked that the collaboration encouraged between workers and carers can produce a revised version of the authoritarianism identified by Goffman (1971) and Laing (1961). In its contemporary form, however, the rhetoric of partnership has replaced that of paternalism.

It is important that participants in the caring enterprise are given space to reflect on the impact of policy climate on their conduct and small work discussion groups can be used to assess this impact critically. As part of this process, practitioners have been encouraged to foster a reflective as well as an involved self. Reflection, as part of practice, facilitates practitioners' awareness of the triangles outlined above and enables them to step beyond exclusive binary relationships. The visually accessible triangles are a relatively simple device that can be used, as doodles or mental images, to foster awareness in practice situations. Thus triangles representing the various parties involved, their alliances and collusions may allow participants to make sense of their position in a relationship (see also Chapter 5 and Chapter 10). Ideas about the complex and shifting dynamics of care can then be held in mind during interaction, hopefully allowing participants to avoid becoming locked into fixed positions and stereotyped role relationships.

References

Bauman, Z. (1995) *Life in Fragments*, Oxford: Blackwell.

Biggs, S. (1994) 'Failed individualism in community care: an example from elder abuse', *J. Social Work Practice* 8(2): 137–49.

Bond, J. (1992) 'The politics of caregiving: the professionalisation of community care', *Ageing & Society* 12: 5–21.

Goffman, E. (1971) *Relations in Public*, London: Penguin.

Khaleelee, O. and Miller, E. (1985) 'Beyond the small group: society as an intelligible field of study', in M. Pines (ed.) *Bion and Group Psychotherapy*, London: Routledge.

Laing, R.D. (1961) *Self and Others*, London: Penguin.

Lawrence, G. (1979) *Exploring Individual and Organisational Boundaries*, Chichester: John Wiley.

10

The hospital in the community

Vega Zagier Roberts

Historically, community care has been associated with hospital closure and this has contributed to the tendency to regard the hospital as separate from – if not inimical to – community care. Now that most psychiatric wards are located geographically within the locality they serve, there is greater opportunity to think about the relatedness of the hospital to community services. Nonetheless, it is not uncommon to hear community-based staff talking about the hospital as if it were far away, unknown and frightening, while ward staff can still feel very cut off from the non-hospital part of their patients' lives. This chapter looks at some of the consequences of not holding the total system of care in mind.

Case study 1

This case study is based on my work with the staff of one of three wards in an acute psychiatric unit which I shall call Blackenwell Hospital. Colleagues known to me were consulting to the other two wards, and yet another colleague was consulting to a residential unit in the community, many of whose residents came there from – and intermittently returned to – Blackenwell.

All three of us consulting to the in-patient wards encountered a similar situation – an extremely demoralized nursing staff working under conditions that made us wonder how they could bring themselves to come to work each day. And indeed, many of them did not. Absenteeism was very high, and over half the nursing posts were vacant, filled by a flow of agency nurses. There were almost daily physical assaults on staff, many of which were quite serious, and constant verbal abuse. Newly qualified nurses arrived full of enthusiasm but quickly became jaundiced when they found that they rarely had more than a few minutes a day to spend with any one patient. They were often promoted within a few months to taking charge of the ward, trying to manage the necessary daily tasks with a handful of regular staff supplemented by agency nurses, spending most of their time 'processing' the constant stream of new admissions and discharges. The older nurses 'soldiered on' but commented often and bitterly on the changes, recalling how until very recently they had had more continuous and meaningful relationships with patients who would return to Blackenwell at regular intervals over many years. Indeed, some remembered further back to when they had worked at Fieldsey, the old Victorian 'bin' some miles away. 'There was a lot wrong with it,' said one, 'but there were a thousand patients and a thousand staff and everyone knew each other. Now I see people in the lift and I don't even know if they work here or not, and I don't know who will come to help if we push the panic button.'

With the closure of Fieldsey and the growing emphasis on keeping mentally ill people in the community as long as possible, the level of disturbance on the wards had increased dramatically. The pressure on beds at Blackenwell was acute. The senior nurse on duty, in principle the person to whom the relatively inexperienced charge nurses looked for support and advice, was often unavailable, tied up for hours at a time telephoning other hospitals to look for beds.

This situation is quite common, particularly in inner cities. At Blackenwell, the stress of dealing constantly with such a high level of disturbance and with the enormous workload associated with rapid turnover (up to half a dozen admissions and discharges in one day) was augmented by the nurses' uncertainty about what was expected of them. They were no longer clear what they were in the business of. For example, they were constantly reminded to respect patients' rights and choices. As a result, many patients spent much of the day in their rooms or wandering the local streets, rather than attending any kind of formal treatment programme. But did patients not have a right to active treatment? Could 'patients' rights' really mean that a patient waiting for housing in the community should be left to spend all day in bed for months if he chose to do so? The nurses felt cut off from the rest of the hospital, receiving little guidance from their managers about these dilemmas, and feeling that their views were not listened to by the clinicians from other disciplines who made many of the clinical decisions. It was as if the ward were a place totally cut off from the rest of the world: the nursing staff often had no idea where patients came from, and little picture of where they went when they left. Although ostensibly discharge planning started at the time of admission, the nurses' experience was of the ward often being used merely as a holding place until either the patient was just stabilized enough on medication not to be an immediate danger to themselves or others, or until more suitable accommodation was found, rather than as a place for real treatment, let alone care. This, more than anything else, was demoralizing, in that it stripped their work of most of its meaning.

My three colleagues and I had, from the start, intended to meet regularly to reflect together on our experiences in our different consultancies, but seemed never quite able to find a time when we could all meet. Since we were all members of the same workshop for consultants, we arranged that each of us would present our work there in turn over four consecutive weeks, reserving the fifth week for discussion of the care system as a whole. This discussion proved very useful for the three of us consulting to the wards, but no reference was made by any of the workshop members to the consultancy to the community-based residential home. It was as if it had ceased to exist: there seemed to be no place for it in the mind while the group thought about the in-patient setting. This we came to see as a mirroring of the experience of the nursing staff of working in isolation, cut off psychologically as well as physically from the wider community. Small wonder that the older staff mourned the old days at Fieldsey when they had been part of a community, however far from ideal.

The system-in-the-mind

I am borrowing here from the concept of the organization-in-the-mind developed at the Grubb Institute (Armstrong, 1991; Hutton, 1997). However, community care does not happen in an organization but in a matrix of agencies. There is no one definite boundary around this system, and there are myriad pressures on workers to narrow their focus to the particular agency in which they work, which – as demonstrated above – is quite complex enough in itself. However, for the work to have meaning and coherence requires holding on to a sense of the interconnectedness of the various care-providing agencies which contribute in different ways and at different times to the totality of the client's experience of care. The evidence from service users themselves is that they see their hospital stays as one part of their experience of their illness – often a very significant part, but not totally separate from the rest of their lives (Barham and Hayward, 1995).

In this instance, it was the person providing consultancy 'in the community' who was most available to hold the whole system in mind and – from her presentation at the workshop – it seemed that the staff of the community-based unit were similarly somewhat better able to hold the hospital in mind than the ward nurses were to feel related to providers of care in the community. But in my experience, this is far from generally true.

For example, in the course of some team development work with a new outreach team, I asked them to draw a 'star chart' (Gawlinski and Graessle, 1988) of their relations with other agencies. They drew a circle in the middle representing their own team, with other circles to represent the other agencies, nearer or further from the centre depending on the importance of the relationship between themselves and each of the others, and with stronger or weaker connecting lines to indicate the quality of the relationship. The hospital was initially left out of the picture altogether, and later found a place only at the outermost edge of the picture. For a long time, the team measured their own success or failure almost entirely by whether or not they succeeded in keeping their clients out of hospital, which in some cases proved a very counter-productive criterion.

However, this equating of readmission with a failure of community care remains commonplace, and is a major contributing factor to the difficulty of holding both locations of care in mind simultaneously. One reason for this may be the historical link between the development of community care and the closure of hospital beds, and the driving force behind the original vision for care in the community as a superior alternative to hospital-based services. A second factor that contributes to maintaining the split in the minds of the people providing services is structural: even now, when most NHS Trusts providing mental health services include both in-patient and community-based services, these are often managed as separate units. In some cases, it may be only the consultant psychiatrist who works across the boundary, while nurses and staff from most other disciplines identify themselves clearly as working either *in* the hospital or *in* the community.

Case study 2[1]

Cannon Fields was the community mental health centre (CMHC) for Northwest Wrexham, where a community mental health team provided on-site individual and group treatment programmes, domiciliary visits and a daily drop-in service. It was one of three such centres – the others serving Northeast and South Wrexham – set up in the mid-1980s to provide mental health services in the community. As each centre opened, some wards at Wrexham Psychiatric Hospital were closed, until finally only three remained open, corresponding to the three catchment areas of the CMHCs. Most of the Cannon Fields team had previously worked at the hospital, which they regarded as rigid, oppressive and suppressive of individuality, and they based their programme planning on their vision of being as different from it as possible. The clients could come and go freely, choosing whether or not to attend formal therapeutic activities. Similarly, staff could work as they thought best, with individuals or groups, chronic or acute patients. It was difficult to set any limits or to enforce any decisions, lest this curtail individual freedom, evoking the spectre of 'the bad old days' on the wards.

The aim of Cannon Fields was defined as 'offering a comprehensive community-based mental health service to residents of Northwest Wrexham with emotional and psychiatric problems, and to prevent admission to hospital'. As a result, admission of anyone in their catchment area to Wrexham Hospital was experienced by the staff as a failure, which they tended to blame on bad management, inadequate resources or incompetence on the part of general practitioners, casualty room staff and other professionals.

Not surprisingly, relations between the CMHC and the hospital's C Ward, to which Northwest Wrexham residents were admitted when they needed in-patient care, were antagonistic. Cannon Fields staff considered attending ward rounds at the hospital a disagreeable chore, and left as soon as the ward round was over, as if contact might contaminate them with something that they had been lucky to escape. They spoke of ward staff with pity, but also with contempt, and were regarded by the ward staff as stand-offish and unhelpful. They behaved as if Cannon Fields were not only a superior alternative to hospital care, as different and separate from it as possible, but as if 'success' would mean doing away with the need for a hospital altogether. The wording of their aims statement – which had been drafted by senior managers before the team were recruited – supported this concept of their task by implying that they (alone) should meet all the mental health needs of the locality and prevent hospitalization.

The management structure also served to sustain this idea. Community psychiatric care was managed as a system quite separate from, and even in competition with, the hospital-based psychiatric service (see Figure 10.1(a)). Subsequently, the management structure was altered to correspond to the three catchment areas (see Figure 10.1(b)). The new boundaries matched and supported the task of providing a comprehensive mental health service, comprising both in-patient and community services, to each catchment area. Patients could then be more readily seen as a shared responsibility, whether they were in the hospital or in the community at any given moment, and the rivalry between the hospital and community lessened. Ward rounds became a central activity for the staff of Cannon Fields as well as of C Ward, involving their working together at assessing the needs of their joint clients.

However, even when community mental health teams and hospital staff make great efforts to work more closely together, there is a constant tendency to fall back on traditional attitudes, stereotypes and defences, with a return of competitiveness and hostility. The fear that ward nurses may feel about going outside the hospital with their patients, and the fear that community nurses may feel about visiting the wards, are often hidden behind their criticisms of each other's practices. Both are also likely to invoke 'pressures of work' as precluding traversing the small geographical distances which now generally separate the two, so that face-to-face contact is kept to a minimum, leaving fertile ground for projective processes to flourish. Even in Wrexham, where so much effort was put into integrating the two parts of the care system, both structurally and 'in-the-mind', there was a gradual return of these old ways of relating. When a colleague of mine began consulting to the Cannon Fields team some years later, the ward had again come to seem very far away and a very bad place to be.

This splitting up of the system-in-the-mind serves to preserve a place for each group to deposit their negative projections and their anxieties about failing their clients. It also makes it possible to 'forget' the clients from time to time: both ward and community teams get a degree of respite from 'exporting' difficult clients to the other subsystem, and can feel understandably reluctant to give this up, as they might have to do if the parts became a

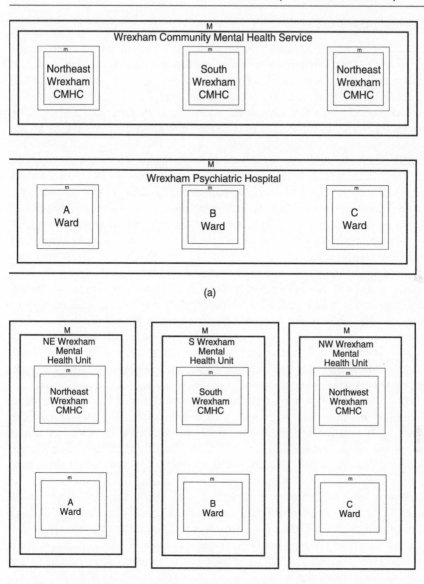

Figure 10.1 Organization of in-patient and community-based mental health services: (a) before restructuring, (b) after restructuring (sectorization)

single system of care in their minds. On the other hand, if workers based in the community cannot trust that something good is being offered when their clients are in hospital, they are likely to continue to feel persecuted by a sense of failure whenever one of their clients is admitted.

Case study 3

A director in a mental health NHS trust asked me to try to improve the increasingly hostile relations between one of the trust's community-based residential units, Evergreen House, and the hospital from which it received its referrals. The staff of Evergreen had been complaining that they were not receiving enough suitable referrals and that they had difficulty getting psychiatric input to their residents when they needed it. Managers at the hospital were complaining that Evergreen took too long to assess referrals, turned down the difficult cases for which the house had been set up, and were too quick to ask for psychiatric intervention and readmission for their residents. This sounded like a fairly straightforward two-party conflict with misunderstandings and different interpretations of the function of Evergreen House on both sides. My initial plan was to have a preliminary meeting with the managers on each of the two sites, and then probably to set up some kind of inter-group meeting.

The hospital managers told me that Evergreen was 'creaming off the easy cases', leaving the more disturbed patients staying far longer than was necessary in hospital, and wondered if the team there were competent enough to undertake the kind of work that the locality needed them to be doing. When I met with the manager of Evergreen House, however, I heard a very different story, so different in fact that I felt for a while as if I were Lewis Carrol's Alice after she went through the looking-glass. He told me that, since opening, the house had turned down only two referrals, one who was too physically disabled to manage the stairs and one who was well known to the other residents and with whom they refused to live. Where was the unreasonableness? Where were the hordes of rejected referrals? This could not be the whole story. Painstakingly, the manager and I went through the files of every single person who had been referred. It transpired that there had indeed been a considerable number of referrals that had not led to placement, but *not* because the Evergreen House team had turned them down. In several instances it was because social services care managers, who were the purchasers of the places in this home, had done their own assessment of the client referred and had not agreed to pay for the placement. In a few instances, the client had turned down an offered place because they preferred to live elsewhere.

It was evident at this point that an intervention based on seeing this as a two-party conflict was doomed to failure. I therefore suggested that, before doing any further work, we set up a steering group comprising representatives from all three agencies concerned: Evergreen House, the hospital, and social services. I had supposed that I would be briefed by this steering group, design an intervention to improve inter-group relations, and then report back to them. Instead, from the very first meeting they became a problem-solving group, and nothing more was required from me beyond facilitating half a dozen further meetings of the group at six-weekly intervals. Over the next few months, they developed a common system for referrals, jointly owning and collaboratively tackling the various issues blocking effective services.

Dependence, interdependence and management in community care

To frame difficulties in dyadic (that is, two-person or 'us-and-them') terms is a common defence. It corresponds to a stage in psychological development referred to by Melanie Klein (1959) as the *paranoid–schizoid position*, where an individual perceives others as all-good (meeting their needs fully and immediately) or all-bad (withholding and persecuting). The more mature *depressive position*, where the individual recognizes others as integrated wholes comprising both giving and withholding qualities, requires tolerating the complexities of ambivalence, that is, having both loving and hating feelings for the same person, and the pain of guilt and remorse for one's own mixture of good and bad qualities. Dyadic all-or-nothing modes of relating can then give way to more complex 'triangular' relations which include a 'third position' (see Chapters 5 and 6).

In an analogous way, groups of people in organizations can display the more 'primitive' defences of splitting – either idealizing or denigrating others, for example managers or other agencies – in which case one could describe them as functioning in the paranoid–schizoid position; or they may be capable of more complex assessment of strengths and shortcomings, both in themselves and in others, in which case one could identify them as functioning in the depressive position. However, neither individuals nor groups ever achieve the depressive position definitively. At times of stress, there is always a tendency to 'regress' to the simpler black-and-white of the paranoid–schizoid position in order to defend against psychological pain.

Since the paranoid–schizoid position involves interpreting one's experience in two-party terms (one good and one bad), bringing in a third party (the 'third position') in itself supports a shift towards more depressive-position functioning. Thus, in the preceding case study, the introduction of social services into what had been seen up to then as a two-agency conflict enabled everyone involved to engage in solving the problem. But how had they come to be left out of the story as told to me?

I think that the common defensive tendency to 'forget' the third position was exacerbated in this case by social services being the purchaser of Evergreen's services. So long as the hospital managers and the staff of Evergreen House could blame each other, they were on familiar ground and could deny the unpalatable fact of their dependence on another agency outside the health service. Conceptualizing the problem as a conflict between two health service agencies provided simplicity, as well as obscuring the dependence of both agencies on the third.

This tendency to define difficulties in terms of pairs – community and hospital, nurses and doctors, purchasers and providers, health and social services – excluding the third corner of the triangle, defends against painful complexities, especially interdependence. However, it also often leads to blaming, scapegoating and stalemate. Bringing in the third position can be a crucial first step.

If we re-examine the preceding case study in terms of a triangle, we can see different defences operating, depending on which corner is neglected:

1   The focus of attention is on the relationship between the hospital and the community-based setting, characterized by intense rivalry and blame between providers. The community-based staff attribute any difficulties they have to the lack of support from the hospital, while the hospital managers blame the residential unit for contributing to their bed blockage. The fight serves to deny the dependence of both on the purchasers, as if resolving the fight would resolve all their difficulties (see Figure 10.2(a)).

2   The focus of attention is on the relationship between care managers and the community agency who collaborate around placements: it is as if the 'right' placement will be permanent (a 'home for life'), with denial of the degree of impairment of the clients and the likelihood that they will need further psychiatric intervention and very possibly further hospitalization (see Figure 10.2(b)).

3   The focus of attention is on the relationship between care managers and managers in the hospital who meet at ward rounds to discuss discharge plans for clients and, as senior professionals, sometimes join in denigrating the expertise of the residential team. In this case, the discussions run as if sufficient expertise is what is needed to prevent relapse (see Figure 10.2(c)).

The way that services are structured and managed can increase splitting or can mitigate against it. This has already been described in case study 2 (pages 119–21) with regard to hospital- and community-based services within a single NHS trust. In this situation, even if there is separate management of community and hospital services in the locality, there is a superordinate management at a more senior level which encompasses both, and there is therefore some built-in opportunity to think about the splits and to seek ways of bringing the different parts of the service together.

Where multiple agencies are involved, as is now very often the case, there is a further level of complexity, since there is no formal superordinate management system. These agencies are often competing for scarce resources. At the same time, the staff in each are defending against the anxieties inherent in the work of caring for mentally ill people, and other agencies provide an endless supply of 'bad objects' which can be blamed for

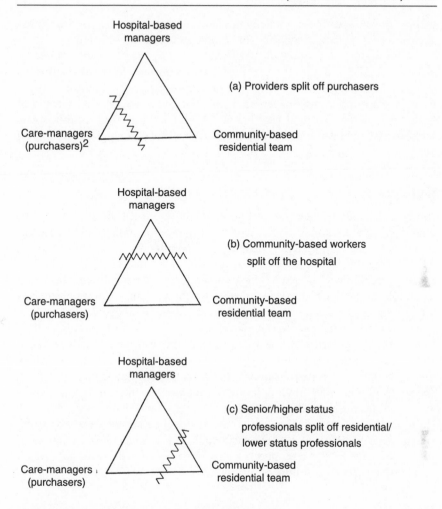

Hospital-based
managers

(a) Providers split off purchasers

Care-managers
(purchasers)2

Community-based
residential team

Hospital-based
managers

(b) Community-based workers
   split off the hospital

Care-managers
(purchasers)

Community-based
residential team

Hospital-based
managers

(c) Senior/higher status
   professionals split off residential/
   lower status professionals

Care-managers
(purchasers)

Community-based
residential team

Figure 10.2 Splitting processes in interagency work

any failure to produce the desired outcomes. Furthermore, where there is no formal boundary around multiple agencies providing different components of services to the population of a designated geographical locality, it is particularly difficult to arrive at any shared 'organization-in-the-mind', that is, a shared concept of the overall task, of one's own particular contribution to this task, or of the relatedness of the parts to the whole. Instead, the different organizations involved in the complex system of care being provided to clients tend to think and behave as if they are autonomous. As shown by the case studies above, the cost of denial of interdependence is high, not only in terms of effectiveness, but also of morale, as conflicts get driven 'downwards' to be acted out between teams or between different agencies, leading to scapegoating and blame as well as to isolation.

Attempts to think about the system as a whole are sometimes made by external bodies set up, for example, to 'reconfigure' (rationalize) such services. An example of a different approach to creating a kind of 'virtual' boundary around multiple agencies is the workshop described at the end of Chapter 16, which brought together staff and managers from health, social services and voluntary sector provider agencies from a single geographical area.

Conclusion

As the case studies in this chapter have illustrated, it is crucial both for the quality of services and the quality of working life for staff that the different elements of the care system – hospital and community – are held in mind. At the same time, there are constant pressures towards splitting, and to the ensuing breakdowns in communication and relatedness. Where there is a formal boundary which includes both in-patient and community-based services, as is the case in most NHS trusts, senior managers need to help teams to work at their interrelatedness. Where there is no formal boundary to hold the components of a service together, and no superordinate management system (and therefore no one person or group to hold the whole mental health care system in mind), the need for the managers within each agency to provide this 'holding in mind' function becomes all the more critical. They need constantly to work at the interconnectedness of their own team or agency with all the others, to make space for thinking about the system as a whole, and to help their staff feel connected with the wider system of care in the community. This must include the hospital, which provides one crucial component of this care.

Notes

1 Case study 2 and Figure 10.1 were previously published in Roberts (1994).
2 In this case, the purchasers were care managers (employed by social services) who were, of course, also themselves providers of mental health services. The dynamics of the case, however, had to do with their having the purchaser role in relation to Evergreen.

References

Armstrong, D. (1991) 'The institution in the mind: reflections on the relation of psycho-analysis to work with institutions', London: Grubb Institute.
Barham, P. and Hayward, R. (1995) *Relocating Madness: From the Mental Patient to the Person*, London: Free Association Books.

Gawlinski, G. and Graessle, L. (1988) *Planning Together: The Art of Effective Team-work*, London: Bedford Square Press.

Hutton, J. (1997) 'Re-imagining the organisation of an institution: management in human service institutions', in E. Smith (ed.) *Integrity and Change: Mental Health in the Marketplace*, London: Routledge.

Klein, M. (1959) 'Our adult world and its roots in infancy', *Human Relations* 12: 291–303; also in numerous collections, including A.D. Colman and M.H. Geller (eds) *Group Relations Reader 2*, Washington, DC: A.K. Rice Institute Series.

Roberts, V. Zagier (1994) 'The organization of work: contributions from open systems theory', in A. Obholzer and V. Zagier Roberts, *The Unconscious at Work: Individual and Organizational Stress in the Human Services*, London: Routledge.

Part III

Learning from the experience of face-to-face work

The chapters in this section are all written from the perspective of working directly with people with mental illness or managing front-line teams. In different ways, they challenge some of the assumptions underlying current policy and practice.

11

Integration or fragmentation

The challenge facing community mental health teams[1]

Angela Foster

Introduction

In this chapter I use my experience of working as a consultant or facilitator with the staff of four community mental health teams (CMHTs) from their inception with the aim of understanding why multidisciplinary work in CMHTs is so fraught with difficulty. The creation of genuinely multidisciplinary teams working outside the institution in the community at large presents us with many opportunities and challenges. However, both managers and workers within such teams feel that their excitement and commitment to the idea is undermined by a sense of being under siege which arises from the demands placed upon them. That these demands often feel impossible to achieve is evident in the literature on such teams, and authors vary in their views as to whether the struggle to provide care through CMHTs is worthwhile or not.

Paxton (1995) claims that 'what we know overwhelmingly is that community mental health teams have been shown not to work', while Tyrer and Creed write:

> The evidence seems to be that long-term community psychiatric care is both good for the patients and satisfying for community teams but we need much more evidence to be certain of this and it would be a great help if we knew exactly what negative factors made some community psychiatric teams fail, sometimes very shortly after they had been set up.
>
> (Tyrer and Creed, 1995: 5)

What is meant by failure is that team members find the demands of working together in a CMHT too difficult and they cease working together as part of the same team.

The purpose of this chapter is to identify those sources of chaos that hinder integrated team functioning, leading instead to fragmentation, and to offer some explanations for this, indicating what is necessary for the promotion of an integrated multidisciplinary service. But first some definitions.

The team, the task and sources of chaos

A community mental health team is usually comprised of a team of community psychiatric nurses (CPNs) and a team of social workers often referred to as care managers (CMs), some of whom will also be approved social workers (ASWs). They are employed by NHS trusts and local authority social service departments respectively, and provide a full-time service in the team (CMHT). Other NHS employees may be full time in the CMHT but are more likely to be part-time. These include psychiatrists, psychologists, occupational therapists and psychotherapists who often have senior status within their professions and within the CMHT team.

The task of CMHTs is to manage staff employed by two different organizations (NHS trusts and social service departments) with a range of professional skills and to coordinate the services that they offer in order to provide the clients with an integrated multidisciplinary service which creates a 'seamless' package of care between hospital and the community.

Sources of chaos fall into four categories. Three are external to the teams and these are the community, the clients and the policies; the fourth, which is internal, stems from the differences between the professions. I will briefly identify the external issues, because they certainly need attention; then I will concentrate on the internal issues in order to offer some understanding about why it is so difficult for teams to process effectively the external chaotic influences that impinge on them.

The community

The community is a more open and chaotic environment than an institution. While many clients undoubtedly benefit from care in the community as opposed to care within an institution because of the freedom it affords them, it is nevertheless the case that people who are feeling fragile often feel unsafe in the community and seek something that would enable them to feel better 'held' – that is, something that would provide them with a feeling of greater security. In addition, the community setting makes it much harder for professional staff to monitor the mental state of clients and, when necessary, to offer firmer 'holding' in the form of providing more intensive care, hospitalization and/or exerting tighter controls on their behaviour.

Clients

The bulk of the clients of CMHTs fall into the group described in the legislation as having 'severe and/or enduring mental illness'. Such illness not only fragments the minds of those who suffer from it; it can fragment the minds of those who care for them, and also systems of care (see Chapter 1). The fundamental nature of severe and/or enduring mental illness, particularly when it is accompanied by a borderline personality disorder, means that those who suffer from it are likely to behave in an unpredictable, disruptive and sometimes violent manner. Their personalities are not integrated and they tend to use mechanisms of splitting and projection as defences against the anxiety and pain in their lives. (See Introduction and Chapter 5). They are quick to decide whether something or somebody is good or bad, and anyone who has experience of working with these clients knows the feeling of being appreciated one minute and hated the next.

While this is always anxiety-provoking, it is also a challenge; these clients can be very appealing and we try very hard to be good for them. We are also flattered by the client who informs us that we understand them better than any of their other workers, past or present.

In a paper entitled 'The ailment', Main (1957) describes how the 'chosen' workers of clients like this often devote seemingly endless hours to their care, becoming exhausted and burnt out in the process while their client fails to improve. Main was writing about these dynamics long before the introduction of comprehensive policies of care in the community and he was able to identify them because the work took place within the defined boundaries of a residential therapeutic community. In the community, such processes between carers and those in their care have always occurred, but the resulting competition between professionals was often encapsulated in rivalry between agencies. In the CMHT, this rivalry comes directly into the teams. All teams have clients who are notorious for the demands that they make on their key workers and also on the team as a whole. When the team is able to manage these clients collectively and effectively, the clients are well contained. This is of benefit to the clients and is also of benefit to other professionals in the client's network of care who are outside the CMHT, such as GPs, because well-contained clients make fewer demands than those whose care is less well coordinated. However, when not managed well – perhaps, for example, when the allocated key worker is on leave – they can generate powerful disagreements and rivalrous feelings, as staff argue about the 'right' way to manage and work with the client concerned. This behaviour produces fragmentation rather than coordination of care, and reinforces, instead of counteracting, the tendencies of the clients towards fragmentation of their own internal worlds.

Particularly difficult clients often appear to take on a role akin to that of team mascot: team members will evaluate their effectiveness by the extent to which they are able to manage these clients in order to protect both the clients and others around them from harm. It is as if the degree of health or sickness of these particularly disturbed individuals is used as a way of monitoring the degree of health or sickness of the team's functioning. Such interdependence and lack of objectivity is unhelpful for all concerned, but there is some truth in the belief that a team's effectiveness is measured in this way by those external to the team.

Policy

The nature of the purchaser/provider split in health and social care is extremely complex (see Introduction). It has introduced bureaucratic splits which, if not well managed, can lead to splits in the provision of care and resulting chaos for both the providers and the receivers of the care. The fact that most practitioners are confused about the actual nature of the contractual arrangements exacerbates this situation. Social workers/care managers, who are employed by purchasing local authority social service departments, clearly have provider functions related to their roles as assessors of need, as care managers in long-term relationships with their clients, and in their role as approved social workers which involves them in using their powers under the Mental Health Act to admit clients compulsorily to hospital care. However, they may also, indirectly, purchase the services of their health service colleagues who are employed by NHS provider units. These provider units are, in theory, in competition with other provider units for their contracts.

In short, CMHT members are employed by two different organizations, each with their own views about the prioritization of treatment and care services, about budget limitations and about how services should be audited. I will take three examples of the chaos that this can produce in the form of the three Bs of bureaucracy, beds and blame.

Bureaucracy

If the two employing organizations fail to agree how staff in a CMHT might integrate the bureaucratic procedures, this leaves staff struggling, like parentless children, to work out how they are to coexist, deciding (or not deciding) among themselves how policies and procedures are to be integrated. While it is possible – with considerable goodwill and motivation for joint working – to integrate the NHS care programme approach (CPA) with local authority systems of care management through the creation of internal team policies, it is equally possible for them to be used, perhaps unwittingly, as a means of disintegration.

Team members must have time to meet in order to work out how to function as a team, but clearly too much time spent trying to resolve conflicts arising from the split in employers diverts time from face-to-face client work. Staff may feel that they need to take this time or, alternatively, they may decide that client work must take precedence. The danger here is that they revert to doing their work as they have always done it, namely, to remain firmly based in their disciplines at the expense of collaborative ventures. This 'split employer' also increases the workload of team managers who frequently complain that their attention is diverted from the responsibility of supporting and supervising their staff (that is, attending to the detail of client work and the anxiety arising from it) to satisfying the demands of their particular employer and dealing with the bureaucratic business of team integration.

In this manner, policies that are designed to monitor and to increase the quality of care that clients receive, thereby reducing the risk to clients, workers and other carers, are in danger of doing the opposite.

Beds

The ability of a well-functioning multidisciplinary team to agree on the need for admission for a particular client, whether via a voluntary or compulsory admission, is threatened if there is no available bed. The shortage of acute and medium-secure beds in psychiatric hospitals, most notably in the inner cities, directly affects the quality of care received by the clients. People are often not admitted until a situation had already become dangerous, leading to an increase in the use of sectioning (compulsory admission under the Mental Health Act) with the resulting loss of liberty for the client. Other consequences of the shortage of beds are that clients may be sent out of their area into the care of people who do not know them, returning to their area only when a bed becomes available (sometimes regardless of clinical opinion about the appropriateness of another move) or discharged prematurely. This exacerbates the considerable difficulty already mentioned of thinking of in-patient and CMHT services as part of a single system of care (see Chapter 10).

The shortage of beds puts great pressure on the psychiatrists (working both in the CMHT and in the hospital) as they attempt to work in the best interests of the patient and also as valued team members of both the hospital team and the CMHT, and heightens the tensions between the two services.

Within the CMHT, this threatens to create a conflict between staff who work wholly in the community and those who do not, most notably the psychiatrists. When good multidisciplinary work that had led to a timely recognition of someone's need for admission is thwarted by the lack of a local bed, with severe consequences for the client, it arouses great pain and impotent anger which introduce chaos into team meetings and team functioning. It is not difficult to see that staff in this situation might prefer to take flight from such meetings, choosing instead to identify with subgroups from which position they can project the uncomfortable feelings of inadequacy and blame elsewhere.

Blame

While it is undoubtedly the case that inter-agency and inter-professional collaboration could be improved and that this would enhance the quality of care received by the mentally ill in the community, we must remain critical of any policy or media reporting that appears to imply that one person can be

held responsible for the behaviour of others. Such a view stirs up persecutory anxiety in practitioners, and can lead to defensive practices such as
paying undue attention to bureaucratic requirements while fearing that the
client's situation remains as risky as ever. In such instances the attention of
the worker can become focused more on what those in authority will think
of them than on the needs of their clients, and this does little to contain the
anxiety of either client or worker.

The Patients Charter (DoH, 1991), which overall represents a positive
step in the direction of patients' rights, can also be experienced as persecuting to providers. In this case it is persecution by the clients that is feared.
Unfortunately, it is often the most difficult-to-manage clients who respond
to a notice, posted on the waiting-room wall, inviting them to complain
about the service they are getting. Some do this in a destructive manner.
This is likely to produce upset, conflict and splits within the team, and
between the team and the senior managers, as investigations take place. The
client, instead of experiencing the presence of a strong and united team
capable of managing his or her destructiveness, experiences individual team
members who are anxious and fragile and who appear to have been
destroyed by it. This confirms the client's worst fears, that he or she is
powerfully destructive.

Internal issues: multidisciplinary working

In the above examples it is possible to see how factors external to CMHT
teams impinge on team functioning in a manner that creates splits between
team members. Difficulties arising from the anxiety inherent in working with
disturbed people in the community can easily set one worker or one discipline against another and these splits, which I would argue are an
occupational hazard, can be fuelled, rather than contained, by policies.
Teams need to find ways of containing and managing these splits in order to
function effectively as multidisciplinary teams. When this is achieved, multidisciplinary work becomes very satisfying and these good experiences are
what motivate staff and enable them to remain committed to this way of
work at those times when being a team member feels particularly difficult. I
suggest that the reason that CMHTs fail is that they fail in their efforts to
contain and manage splits, and therefore fail to become integrated teams.

Why should this prove so difficult? Why do members of CMHTs
constantly complain about the difficulties and the demands of the work,
both loving it and hating it?

When CMHTs are formed, staff come not only with their own personal
culture and history, but with their professional culture and history. Staff
used to working within hospitals are familiar with a culture of benign
patriarchy with the doctors at the top. At different times this might have felt
kindly, *laissez-faire*, supportive, attacking or wasteful, yet the hospital as an

institution was able to protect the thinking task from too much onslaught from the outside world. It acted as a container for staff and patients and met their dependency needs. It was also prone, when anxiety was high, to anti-task defences (Menzies, 1959) such as dependency, not thinking for oneself and, at worst, was cruel to patients and felt stultifying for staff. Some workers would 'escape' to outposts in the community in order to feel freer.

Within social service departments, where fieldwork in the community was the major occupation, workers were 'held' by statutory obligations and by supervision and management systems that monitored this. There was a vitality that came from being buffeted by the daily demands and the unpredictability of the outside world. When anxiety was high, the culture was prone to anti-task defences of fight and flight (high turnover of staff, confrontations and strikes) and workers would feel alienated. Some would 'escape' to outposts in the health services in order to find a more protected space in which to think and to develop their therapeutic work (see Stokes, 1994).

The formation of CMHTs places all these people (some willingly, others unwillingly), in the community where, it can be argued, the dominant defence against the anxiety of working with disturbed clients in this setting is one of fight or flight. There is no shortage of opportunity for staff in CMHTs to fight each other as the team includes workers from different professional disciplines who would previously have worked in separate agencies with different cultures and different defences. We can all recognize a tendency in ourselves to preserve the goodness of our discipline or team by projecting the conflict and having the arguments with people who are outside this. However, when we acknowledge those people who might conveniently have been 'our enemies' in the past as 'part of us', we have to struggle with the discomfort that this produces (see Figure 11.1).

From the point of view of the outsiders to the CMHT – GPs, other agencies and the clients – CMHTs are an advantage in that they only have to make one telephone call instead of many and if they receive a team response to their requests. The staff of the CMHT are required to think and to work together in order to provide this.

When the differences between staff feel unmanageable, there are two obvious defensive strategies of flight to which people can resort. The first is to revert to old tried and tested methods of work which lead each individual or discipline to 'keep their head down' and avoid the conflict situations by avoiding meetings and 'getting on with working with their clients' in the same way that they always have. While they may be offering a valuable service, they are not working as part of a multidisciplinary team and they are in danger of providing a fragmented rather than an integrated service to the client. The second flight defence is to avoid struggling with differences by behaving as if everyone in the team were the same. This is flight from multidisciplinary working, resulting in staff functioning at the lowest common denominator of sameness, giving up the satisfaction that comes

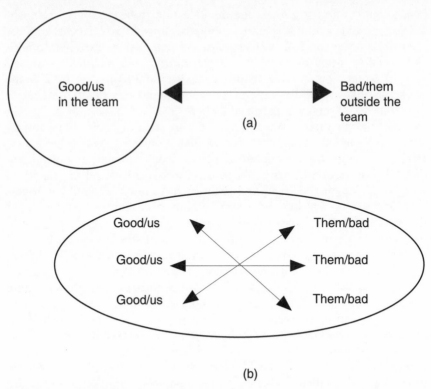

Figure 11.1 (a) Dynamic prior to CMHT formation; (b) dynamic post-CMHT formation

from professional expertise in favour of team cosiness. This defence obscures the value of difference and drastically reduces the options available to the client.

It might be argued that these two team defences of fight and flight are so powerful because they are ways of avoiding the challenge of integrating the skills of different professions into a comprehensive service. Tyrer and Creed (1995: 6) argue that 'The training received by each discipline is different and the combination of beliefs and attitudes inculcated is such that when these disciplines are put together later and asked to work in a community team a potentially explosive mixture is produced.' There is no agreed philosophy about the nature of mental illness – its causes or its treatment – and the failure of psychiatry to find a cure means that the medical profession is no longer automatically seen as the expert profession in the field. There are inherent conflicts in the concepts of treatment and social care; of care and control and of managment and empowerment. While it can be argued that, in order to provide appropriate care for those with severe and/or enduring mental illnesses whose needs change over time, professionals need to find, and constantly re-find, appropriate balances between these approaches, this poses real challenges to the multidisciplinary team.

In psychodynamic terms the team is required to function in the depressive position (see Introduction). Staff have to be able to value their differences, feeling secure enough to recognize their individual strengths and weaknesses as well as those of others and to recognize and value the specific contributions of each discipline. When a team is able to take up mentally a position of observation – thereby creating a reflective space – it becomes possible to do this. When anxiety, related to particular clients or to particular policies or both, is too high, the team will revert to paranoid–schizoid functioning where such openness feels too threatening because it is no longer possible to hold in mind the strengths *and* weaknesses of one's own or anyone else's work. Each team member then fears attack because there is a need within the team to locate all the 'bad', unwanted aspects – the doubts, insecurities, inadequacies and failures – in someone else (see Chapter 5). See Figure 11.2.

Position of observation

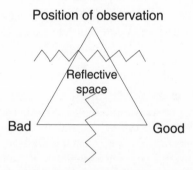

Bad   Good

Figure 11.2 Teams oscillate between fragmentation and integration: the *reflective space* represents the possibility of depressive-position functioning and healthy integration; the *jagged lines* represent the fragmentation that occurs when workers fear being overwhelmed by the demands of policies or clients

Management and authority in the team

Pressures on effective team functioning are severely increased because the task of deciding who should have responsibility over what is left to each team to work out for themelves. The Department of Health issued the following guidelines:

Teams must be managed efficiently if the service is to be effective. Individual teams will need to decide how the management tasks . . . are carried out. The team may be non-hierarchical, or conversely led by a single individual; what is essential is that, once again there is *clarity* about respective roles and lines of accountability. Making sure that the management structure is right is not an optional extra for teams, but an essential part of effective working.

(DoH, 1995: 36)

One could argue that this denotes an abdication of responsibility by higher management from the Department of Health downwards. Teams can spend enormous amounts of time trying to agree on operational policies which, at the end of the day, stand or fall depending on the personalities and the goodwill of the team members. While this is frustrating and difficult for all, the role of psychiatrists is a particularly complex one. They still carry considerable clinical responsibility and if team management structures are either unclear or unsupported by team members then there are likely to be times when team members behave as if they were operating within the old hospital model of dependency on the medical profession. Psychiatrists, who are trained within such a system, may find it easier to collude with this than to challenge it, but this ultimately leads to conflict. A survey of the organization and operation of CMHTs (Onyett *et al.*, 1994) found tentative evidence for lower turnover of staff among less medically dominated teams.

Toxicity

Wykes (1995: 103) examines the aims of community care and states that services should not be toxic: 'Staff should not experience more burnout, sickness, turnover, danger (violence from patients and from the public in carrying out their job).' Yet clearly many staff in CMHTs do experience their service as toxic. The untreatability of many of the clients (see Chapter 1), the complexity of the multidisciplinary approach, and the lack of or the unworkability of management structures, together with the constant pressure of work and limited resources – all contribute to the feeling that the work gets inside the individual worker in a manner that can feel dangerously malignant. In order to tackle this – so that a team can function well together, providing job satisfaction for individual team members and effective services both for the clients and for other professionals in the networks of care – teams must find a way of dealing with the toxicity. Toxicity, if not managed by the team, becomes, in itself, a source of fragmentation and chaos as the team members appear to fall apart, becoming disturbed by their work, taking time off or leaving. When this happens it genuinely feels as if something both contagious and malignant has got into the team and this is anxiety-provoking and upsetting for everyone as they worry about their own fitness for the job, their ability to survive this 'epidemic' and whether or not the team, as they know it, will be destroyed by it.

An effective staff support group is one way of attempting to deal with the toxicity that is, in many ways, an occupational hazard. Even though some staff will attend only irregularly and others never, the fact that, alongside other meetings, a time is allocated specifically for the purpose of dealing with those issues that the team find distressing and difficult to address is significant. Issues might include the death of a client, the leaving or the sickness of a valued team member, dangers in the work, irritations about multidisciplinary functioning or rage at the latest policy initiative. At quieter times it might be thoughts about collaborative research or how to promote their work more effectively. All such issues benefit from thinking time that is not dominated by a busy business agenda even though they may subsequently be placed on the agenda for a business meeting. It is a space to think together in which differences of opinion can be held in mind and considered. It is a space in which it is possible to address differences and to appreciate others because it is protected from the pressure to make hasty decisions. In short it is a space in which fight/flight defences can be examined and the move towards greater depressive-position functioning can take place.

Conclusion

The CMHT, it seems, is often left to find a way of coping with and managing what feel like impossible demands both from clients and from policy. The struggle to do this collectively can be avoided through fight or flight, or addressed through finding ways of containing the pain and suffering that is generated by the nature of the work but not contained or openly acknowledged either by the clients or by the policies.

The idea of a wholly integrated team is a fantasy which parallels that of a wholly integrated individual. The demands of the work are such that toxicity will always be present and one can only hope to do a good enough job most of the time with the support of one's colleagues. Many staff in CMHTs believe that they are managing to do this. A staff support group that begins with feelings of desperation and despair often ends with members valuing and appreciating their work and their colleagues acknowledging that they are offering a good enough service delivered by committed and skilled professionals. This is possible because staff are prepared to give time to working on the anti-task defences as they arise, and to face up to the reality of the limitations of their work and to the painful realities of the lives of their clients. It is so much easier to flee from the feelings that these realities stir up than it is to face the pain of it all. Yet it is through facing this that staff hold on to their humanity and thus are able to continue doing the work that offers continuity and meaningful care to their clients.

Note

1 The author wishes to acknowledge the valuable contributions of Viv Igel and

Naomi Landau who were joint authors with Angela Foster of an earlier version of this chapter, given as a paper entitled 'The management of community mental health teams: integration or fragmentation', at the Ninth Annual Conference on Psychoanalysis & The Public Sphere, London, 1995.

References

DoH (1991) *Patients Charter*, London: HMSO.

DoH (1994) *A Framework for Local Community Mental Health Charters in England: Consultative Document*, London: Department of Health.

DoH (1995) *The Health of the Nation. Building Bridges: A Guide to Arrangements for Inter-agency Working for the Care and Protection of Severely Mentally Ill People*, London: Department of Health.

Main, T. (1957) 'The ailment' (paper given to Medical Section, British Psychological Society), in J. Johns (ed.) (1989) *The Ailment and Other Psychoanalytic Essays*, London: Free Association Books.

Menzies, I.E.P. (1959) 'The functioning of social systems as a defence against anxiety: a report on a study of the nursing service of a general hospital', *Human Relations* 13: 95–121; reprinted in I. Menzies Lyth (1988) *Containing Anxiety in Institutions: Selected Essays*, vol. 1, London: Free Association Books.

Onyett, S., Heppleston, T. and Bushnall, D. (1994) *Organisation and Operation of Community Mental Health Teams in England*, London: Sainsbury Centre for Mental Health.

Paxton, R. (1995) 'Goodbye community mental health teams – at last, *J. Mental Health* 4: 331–4.

Stokes, J. (1994) 'The unconscious at work in groups and teams: contributions from the work of Wilfred Bion', in A. Obholzer and V.Z. Roberts (eds) *The Unconscious at Work*, London: Routledge.

Tyrer, P. and Creed, F. (eds) (1995) *Community Psychiatry in Action: Analysis and Prospects*, Cambridge: Cambridge University Press.

Wykes, T. (1995) 'The toxicity of community care', in P. Tyrer and F. Creed (eds) *Community Psychiatry in Action: Analysis and Prospects*, Cambridge: Cambridge University Press.

12

Beyond keyworking

Trinidad Navarro

In this chapter I will be discussing why I think the model of keyworking as an approach to the care in the community of severely mentally ill people cannot adequately provide for clients' or workers' psychological containment. This situation is in part due to a pervasive systemic denial of the enduring nature and the severity of the disturbance in these clients, and of the impact of the loss of the psychiatric institutions. There is no doubt that there is a need for a system that can manage and monitor as well as treat clients within the community. However, I will argue that this can be done better if the responsibility for clients and for the therapeutic work with them is conducted through a team approach, using psychodynamic principles.

I use the term 'containment' in two ways. First, I use it as defined in the *Concise Oxford English Dictionary*: contain – 'hold or be capable of holding within itself, include'; container – 'a vessel, box, etc for holding particular things'; containment – 'the action or policy of preventing the expansion of a hostile ... influence'. And second, I use it as a specific psychoanalytic concept (Bion, 1967) to indicate the need for the 'vessel' in the form of the community and worker to be able not only to hold on to the disturbance but also to 'digest' and process it (see Introduction for an explanation of the psychoanalytic theory of containment).

The client group to whom I am referring have long histories of intermittent psychiatric hospitalization; most will have a diagnosis of schizophrenia or one of the other psychotic illnesses. Prior to the onset of illness, these people have had, at best, a history of emotional, psychosocial and socioeconomic deprivation; at worst, sexual, physical and/or emotional abuse. Their early environments were invariably characterized by familial breakdown, such as desertion by one parent, violence, mental illness, unemployment, poverty, poor housing, etc. This frequently resulted in the clients having been taken into foster care as children or young adolescents, or receiving some other form of professional intervention, thus beginning a lifelong experience of broken relationships and attachments. Many are from ethnic minority groups and in particular from the black African Caribbean community. For these people the above experiences are even more confusing and distressing when they have had the added complication of being fostered by white parents. In my experience, the resulting identity confusion, personal and cultural, when experienced within a predominantly white psychiatric system such as obtains in the United Kingdom, further aggravates the illness.

People with severe mental illness have very few, if any, internal resources upon which to draw. When psychotic breakdown occurs, both the internal and external environments are experienced as hostile and persecutory and are treated as such by the client, often resulting in violent acts directed towards the self or others. In many instances the psychiatric hospital itself has been the only experience of security and consistency in their lives. A report of the confidential inquiry into homicides in England and suicides in England, Scotland and Northern Ireland by mentally ill people states that 94.9 per cent of these homicides are committed by 'discharged in-patients and out-patients' and 76.8 per cent of suicides have also occurred away from the hospital (Boyd, 1996). I have been involved in two cases where clients have presented themselves for admission having just committed an act of violence, in one case homicide.

Problems inherent in keyworking clients

Given the nature of this client group, I would argue that they cannot be adequately looked after by the keyworker system. In the first instance, they have reached such a stage of cynicism that the promise of a special one-to-one relationship as part of a care package is meaningless to them, for they have experienced the loss of numerous relationships which have been initiated in this manner. Not only have they lost the worker permanently at some point but they have often lost the service that was provided on a regular basis while the relationship with the worker existed. The impact of 'ordinary' annual leave and sick leave on the client cannot be underestimated within a keyworker system. Typically, in the absence of the keyworker the service simply ceases for the client as well as for the other professional agencies that may be involved in their care. Sometimes the consequences are so drastic that they appear to result in clients acting out their internal worlds, at times ending up committing grievous bodily harm, homicide or suicide. The aforementioned report of the confidential inquiry speaks to the finding that 'changes in the pattern of care are well recognised risk factors ... discharge from in-patient status, change of keyworker necessitated by resignation or holiday, and so on'. It further states that 'the patient may interpret the change as a rejection and a response should be made to these concerns' (Boyd, 1996).

A less dramatic but equally damaging consequence is the way in which this system feeds into a sense of crippling dependency where the ability to deal with reality and the external world is located in another person (see Chapter 1). For instance, something as simple as dealing with a final demand on a domestic bill can escalate into a full-blown crisis, and occurs when adequate support is not available and when the client does not have sufficient internal resources on which to draw.

Example 1

The final demand arrives. The keyworker has all the information relevant to this back at the office in the client's case notes. The client telephones the keyworker (or another agency telephones on the client's behalf). The person who answers the telephone takes a few minutes to register who the client is and then to put the caller through to the right department. Someone else answers on the correct extension. The client (if it is the client calling) wants to speak to their keyworker. She is informed that her worker has not returned from annual leave yet because she is now on sick leave; no one quite knows when the worker is expected back. The client begins to feel panicky and asks if someone can help her with her problems. The person on duty, who may have very little knowledge of the client's situation and who may never have met the client before, can only offer limited help.

Keyworking gives life to the pre-existing ideological notion that a two-person relationship is the fundamental basis of therapeutic practice. In this system, workers often behave as if it is only the keyworker who can understand the client, be responsible for her and ultimately have 'ownership' of the case.

In the meantime, intense feelings are often stirred up in the client by this type of situation. Fear, rage and a sense of persecution can arise when the primitive desire to belong and be totally dependent on another is frustrated. Suddenly the same person who was able to think about who to ask for help is now completely unable to think. She does not know what to do with her feelings so that they are inevitably acted out until conventional control is provided in the form of hospitalization, medication and so on.

But even when a keyworker is present there is a lack of psychological containment for this client group, for the keyworker system is, in my view, full of contradictions and paradoxes. Its essence is about providing a 'trusting' one-to-one relationship, through which the client and worker work on the client's achieving the various goals set out in the care plan, the ultimate aim being to 'make the client more independent'. This latter term has become a mantra for community care. Although it reflects the ideology of policy-makers and the idealism of practitioners, it actually prevents the understanding of what this client group needs, which is, in the first instance, to be understood as suffering from serious and enduring mental disturbance. The client's illness is going to last longer than the keyworker.

The denial of the severity of clients' disturbance is understandable as a defence for workers against the pain associated with the rejection by clients of the help and understanding that they attempt to offer. This realization is particularly painful for individuals who have entered the field in order to make reparation for relationships that they feel they have damaged in the past (Klein, 1988). This denial is, of course, colluded with, indeed set up by, the wider system (community) which cannot tolerate the anxiety that the presence of severe mental illness in the community stirs up. Another good reason for the keyworking system to deny the severity of the problem is that it is simply not possible for one individual to tolerate this level of incessant disturbance. Thus, another contradiction is in the practice itself. The trusting and therapeutic relationship is, in reality, one of containment through management as in the dictionary definition rather than one of therapeutic containment in Bion's sense.

From the client's point of view, the lack of safety is nothing new in itself. However, what is different from their earlier experiences is that in the keyworking situation there is the appearance of a special relationship giving rise to a belief that therapeutic containment is possible. The reality of keyworking is a far cry from the idealization of a special two-person relationship, and workers who have been drawn to it in fact frequently end up disappointed, resentful and burnt out.

Furthermore, as recent changes in policy emphasize the management aspect of the keyworker's role, the individual keyworker has become increasingly burdened with the responsibility of controlling and tracking clients. For example, supervised discharge requires the keyworker to have and execute the following powers:

1   require the client to attend for medical treatment and rehabilitation
2   require the client to reside in a specified place; and
3   to convey the client to a place where he or she is to attend for treatment.

The experience of keyworking moves closer to social policing than to a therapeutic interchange between two people. Even the management of these clients is superficial. The contact and resources required to keep a 'finger on the pulse' are greater than any individual can hold. What is required of keyworkers is that, in the event of a serious crisis, they can be seen to have done their job. That essentially means that the worker needs to know where the client is and where the client should be; that clients have received their medication; that their basic health, nutritional and housing needs are met; and that the worker has contacted the right people, say, a psychiatrist or CPN, in the event of an impending crisis or breakdown. Other aspects of the care plan – goals such as repairing family relationships, learning to cook and shop, and so on – take second place.

This system inhibits the development of both the client and the worker.

The therapeutic potential of working alongside the client on the everyday tasks is never realized. A worker who is full up with anxiety about their management responsibilities does not have the mental space to process their own experience of doing the job, nor to think about and process the confusing dynamics between themselves and their clients. It is difficult for the worker to fully experience, think about and process their interaction with and reaction to the client, as this involves experiencing a high level of psychotic disturbance (which is very difficult to do without adequate professional support) and the keyworker often feels isolated in their role.

The Team Approach

In order to work effectively, we need to start from the premise that this client group will never become completely 'better' or independent of professional services. This then requires a mental health service that does not demand progress and that does not close 'the case' when progress is made. The service needs to be able to tolerate and 'digest' the disturbance as well as manage it. In other words, we need to be able to contain the disturbance therapeutically. This is no simple task, and services often defend against the impact of the disturbance by becoming omnipotent in their thinking and consequently ineffective in their practice. Facing this reality requires the team and the workers to know and work within their limitations. Limitations can be reduced and the capacity for containment and management increased if the work and the experience of it is shared among a group of people, i.e. the whole team. This is referred to as the Team Approach, a system of care that acknowledges the severe and enduring nature of the disturbance and attempts to work with the loss of the psychiatric hospitals and to replace them with a sense of an 'institution in the mind' (Armstrong, 1991). The intention is that the team will be in existence for as long as the client needs their services. Since the team is more enduring than any one individual worker, to shift the keyworking relationship from one between an individual client and an individual worker to one between the client and the team (or service) offers greater long-term dependability and therefore greater containment.

A Team Approach to community mental health work was first introduced in Wisconsin, USA, and then worked with in Thresholds, Chicago. This model was brought to London in 1990 by Tulip, a voluntary sector community mental health service, and has been considerably adapted so as to incorporate a psychodynamic perspective. The team as a whole assumes responsibility for each client and all team members know and work with each client. All direct work is carried out in the community, each client receiving a minimum of one visit at the same appointed time each week. The use of this model facilitates the operation of a no-close policy, i.e. in theory clients' cases are not closed or reassigned.

The overall aim of the Team Approach is to create a therapeutic milieu within the community where clients feel held in the mind of the team, and the team is in the mind of the client. The team brings into the community 'an environment that provides highly reinforcing opportunities for new patterns of talking, feeling and acting, as well as expression and examination of old patterns and motivations, and this environment (should) exist both for patients and the care providers' (Whalley, 1994: 461).

In Tulip, the Team Approach is used in both residential and outreach services, but for the sake of clarity I shall be referring to the work done by the outreach teams. In order to allow for dependency on and attachments to the service rather than to the individual, and yet not overwhelm the client with lots of new faces, the introduction to the team is made gradually. This process starts with two team members visiting the client together. On the following visit one of the original two is accompanied by a new person and so it goes on until the client has met all the workers, all introduced by one of the two original team members. When this process is completed and so long as it is judged to be safe, workers visit on their own on a rotational basis. To enable the client to experience the team as a cohesive and consistent service, structures and mechanisms for sharing information and ideas, and for decision-making and planning, need to be in place.

In a clinic or hospital, containment is provided not only by the building but also by the structure of the day: meetings at set times in set places, to address set tasks in predictable (reliable) ways. In outreach work, many of these traditional sources of containment for the worker are stripped away in order to provide a richer, more accessible and in-touch service. Outreach workers do all their direct work with clients in the environment in which the clients live. Workers are constantly moving from one environment to another and from one disturbance to another without contact with colleagues for hours on end. But structure and containment are still necessary, and therefore alternative ways to provide these must be found.

At Tulip, meetings take place at the beginning and end of each day. The morning meeting is a check-in system which addresses practical and administrative issues, such as rearranging a visit due to workers' sickness or arranging for a worker to attend a ward round at short notice. The focus is on what needs to be done and by whom. On one day a week this time is used to plan and allocate the week's work, so that subsequent meetings serve to update and rearrange plans where necessary. Information about clients is confidential to the team as a whole, not to the individual worker, and this is understood by the client. If staff felt that they had to keep information to themselves, the model would not work. The evening meeting provides a space for workers to debrief as the day's work is reported and recorded. This includes work done on behalf of clients, contacts with other services, as well as direct client contact. Workers report on both the factual information and their own emotional experience of doing the work. The factual and experiential information is discussed, reflected on and recorded and any subsequent action that needs to take place is also recorded and put on the timetable. These meetings focus on what has been done, how it was done and on what may need to be done as a consequence. Both meetings require a strong management presence to lead the process and contribute to its content because this is where the disturbance experienced by the workers in the community is 'digested'. It is also the place where workers' differences, and issues around being an individual within a group, are negotiated. The group could not maintain this level of peer supervision without the general sense of holding provided by the manager's authority and direction.

Of equal importance is regular consultancy to the team provided by an outside consultant (see Chapter 5). In this space, workers are not under pressure to take action and can explore freely, weekly or fortnightly, their counter-transference reactions as individuals and as a group to the clients. Similarly, just as clients have transference reactions to the team, the individual workers and the team as a whole have a transference relationship to the organization and to the clients. It is very important to explore and disentangle these dynamics, as put so eloquently by Whalley: 'The empathetic response is compromised when the treatment provider's dilemmas parallel or complement those of the client. Conversely, examination of the counter-transference feelings can provide insights into clients, thoughts, feelings, actions' (1994: 459). I will give an example of this below.

There are a variety of important processes that work in tandem with the Team Approach and these are located in the two meetings, which are essentially interdependent, addressing both the practical and psychosocial aspects of the work as they are expressed consciously and unconsciously by the client, the individual worker and the team as a whole. For example, work allocation is not simply a matter of rotating the tasks and visits equally and without thought; it is about making use of the experiential, cultural and professional differences as applicable to the work.

Example 2

On one occasion, the team received a telephone call from the local police, asking us to intervene in a situation where they had arrested Terry, a young black client of ours, for shoplifting. We were lucky to have a choice about who in the team would be best placed to deal with the situation. As we had to act quickly, we needed to think quickly about what we wanted to result from the intervention and therefore what attributes were needed. We knew the client well and guessed that he was acting out (he was generally a quiet and often very depressed young man) and therefore needed to feel safe. We needed to send somebody whom he respected, who could advocate for him as well as challenge him and set some limits on his behaviour. The person would also need to project a sense of authority so that she or he could negotiate with the police. We decided that John, the black male worker in the team, should go for all the above reasons, but also to provide the client with a role model while challenging the stereotypical view of young black men. This was not an easy decision to make or to execute. It never is, as it involves dealing with emotions such as jealousy and envy; in the end, as the manager, I had to make it. However, it was possible to take this decision and for it to feel right to the group because the team had a historical knowledge of the worker's qualities and skills, of the client's psychopathology and of the quality of relationship between worker and client.

At the evening meeting that same day, John reported back on his experience. He said that he had negotiated with the police to allow Terry to be let off with a warning. He then accompanied Terry to his flat and spent time with him thinking about what he had done, while helping him to clean up his flat. Terry had stolen a pair of shoes that he did not need and he had done this in such a way that he would inevitably be caught. John explored with him the possible reasons for his doing this at this time. Terry said that he was fed up because things were not going well with his father: they had had a row the night before.

In the meeting, John thought further about his feelings while with Terry. He said that at times he had felt very angry with him, and at other times very sad; and that Terry had seemed quite cut off from his own feelings. Other members of the team contributed by thinking about their recent experiences of Terry and also about what they felt as John was reporting back. There was a consensus that this behaviour was out of character and that there seemed to be a lot of anger about. It was decided that Terry should be visited again the next day by a different member of the team and that the team's thoughts would be explored with him. It was also decided that the team would inform Terry of their plans to make contact with his psychiatrist, and that they would arrange for a case conference and to visit Terry's father to find out more about the row.

It is of equal importance that team members should consider the meaning of their different experiences of the client.

Example 3

Jackie returns from a visit to David. At the evening meeting the same day she relates details of the visit and adds that, for no obvious reason, she felt quite unsafe while with him. The team have worked with this man for three years and up until then no one had expressed such a feeling. Another woman in the team says, 'It's funny you say that. I felt a bit uneasy when I saw him the other day.' Various male members of the group add that they have never felt threatened by this client and one adds that he gets the sense that the client is feeling frightened, and frightened by women in particular. Another member of the team reminds them that, in fact, this client has in the past assaulted his mother which led to his being compulsorily admitted to hospital. This feeling of unsafety among the female workers might be evidence that David was heading for another breakdown. The team can then take a number of actions simultaneously. For instance, they may make contact with other professionals involved with the client to see if there have been any difficulties recently, or they may decide that one of the male workers should check him out later in the evening. The next day, one or two workers may visit him to discuss the team's concerns, and so on.

It needs to be acknowledged that for workers the pressure to hold large numbers of clients in mind is enormous. At the same time, there is the sense of loss that comes with not being able to form and work with individual attachments on a long-term basis. Clients too have reported their dissatisfactions with this model. There are occasions such as bereavement when it is inappropriate for several workers to visit the client. In such instances one worker is allocated for a set period of time. This is an area that needs further research and which may result in a modified version such as smaller teams with smaller client groups.

Gauntlett, in his evaluation (Gauntlett *et al.*, 1996) of three community mental health teams, reports that the Tulip outreach team workers reported 'the highest intrinsic and extrinsic job satisfaction; and the lowest levels of burnout on nearly all dimensions'. These findings, I think, are due to the constant process of peer supervision, facilitated by management, in the various forms that I have described above. As well as clarifying workers' skills and strengths and sharing responsibility and decision-making, workers' disturbing experiences are demystified and are therefore less frightening. For example, in the case of a woman who feels threatened, by sharing this information with the group she can feel contained enough to be able to hear and think about the possible meaning that this may have for the client. Even something as subtle as the idea that she may have felt frightened because that was how the client felt will help her to experience her feelings as understandable and usable (Navarro, 1996).

Clients, in turn, can be provided with a relatively unconditional, lifelong service. One client said:

> I thought it was going to be a short-term thing, but to my surprise they say 'No, we will continue with you as we feel we need to', and I felt that as well. I wanted to. I thought they were going to stop all of a sudden, and I got into a panic a little, but they assured me it was ongoing, as long as it takes. I was quite pleased with that. I've never said that to anyone, but deep down, I'm quite pleased about that.
>
> (Gauntlett *et al.*, 1996: 44)

They have the opportunity of having a team as well as the individuals within it to relate to, learn from and to use as a transference object. As another client said with great insight when interviewed:

> Every time someone came, it would be someone different. I've met a lot of people, and they have given me a lot of encouragement. Personally, I think it would have been a bit heavy for one person to come every week, for them, it would have been unfair for one person to take all that on, even though it's their job ... I find that every one of them is different. They've all got their own way of approaching me and talking to me, but basically they're all saying something the same, especially when it's coming to give support.

Clients can also feel much safer when violent, hateful feelings are uppermost. For example, there have been a number of occasions when clients have left messages on the answerphone such as, 'You're all f****** bastards, you're all useless, don't bother coming to see me again.' When such messages are received, the reactions of all team members are listened to and thought about with the intention that the client can then be responded to in a helpful and thoughtful manner, rather than in a reactive, punitive or passive way. Counter-transference reactions such as rage and a desire to close the case, or a sense of hopelessness and despair, can be seen as different aspects of the client's experience. Pulling these feelings together and communicating them back to the client in an integrated and simple form helps the client to feel understood and to know that their destructive feelings have not in actuality destroyed the relationship with the team. Contrary to assumptions that a Team Approach means the loss of a relationship, then, clients are provided with a therapeutic milieu within the community through a rich matrix of relationships.

References

Armstrong, D. (1991) *The Institution in the Mind: Reflections on the Relation of Psychoanalysis to Work with Institutions*, London: Grubb Institute.

Bion, W.R. (1967) *Second Thoughts: Selected Papers on Psychoanalysis*, London: Heinemann Medical Books; reprinted (1984 and1987), London: Karnac Books.

Boyd, W. (1996) *Report of the Confidential Inquiry into Homicides and Suicides by Mentally Ill People*, London: Royal College of Psychiatrists.

DoH (1995) *The Health of the Nation: Building Bridges*, London: HMSO.

Gauntlett, N., Ford, R. and Muijen, M. (1996) *Teamwork: Models of Outreach in an Urban Multicultural Setting*, London: The Sainsbury Centre for Mental Health.

Klein, M. (1988) *Love, Guilt and Reparation and Other Works 1921–1945*, London: Virago.

Navarro, T. (1996) 'Group supervision and the Team Approach', unpublished paper.

Whalley, P. (1994) 'Team Approach to working through transference and counter-transference in a paediatric/psychiatric milieu', *Issues in Mental Health Nursing* 15: 457–69.

13

Help to do the ordinary

The place of counselling in community care

Angela Foster

Introduction

In this chapter I draw on my experience as a psychotherapist and as a consultant to staff working with the mentally ill in the community, with particular reference to my work as supervisor to a MIND counselling project operating in an inner city area. This project was created to provide a service to people with histories of mental illness who are often denied counselling by other services. Such a counselling service can be seen as a brave initiative or as a naive and foolhardy exercise, depending on one's point of view: a brave initiative because it is not easy to counsel these clients; a naive and foolhardy exercise because there are some sound reasons for believing that, while counselling might be what these clients want, it may not be what they need or are able to use. It may even be bad for them.

People who have enduring mental illness find doing ordinary things difficult, for example working, travelling and sustaining relationships, and their difficulties tend to be long term rather than temporary. Such people are now spending most of their lives in the community. The host community did not request their presence and for a variety of reasons they tend to ignore them, shun them or even persecute them (see Chapter 2). The community 'out there', especially in our inner cities, is more demanding and alienating than that which existed in the long-stay psychiatric hospitals which are now closed. Many people with mental illness who are now in the community have experience of such hospitals which, for all their faults, offered asylum to the vulnerable within a permissive culture that accepted and contained odd behaviour and provided long-term relationships. The mentally ill who make the move into the community from these hospitals, and also those who have only experienced short-term hospital care, frequently defend themselves by avoiding contact with others. They are often lonely, leading lives that feel empty and directionless. They are frequently disillusioned with their drug treatment and, when asked what sort of service provision they would like, often request counselling. The aim of the MIND service is primarily to enhance the quality of life of such people; in other words, to help them to do the ordinary.

The client and the worker

Anne and John are representative of the people with long-term illnesses who have requested counselling from the MIND project. Anne has a diagnosis of chronic schizophrenia. Having lived rough, she is now successfully living in her own flat. She hears voices and is prescribed major tranquillizers which she takes responsibly. She is an intelligent woman who is well informed about mental health services, well known to service providers and keenly aware of what she feels is lacking in her life. She sought counselling because, although she has friends who are also service users, she lacks any meaningful relationships in her life and wanted the opportunity to talk with someone.

John presents as if he were homeless, although he is not. He describes himself as confused and muddled, yet is very clear about what he wants to say, having spent all day thinking about his appointment. He has had psychotic breakdowns every two or three years for ten years, yet each time they seem to take him by surprise. Prior to his breakdowns he had a professional career and, although he had to leave his job, he compensates for the bleakness of his marital relationship (and the bleakness in his own life) by working as a volunteer helping others. He requested counselling because he thought he was due to have a further breakdown and wanted to try to anticipate and understand this with a view to avoiding the need for hospitalization.

Hinshelwood (see Chapter 1), describing the experience of workers with psychotic clients, notes that the clients communicate a sense of hopelessness and despair in an indirect manner which gets 'inside' the worker, often causing the worker to feel that there is nothing they can offer. Such clients also communicate a feeling of fear that something out of control might happen, for example madness or violence, and that the worker might somehow become contaminated by this. This can cause the workers to distance themselves from such clients who, as a result, may be treated as if they were barely human or not properly alive. Not surprisingly, clients often complain about this treatment, indicating that they want better relationships with their workers.

However, as Hinshelwood suggests, there is something about the manner of relating to others by these clients that may ensure that others keep an emotional distance. Related to this is the notion that the clients may in fact require this to be the case. We know that psychotic people do not do well in highly emotionally charged environments, and we also know that they frequently miss appointments as if they were themselves monitoring the degree of involvement. In other words, the transference and counter-transference with these clients may be thought of as determining an appropriate degree of involvement for both worker and client. Anne, for example, limited the extent of her emotional involvement by distancing herself from the pain in her sessions and John limited his by messing up arrangements for sessions and by projecting his anxiety into his counsellor so that he too messed up the arrangements (something that the counsellor did not do with his other clients).

The current legislation on community care of the mentally ill would appear to support limited emotional involvement as it promotes the management of clients above all else. Those workers who could offer counselling to their clients and who, in some cases, would like to do so, often claim that their therapeutic skills are devalued and that they are denied the opportunity to work in this way. It is easy to see why organizations like MIND want to offer counselling to such clients, because it seems unfair that they are denied access to it elsewhere; and it is also easy to see why counsellors would want to offer a service to clients whom all others seem to have failed, hoping that their particular brand of engagement will be put to good effect by the client. But how omnipotent is this? Certainly to engage emotionally with these clients makes the work much more difficult for the worker and probably for the client too. Nevertheless Anne and John managed to instil in their counsellors (and indirectly in me as the supervisor) a desire to offer them fifteen weekly sessions.

It may be that an unspoken reason for refusing counselling to clients like these is that it is too disturbing for the counsellor rather than its being too disturbing for the client. Workers are aware that pain, which is put out of mind by clients, gets lodged inside them. They worry that if they are not in touch with it and able to find a way of processing it, they will be damaged by it. It feels malignant. On the other hand, if one remains in touch with the pain of the day-to-day work, how can one bear to continue doing it?

I will use my experience with Sue to examine in greater detail the disturbing processes that take place within sessions. I have worked with Sue, seeing her once a fortnight, for a number of years. She is a musician who is unable to work for long periods. She describes her condition as facing in on herself, and this seems to be a good phrase to describe her severe narcissism, that is her absorption with her inner world which limits her capacity to be objective. She is known to the statutory psychiatric services, takes prescribed drugs (minor tranquillizers) irresponsibly, and has been hospitalized twice for overdoses in the past. She feels very vulnerable, says that the drugs do nothing to change this, and is extremely reluctant to use services that would require her to mix with others. Unlike Anne and John, she has never had a psychotic breakdown but would be diagnosed as severely borderline and therefore presents similar difficulties for the worker in that, like people with psychotic illnesses, borderline clients also function almost exclusively in what, in Kleinian terms, is referred to as the paranoid–schizoid position (see Introduction).

Sue is in no doubt that while other mental health professionals might 'have their hearts in the right place', they simply go through the motions when talking to her and she prefers what she refers to as psychotherapy. What I understand by this is that she feels that she needs a more containing relationship: a relationship in which she feels held and understood.

Sue attends most of her sessions and manages to arrive promptly, despite a long journey which she finds difficult. She is pleased to arrive and usually begins her sessions by giving me an 'up to date' account of her mental state. This account, which is accurate, as far as I can see, rarely changes, and I frequently feel extremely sleepy in her company. In other words, something happens which causes me to close my mind to her emotional situation.

My sleepiness with Sue does not feel like my own: in other words, it is not a reflection of my state on any particular day but rather it is something that comes and goes with Sue. It can be described as a deadened and deadening state of mind that comes into the room and into me via Sue. In response I feel the urge to become unusually animated in an attempt to keep myself awake, if for no other reason. On the occasions when I catch myself doing this, it feels like a rather inept way of trying to bring her, and me, back to life and, as such, it may be preferable for Sue than the hopelessness of sitting with a deadened therapist.

Psychoanalysts have identified two forms of projective identification – one that is essentially benign and aims to communicate something to another person, and another that aims to find relief by evacuating something unwanted into the object. I am concerned primarily with the second kind, which is nonetheless a form of communication, if only we can pull ourselves together sufficiently to understand it.

My desire to become animated with Sue is not an example of processing and understanding. In spite of my recognition of this, I am aware that I still do it sometimes and I believe that I do it in order to survive the situation which is, after all, a prerequisite of being able to work with these clients. It is better than becoming angry and attacking, which would be experienced rightly as retaliation, and it is also better than appearing to be killed off. Nevertheless, it is an attempt on my part to put something back into my client and as such is likely to be experienced as intrusive and inappropriate. It is an avoidance of the pain of the deadening state of mind that is inside Sue and is experienced in the session and in me.

Clients who use projective identification as a form of evacuation feel empty as a result. It is as if there is nothing left inside with which to work. Sue is well aware of this. She wants psychotherapy to help her to get back in touch with her internal world because she believes that she can only mix with others if she has some substance.

Another result of excessive projective identification is that the client feels that there is no boundary between themselves and other people because the process of projective identification is one of entering others and of being entered, in a manner that is not openly negotiated, but rather is done without warning and without permission. Sue describes herself as being without a skin and therefore in too raw a state to be with other people. Her experience of being with others is that sooner or later they invade her. She experiences this as abuse, as if someone has seen that she has no outer protection (no clothes on) and has then chosen to abuse her by getting right inside her. When she is feeling empty and exposed to such assaults, she loses her identity. She sees herself as the victim rather than as both the victim and the abuser, but one can speculate that this is the nearest she gets to being in touch with the manner in which she too abuses others by getting inside them in an indirect and psychologically violent fashion. Anxiety about annihilation would appear to be preferable to the anxiety that would emerge if she were to own her violence to others.

What she can own is her violence to herself. She knows that she loses the contents of her internal world. She not only loses what she gains in the sessions in the spaces between them, but she also loses touch with any of her positive attributes or successes. It is only late on in our sessions that she is able to be in touch with anything she has managed to do, such as creative work or socializing. She can only connect with her achievements when the setting feels safe enough for them to be held in mind and protected from the destructive attacks that originate in her internal world, that is, when both she and I have survived and overcome the destructiveness (in the form of sleepiness) which has threatened to engulf us in the session. However, most of the time I am left to think that her internal world and external life are equally empty. I have no doubt that it is important that I should feel this in the sessions in order that I should not become too hopeful, because when she loses these aspects of herself she is left with nothing and has nothing on which to build, no foundations and no substance.

The rationale behind the work

I now want to address two questions. First, *how* do I work with this woman; and second, *why* do I work with this woman? With regard to the first, I have known her over a number of years. The fact that I have evidently survived this experience and that as a result I know her very well, is of great importance to her. I do not retaliate except by looking very sleepy sometimes which she notices and I acknowledge, or by becoming over-animated at others, something she appears to put up with. I am therefore trusted as someone who can put her back in touch with herself in a way that feels safe to her. I listen, make connections and sometimes offer explanations. I enable her to look at herself from the outside as well as from the inside – that is, to gain some objectivity – and thereby Sue gains a sense of perspective. Our sessions provide her with a renewed sense of her own identity and a feeling of substance. She usually leaves with ideas about what she could be doing and a feeling that she is able to do something. This is markedly different from her position when she arrives for a session, when she describes the alternatives available to her but is unable to choose between them and feels paralysed, unable to do anything.

On the other hand, Sue thinks that I am pretty useless since, because she is rarely able to hold on to what she has gained in sessions, nothing changes. It seems that fundamentally she is faced with a choice between unbearable anxiety and emptiness; and time and again she opts for emptiness. Essentially, I am performing a holding function while we both engage in a process in which the outcome remains unknown. The future for Sue is genuinely unknown and she needs a worker who is able to bear the anxiety of not knowing.

Sue is not getting better and – in my view and that of her psychiatrist and keyworker – she has little chance of improving unless she is able to take the risk of coming off tranquillizers and engaging in some form of rehabilitation. It was with great difficulty that I informed her of my unwillingness to continue working with her unless she made better use of the statutory services available to her and saw me as part of her network of care because I felt that both she and I needed this. My difficulty arose from an anxiety that if I attacked the fantasized, exclusive nature of our relationship, Sue would become violent. On reflection, it seemed that I had to be courageous enough to insist that I became a part of a wider network of care that could offer greater containment. I had to avoid colluding with her fears that the wider professional community was too dangerous with which to engage, and to overcome my fear that any change in our arrangements (and any change in her) would be deadly. In the event, when I put this to her, she reacted with mild acceptance and perhaps with some relief. I was subsequently invited to her care reviews and attended as often as I could. I felt better once I was in touch with others who also took some responsibility for Sue's wellbeing.

I continued working with Sue (and this may be my omnipotence) because I think that she would have found it too difficult if I had not. She, with her own omnipotence, is generally well defended against her dependence but she did become very disturbed when her previous GP decided that he would no longer work with her after having done so for many years. It was only when I identified her extreme feelings of loss that she was able to make sense of her disturbance. This was one of the very few times that she has cried in a session. I am aware that I often think of my work with Sue as second-class work, and about her as a second-class client, and that in this manner I too devalue the work that we do. This is, no doubt, in part due to persecutory ideas that we all develop while training and in supervision about what constitutes 'proper' work, but it is also the case that projective identification and counter-transference are very powerful processes. However, Sue has had periods of successful, creative work and manages to maintain an independent existence in the community, largely avoiding the need for hospitalization.

Like Sue, many of the clients of the MIND counselling project also use projective identification as a way of ridding themselves of what feels unbearable. They present with what the counsellors and I have identified as an 'unbearable lightness of being'. By this we mean that the client feels light, superficial and empty. We have noticed that these clients rarely cry in sessions;

the box of tissues never needs replacing. It is the counsellors who feel the unbearable pain of their clients' lives. The non-verbal way in which unbearable feelings have been communicated quite rightly make the counsellor reluctant to confront the client with the extreme pain of what has been projected. But how is the counsellor to inject more substance and liveliness into the situation? Or is the task simply to bear the unbearable and the unknowable?

Anne attended her sessions religiously. It seemed that there was a lot with which she was unable to be in touch and she was undemanding in the sessions, seeming to be satisfied by a fairly 'watered down' weekly 'feed'. As time went on, she appeared to be more at ease in the agency and with herself. Although she felt that she would need weekly feeds for the rest of her life, on balance she considered fifteen sessions to be better than none. She came for her follow-up interview looking good and reported that she had referred herself for longer-term psychotherapy elsewhere. We doubted that she would be taken on by the other agency and noted her real sadness at the ending of the counselling and her desire that her counsellor should not forget her.

John was more like Sue. His counsellor's counter-transference was also one of sleepiness, of not being able to think. We considered this in relation to psychotic processes that attack linking and thought processes. We knew that counselling could not prevent John's next breakdown but thought that it might be possible to enable him to do some work on linking so that he could begin to know and understand himself better. The first half of the work with John was dominated by evidence of psychotic processes which at times caused the counsellor to feel quite devoid of any relevant skills and helpless in the counselling situation. In other words, the counsellor would feel as if he had had the unexpected breakdown. The aim of the work in these sessions was to contain and process some of this chaotic material which, however, was acted out on the boundary of the sessions by both John and his counsellor in confusion over the times of appointments and even rooms.

The second half of the work was much better contained, and John shifted from being an emotionless man to someone who was in touch with his feelings and talking about these, including anticipating how he would manage the termination. He made plans to travel. We might consider whether this was brave or foolhardy of him as he now recognized that his breakdowns often followed holidays. However, he felt ready and able to take on more. His appearance changed; he looked much better and he began to go for job interviews. He ended the counselling well; however, in his follow-up interview he looked less well, and seemed not to be in touch with this. His holiday had been a success. He reported that he had valued the feeling of being looked after that he had experienced in his counselling, and acknowledged his sadness at its ending. We felt that he had indeed gained something from the experience, although he subsequently had his breakdown.

Evaluation

The MIND service has been evaluated by an independent researcher. The number of clients interviewed was small and not all of those who referred themselves for counselling and who were offered it suffered from long-term mental illness – I will therefore not cite figures. However, over half of the clients reported that they had found counselling helpful. The main reason that people gave for its not being helpful in the long run was not related to the quality of the counselling on offer but to the time-limited nature of the contract. With reference to the comments made by those clients with long-term illnesses, the researcher states that, 'The heavy feelings of loneliness and depression were not resolved in that short period of time.'

As providers of the service, the counsellors and I would not expect such feelings to be resolved. We would argue that counselling is valued by these clients because it fosters greater containment in the form of a relationship in which the client feels held and understood and which offers the possibility of owning more of oneself and therefore feeling less empty. This enables the client to feel that more is possible in life and so reduces frustration and loneliness. However, it is very difficult for those people described here to retain the benefits of counselling after its termination. To end a contact after fifteen sessions when the disturbance is ongoing can be experienced by both counsellors and clients as a cruel form of torture.

Clearly, we do not have the resources, financial or emotional, to offer individual sessions on a permanent basis and, although many clients request onging work, many others would be daunted by such an offer. In view of this, the counsellors and I have argued that we should recognize the ongoing dependency needs of this client group through the provision of open-ended groups that are appropriate to their needs and abilities. Such groups would serve the same humanitarian functions as the individual counselling in the form of a weekly opportunity to meet with others in a community where they would be known, valued and understood. They would be based on a therapeutic community model providing communalism, democratization, permissiveness and reality confrontation (see Chapter 15).

When providing this sort of service, whether individually or in a group, to such needy people, the value of psychoanalytic theory is not in its use *per se* for the client but rather, through supervision, to help counsellors to bear the pain of the work. In supervision the counsellors are able to make sense of the projected material inside themselves and to think about their clients, which can be very difficult to do in the session with the client. This process then informs their practice in future sessions. Healthier clients are able to learn from this process and to introject the skills of the counsellor, thereby gaining an *internal* resource for making sense of themselves. However, as I have indicated, these clients have great difficulty in internalizing this process and therefore need ongoing help. Within the security of the consulting room the clients that I have described feel that they have substance and life but they were only able to retain and to use a small part of the work when they were separated from the worker. Their internal worlds are so chaotic that they could not derive any lasting benefit from good 'feeds' because they could not internalize 'an object capable of containing and dealing with anxiety' (Segal, 1975: 94–7).

Through offering a group in addition to the individual counselling service, MIND would be able to provide ongoing help of the sort that I offered to Sue, with the additional benefits of peer support. But what about the wider networks of care? We are trained to think of counselling relationships as highly confidential and it is not our practice to engage with others in our clients' network. In this context it is interesting that, in the year since I joined in Sue's care reviews, Sue has felt able to move away from me. I do not know why this is. I suspect that my engagement with her community, which largely consists of her professional network of carers, has felt both rejecting and empowering – rejecting because it ended the illusion of exclusivity in our relationship, and empowering because it liberated her from the fantasized cosiness and limitations of our rather stale relationship. It may well be that, when working with severely damaged clients, we need to be more active in demonstrating that the world out there is safer than they think. We need to go with them in the same way that we would go with a young child as they venture out into the wider world to facilitate effective links between these clients and their community. I did this by being with Sue in her care reviews. My contributions, based on my knowledge of Sue, added another dimension to these reviews. There was more engagement and less of the 'going through the motions' that Sue had so often described. The resulting care plans were little changed but it would seem that Sue felt some change within herself.

Conclusion

It is my contention that, when working with severely damaged people in the community, we need to create and keep alive systems of care that can provide an ongoing containing function for the clients. We do this through counselling, group work and appropriate supervision. We need to ensure that the work is contained properly within our agencies and to make effective contact with other agencies involved in our clients' community of care so that these systems can benefit from our experience and our clients can benefit from our links with their community. Thus containment is provided both internally and externally. As Hunter and Riger (1986: 64) state, mental health programmes need to direct attention 'not simply to individuals' needs nor to community capacities, rather to the relationship between the two. Working on the "fit" directs one to both counselling in terms of individuals and increasing capacity in terms of communities.'

Bulmer (1987) urges us to examine the reality of such nebulous terms as 'community' and 'network' in order to reach a better appreciation of the complexity of the interrelationship between formal and informal care. We do not automatically think in terms of the wider systems of care that these clients need. We are bounded by policies that stress a 'treat and move on' philosophy which is at odds with the hopeless feeling accompanying chronic illness and with the inability of many clients to process therapeutic help in a way that would foster lasting emotional development and the ability to move on.

A sense of community for these clients is dependent upon the existence of a system of care that offers both reliability and continuity and which can function as an effective container for their projections. I suggest that, implicit in the concept of community care, if it is to be viable, is a requirement that the community is able to provide some sort of reasonably effective containment for most mentally ill people for much of the time and that we need to offer counselling and a related form of group work because these provide a humane form of containment which, provided it is linked with other services, enhances and complements what is offered.

References

Bulmer, M. (1987) *The Social Basis of Community Care*, London: Allen and Unwin.

Hunter, A. & Riger, S. (1986) 'The meaning of community in community mental health', *J. Community Psychology* 14 January.

Segal, H. (1975) 'A psychoanalytic approach to the treatment of schizophrenia', in M. Lader (ed.) *Studies of Schizophrenia*, Ashford: Headly Bros.

14

Community, care and quality
A lesson from group psychotherapy

Naomi Landau and Michael Wallbank

Introduction

In this chapter we reflect, from our perspectives as a senior social worker/care manager and community psychiatric nurse respectively in a multidisciplinary community mental health team, on our work with those who have both acute and continuing care needs. We give an account of a clients' evening psychotherapy group which we co-conduct, as illustration.

We welcome current moves to target vulnerable people and ensure that they receive coordinated quality care. Care management and the Care Programme Approach (CPA) offer opportunities, especially on the macro level, for organizations to purchase services in response to identified needs. The attempt to develop a system of care based on need rather than on resources available is an admirable one, if one that remains difficult to convert into reality.

At the same time, we acknowledge that in any system of care there are dangers which can undermine the very objectives that they seek to achieve. In this chapter, we identify some of these. We suggest that working practices easily become defensive measures for psychiatric services, reinforcing fragmentation rather than helping clients to make the necessary connections, both internally and with their outside world.

We argue for the importance of retaining a therapeutic ('provider') role with clients. Recent writings on risk management emphasize the importance of the relationship between worker and client (Crichton, 1995). Therapeutic involvement is essential to engage disturbed and chaotic clients in the process of assessment at all. The danger with splitting commissioning and provision for such a fragmented client group (people with severe and enduring mental illnesses, targeted by statutory services) is that it can lead to reinforcing the internal fragmentation of the client group. Engagement with one worker proves difficult enough for most clients, let alone with a barrage of workers from different agencies. It is impossible to implement or review a care plan without an involved, trusting relationship with the client.

A second important split occurs when we identify a high priority group of clients to meet the criteria designed by the local authority for care management/CPA (DoH, 1990a), and for the Supervision Register (DoH, 1994). Everyone is aware of much-publicized failures of the system to meet the needs of some vulnerable and difficult people. Increasingly, only people who suffer from the most serious of psychiatric symptoms have access to resources. In terms of group treatment and support, this means that they have access only to each other. This reinforces the generally perceived split between those who are 'mental' and the rest of the community.

This splitting off impinges dramatically on the very clients identified as most vulnerable. Where they link into group support and group treatment, they will have less opportunity to have contact with less disabled clients. Workers who traditionally used a range of resources and therapeutic skills are less likely to have access, for example, to training in psychotherapeutic responses to the needs of their more disabled and difficult clients, as these skills are seen now as relevant only to the less disturbed. A significant number of staff with therapeutic knowledge and experience are being moved into the role purely of providing 'packages' of care. Some workers, who trained, after all, as providers of a range of therapeutic interventions, move away from the statutory sector into other agencies where they can use them, but with a less exclusively vulnerable and difficult client group.

We argue, and do so through the example of the psychotherapy group, that our job is not to separate off but to integrate. Psychiatric services and interventions should be developed with this in mind. Otherwise, in the move away from an asylum-based system towards a community-based one, we create structures that bring about yet again a divide between people with mental illness and the wider community. We use the psychotherapy group as one example of a service that was offered as part of a package available to clients, and of how a group can be an agent for integration and connection, rather than fragmentation, when it becomes a place where clients with different needs and abilities engage with each other, and where the assessor (care manager) is actively involved in ongoing provision (treatment).

What do we mean by community, care and quality?

The thrust of this chapter is to expand on terms like 'community', 'care' and 'quality'. These are terms to which we all attach some meaning, with little awareness as to whether this meaning is shared. We can become glib in our use of them as a way of avoiding the enormous difficulties for our clients, and also for us, in making the terms a reality.

Community

Recent UK legislation – the NHS and Community Care Act (DoH, 1990b) and accompanying Department of Health circulars – provides a legislative framework for the move in psychiatry towards mentally ill people receiving their care in the community. Inherent in this move is the assumption that there is such an entity as community. It is not one readily available, however, for our clients to use. In a very real sense, there is no such thing as community for most of them. It needs to be created both internally and in the outside world. Most are out of contact with themselves and others, and through mental illness they become marginalized and increasingly isolated. Hospitals provided an institutional community identified with a building. Without such a container, the notion of community becomes much more tricky.

Care

This is not something that clients can easily receive. Very often, those with mental disorders and illnesses have had very poor experiences of care, and their internal worlds are littered with attacking and rejecting objects as a result of their early experiences of inadequate care. Clients can feel neglected and workers can feel anything but caring: rather, they can feel hateful and attacking in return. The policy of care at arm's length – care management – can serve as a defence, to increase the emotional distance between client and worker. We would argue that quality care for what is a very fragmented and out-of-touch group of people can be provided by professionals only if they have a thorough understanding of the processes of mental illness, and bring a reflective and planned approach to the work.

From our experience, the effect on workers of focusing exclusively on people with severe and enduring mental illness is ultimately detrimental to clients. Many of those targeted as being high priority are not willing participants in care (a consideration often overlooked in ideas of a client-led package of care). A large minority enter the care system via compulsory admission and have gross problems in engaging, often attacking that so-called care and the care managers, rejecting contact and intimacy. When these are the only people targeted, the effect can be numbing for workers – creating a 'caring' group that is numb, rather than alive and sensitive to the issues and demands that this work requires. It can produce a defensiveness that leads to poor practice and care. The danger of current trends is that skilled workers with expertise in many fields leave the public sector, leaving behind a demoralized and defensive service (see Chapter 1).

Quality

There is a widespread desire among politicians and managers (and indeed clinicians) to find ways of setting standards, of measuring the value or effectiveness of care. However, the danger is that, in attempting to define concrete measures of quality, we lose the very quality we seek to ensure. The system that attempts to measure quality is defensive and ends up emphasizing quantity. The legislation is born out of a very real anxiety about caring for large numbers of psychiatric patients in the community, following drastic reduction in the number of beds available to mental health teams. It is an awesome task. Attempts to package care and to quantify interventions are a way of coping with the anxiety generated. The systems developed so far can mask the very complex issues involved. Foster (1993; see also Chapter 5) talks of how the system itself becomes psychotic – taking flight into unreality as a dysfunctional way of coping with the anxiety aroused. Attempts are made to deal with anxiety by prescribing numerical measures, e.g. response time to referrers, numbers of face-to-face contacts with clients, rapidity of response, etc. Our experience as workers is that staff time and preoccupations become focused on producing these statistics. Driven by the new anxiety of meeting statistical targets, workers lose the capacity to reflect together on effective ways of responding to the real needs and confusion of the clients. In the current debate, quality – as opposed to quantifiable measures – gets squeezed out.

Nonetheless, it is important to have a concept of quality, and to attempt to measure the value of interventions. We believe that this can be done in a meaningful way by attempting to examine outcome measures. This is what we have attempted in evaluating our group (see pages 172–3).

The history of the group

Foulkes (1990) wrote: 'The community is represented in the group.' We are working with clients whose disturbances are, at root, problems in communication, in connection and in belonging. We work in a team which aims to provide clients with a sense of community. We do this through the use of a local community centre – running mainly activity-based groups there – and through our networking and the commissioning of care. We would argue that the team also does this in all aspects of its therapeutic interventions, not least through the psychotherapy group.

The group is a slow, open one: that is, new members are able to join the group over the course of its lifetime – and some members leave – but the group is given time to prepare for these changes, and due consideration is given by the group coordinators as to when the group is ready for them.

Work for us began with joining a weekly supervision group at the Institute of Group Analysis (IGA). That work was crucial to the subsequent life of the group, helping us to plan and reflect on the continuing process. We agreed to meet with potential members three times before they joined the group, to assess and to prepare them for the group. We put advertisements and notices for the group in places that our clients frequent, such as drop-in centres and GP surgeries. We assessed a total of seventeen people with a broad range of need, from those requiring care management (diagnosed as suffering from severe and/or enduring metal illness) to others with less severe problems. Of these seventeen, nine were not allocated places, either by their own choice, or because we felt the group did not meet their needs, or because the needs of the group as a whole contra-indicated their joining. Of the original eight people who joined, three dropped out earlier than we recommended: we knew there was a risk of people leaving in flight, thereby repeating established patterns in their lives.

However, most group members, including those who left, have seen marked changes in their functioning. At the time of writing, the membership includes clients who have recurrent and long-standing mental illnesses and qualify for care management under our local authority's eligibility criteria; others with severe and long-standing personality problems (borderline/psychotic, or anti-social personality disorder with depressive symptoms); and one with some personality problems who suffers from crippling anxiety.

The life of the group: the group process

The group members

Members bring into the group current difficulties in their work, accommo-dation, intimate relationships and families. They bring a history of such difficulties from the past, and an account of their first significant relation-ships with their families of origin or substitute families. They bring their experiences of not coping and of illness. Neglect and abuse feature promi-nently in their histories, as does a pattern of repetition in their relationships.

Within the group they encounter feelings in relation to the group as a whole, to individual group members or to the conductors, which are often familiar feelings for them. They use a variety of mechanisms – denial, projection, displacement – to keep these feelings at bay. They nonetheless communicate these feelings in very powerful ways. For instance, one member has been consistently muddled about the timing of breaks – missing sessions immediately before and after, and attending the centre during the break – while denying having any difficulty with separation.

The role of the staff/group conductors

Our role as conductors has been to transform these unconscious primary processes into conscious experiences and feelings. In the above example, the group member is, in fact, repeating an experience of gross neglect. He was abandoned by his natural mother at birth and experienced abuse in a variety of institutions. In letting the group down so consistently, he is attempting to displace these powerful but most uncomfortable feelings onto the group as a whole. In turn, the group denies experiencing being rejected or let down by him, as they too share unacknowledged experiences of rejection and neglect.

In the group we have looked at how this client's feelings about breaks are being expressed in this acting out, which reflects recurring patterns in his experience of work and in his relationships which are often very damaging to him. He anticipates loss, rejection and abuse by initiating separation himself, and in turn provokes the hostility of the group through his actions.

There is resistance to our attempts to interpret the content of the group. Such denial is understandable; these are very isolated people for whom connection is terrifying because of their history of being repeatedly let down. However, as group members continue to bring material that confirms these patterns, so their resistance lessens and they begin to own and recognize in themselves and in each other these previously unknowable feelings.

It is the role of the conductors to nurture this sense of connection, and of meaning to be found in relationships within the group – i.e. to create a sense of community. The group is reluctant to examine the meaning of absences because the sense of the absence of good primary objects is so painfully present in their lives. By paying attention to the minutiae of the comings and goings of this 'community', we attempt to create their own internal 'packages of care'.

The role of supervision

We derived important insights from the fact that supervision itself took place in a group, with issues for us as co-conductors often mirrored within supervision. We were able to explore our own counter-transferences in the group itself, within the safety of supervision. For instance, during the assessment process, we disagreed over the suitability of one applicant, and were able to look in supervision at how this disagreement reflected the client's own ambivalence about joining the group and wanting to change; a conflict that culminated in his not returning for his final assessment appointment.

Another time, we brought our extreme anxiety about one group member who expressed self-destructive and suicidal ideas. This was a client with a long history of breakdown previously framed solely in terms of a psychiatric diagnosis of manic depression with a consequent need for hospitalization. In the group, she began to explore alternative ways of understanding her experience, most notably the way that she might be using her role as patient to avoid looking at painful, angry feelings. The work brought her enormous rage to the surface, which was expressed both towards the group and then turned inward against herself. In supervision we found ourselves at times reproaching each other, albeit subtly, about our own interventions, and considering additional psychiatric assessment. We came to recognize that, although we had to take her suicidal thoughts seriously and liaise with her GP and psychiatrist (something that we always discussed with prospective members of the group, and within the group itself), our counter-transference feelings could also be understood as our colluding with her powerful need to see herself and the group as requiring protection from her destructive feelings. It was vital that we and the group contained her – tolerated, understood and helped her to think about these feelings – rather than merely getting rid of them and, most dangerously, getting rid of her from the group.

The value of working as a group

Working with such high-risk clients, who project destructive fantasies onto the group and onto the conductors, demands an ability to provide containment while our own counter-transferences are so hard to bear. Their impulses are to reject and spew out rather than stay with and reflect. We, as conductors, were often identified initially as the only people in the group capable of containing such feelings so as to be able to reflect on them. Our task has been to trust the group to do that work, to allow the group members to model for each other ways of providing such a thinking capacity.

We have made the point that people in the group come with different histories and differing experiences of psychiatric services: some with a long history of major mental illness; others experiencing recent crises, driving them to begin confronting vulnerable aspects of themselves. In addition, some are apparently enthusiastic to work, and grasp at the process eagerly, while others show their ambivalence more clearly. Most are defended and confused. By trusting the group to do the work, we as conductors allow connections to be made within the group at the individual members' own pace.

For some of the group members, one of the most difficult things to face has been that problems that have been previously always framed in terms of illness can be understood in other ways; ways that do not deny the reality of illness, but nonetheless give them more control – in itself a frightening prospect. They do this by making connections with other members of the group. Some of those other members share similar problems in relationships and in taking control of their lives, yet do not have the same illness model on which to fall back, and, what is more, insist on 'normalizing' many of the experiences of their 'ill' co-members. One result can be that group members who previously explained all their difficulties in terms of mental illnesses are forced to look again at how they view themselves.

If the group were composed wholly of those meeting care management criteria, it would function (if at all) in a very different way – the learning and modelling would fall far more onto the conductors rather than on the group as a whole. The main, or only, reflective role would be ours, and this would work against the group learning process. It would not provide the same opportunity to the more damaged members of understanding and recovering through the insights of others less ill and less prone to psychosis. It would be more difficult to move to a position where health would be seen as located not just in the conductors but in the group as a whole.

What must be apparent to the group members is our own trust and confidence in each other as co-conductors, developed through the supervision that we receive. Good coupling, bad coupling and failure to couple at all have been issues for all group members. One member joined us when she was suffering from crippling panic attacks and delusions about her body. She attributed her current problems to a history of unsatisfactory, casual sexual relationships, alternating with longer-term relationships with men who were abusive or neglectful. She used her relationships in the group – with us as longed-for parent figures, and with her 'siblings' in the group – to reflect on these patterns, and on the connections between them and her family history of relating to a neglectful father, an alcoholic mother and a sister of whom she felt deeply envious and resentful. She also explored her difficulty in forming adult relationships with non-abusive, caring men, which have proved unexciting. Doing this work, she has been able to settle down and marry a man who is providing her with the care for which she has longed. There are still difficulties, disappointments and challenges, for example her reluctance to address her own desires to punish and abuse, but she continues to use the group to reflect on these. Meanwhile, engaging with her struggles helps other members to make connections with their own. Another group member, with a long history of manic depressive illness, has formed a close identification in the group to this woman, and has begun to look at the function of her own illness in providing her with a way to cope, with her own dysfunctional family relationships and with an inner world in which she too is able to enter into relationships only with men who abuse and reject her.

The connections are not all one way. This same pair in the group brought about another shift when one of them told the group for the first time what her experience of acute depression had been like – a moving moment in the group. For the other woman, however, it was also a terrifying moment, for she recognized her great fear of becoming psychiatrically ill like her own mother, and how she had fought hard throughout her life to keep this fear at bay. For a while she began to suffer severe panic attacks again, even missing work for a few days. However, she came determinedly to the group and worked on this, facing and trying to understand her own depression. As she did so, the panic subsided, and she was able to return to her job.

A man in the group has suffered from recurrent depressive illnesses, and presents as very passive in the group – listening, sometimes offering helpful comments, but often unable to remember details from one group meeting to the next, and very rarely intervening spontaneously to share his own experiences. This behaviour was pointed out to him in the group. His first response was to absent himself from the group for a week because he felt too depressed to come. The following week he returned, stating a determination to look at how his behaviour in the group – listening, apparently caring, but essentially withholding himself – reflected what he did in his relationships outside the group, and to try to understand why. He has begun to make connections between his own experience and other people's accounts of themselves in the group, and in particular to see how his own story of abuse and neglect by his family connects with what others tell of their histories and current experiences. He is making contact with his own feelings of loneliness and longing for relationship, from which he had previously been cut off as a way of protecting himself against further experiences of hurt and rejection. He has also begun to recognize parts of himself that reject and attack other people.

Outcomes

Psychotherapy is often seen as an expensive option. Setting aside the relative economy of group work as opposed to individual, we would like to consider the effect of working in this way on three other areas of expense: hospitalization, use of medication and time spent with GPs and other professionals.

Use of psychiatric services

The majority of members have made use of psychiatric services, including some who had embarked on major psychiatric careers as in-patients, day-patients or out-patients prior to joining the group. In the current lifetime of the group, all members have avoided those patterns, and the group has been the single point of contact with services. Two members who previously had hospital admissions, in one case lasting many years, have not needed such care.

Contact with GPs and others

We are in regular contact with local GPs and other referrers, and their feedback suggests that the demands made on them have greatly diminished, group members either not seeing them at all or using their time less frequently and more appropriately.

Use of medication

All group members were on medication of some sort – anti-depressants, lithium, and major and minor tranquillizers. Now, only the member prescribed lithium remains on this treatment. We have looked at the options that individual group members have, including medication, especially when they encounter difficulties. In fact, apart from this one member, for everyone the group has become the *only* treatment.

We looked at changes in the quality of life of group members over the lifetime of the group using the Global Assessment of Functioning (GAF) as an overall measure prior to their starting with the group, and again two years later. In so doing, we were looking at the increased capacity of our client group to do more than just survive. All demonstrate improvement. Some more damaged people came with very low levels of functioning and have demonstrated a major shift, whereas those with higher ratings to begin with showed a less dramatic but nonetheless significant increase.

Of those currently in the group, only one member was previously in full-time employment, and was finding this difficult to sustain. Now that member has achieved promotion. The others are all in full-time or part-time employment with the exception of one who works in a sheltered work scheme and another who is a full-time student.

All but one previously lived alone and all reported a history of difficulty in sustaining close sexual relationships. Two have married, one to her first non-abusive partner. All use the group to explore the meaning of sexual relationships in their lives.

What we describe in this section can be summed up as a growing ability for the group members in making connections with their outside world – with a community – and this mirrors the process that we have seen in the group where they have made increasing connections with each other, and with and within themselves. In other words we are talking about real 'quality' of care – care that has as its aim more than mere survival.

We do not claim that these changes are solely the result of our group meetings. Our contact has been part of a process over years, involving different mental health care professionals, GPs and others. All have played a part in the group members' internal developments. Nor is there any way that we can say whether these changes would not have taken place anyway, that is without the intervention of the group. Nevertheless, the differences over the lifetime of the group are striking when compared with the usual histories of people like these.

Conclusion

The main thrust of our argument has been that any discussion of the concepts of 'community', 'care' and 'quality' must take on a more integrated and integrating approach. We urge the necessity of more flexibility in using the strengths and skills of workers, targeting the more vulnerable but not excluding other needy clients.

We wish to avoid an approach that targets only the severe and enduring mentally ill, excluding the less ill – colloquially, and perhaps contemptu-ously, known as the 'worried well'. Present shifts concern us because they further cut off the most seriously ill from their actual community, and from that sense of community that is so elusive for them anyway.

In the group, we ensured that the criteria for membership encompassed a broad spectrum of need. We have argued that our job is to work with our clients towards integration and connection. This takes place at two levels – in the inner world of our clients and in their relationships with the outer community. But the two levels are connected. This is what quality of care in the community is about. It *is* about care that connects and integrates rather than cutting off. It is *not* about replacing one system – a hospital which responds to patients' sense of disconnectedness by disconnecting them further from the rest of society (but which at least had the virtue of providing an institutional community) – with another which abandons people within a terrifying so-called 'community' and reinforces their sense of isolation and confusion.

In attempting to deal with anxieties about meeting health care targets for the mentally ill, statutory bodies can work against this integrative approach. In developing policies and strategies that are designed to defend them against attack, they produce a less integrated, less flexible service for their clients. In its 'flight into unreality', the system leads to fragmentation among professional carers and ultimately reinforces the fragmentation of our clients. The strategies that split off care and provision, and the 'mentally ill' from the 'worried well', deprive the most vulnerable of the care that is provided by access to an important range of therapeutic approaches and techniques. Increasingly, only those interventions susceptible to a 'quantitative' system of measurement become acceptable within such a system.

We believe that, rather than developing more policies and procedures, the emphasis needs to shift now towards supervision, support and training for therapeutic work. By developing opportunities for staff development, and creating an environment that encourages the growth of a diversity of approaches, we can challenge and enliven, rather than 'numb', workers and clients alike. Thoughtful care is quality care. Reviewing the outcome of that care, rather than just collecting numerical statistics, is a worthwhile measurement of that quality. Measuring quality of care must take into account the extent to which it genuinely facilitates integration and the development in our clients of that elusive concept of community.

References

Crichton, J. (ed.) (1995) *Psychiatric Patient Violence: Risk and Response*, London: Duckworth.

DoH (1990a) *The Care Management Approach*, Health Circular (90)23/LASSL (90)11, London: HMSO.

—— (1990b) *NHS and Community Care Act*, London: HMSO.

—— (1994) *Introduction of Supervision Registers for Mentally Ill People from 1 April 1994*, *Health Service Guidelines* (HSG(94)5), London: HMSO.

Foster, A. (1993) 'Psychotic processes and community care: the difficulty in finding the third position', *J. Social Work Practice* 7(2): 129–39.

Foulkes, E. (ed.) (1990) *Selected Papers of S. H. Foulkes*, London: Karnac Books.

Part IV

Initiatives for empowerment

Current structures and policies can be disempowering not only for users but also for staff and managers. The chapters in this section consider various approaches to facilitate their taking a more proactive stance, and how reflection on experience can be translated into action.

15

A potential for partnership?

Consulting with users of mental health services

Helen Morgan

Introduction

A review by the King's Fund of adult mental health services in three West London boroughs for the purchasers of one health authority highlighted the need to consult with stakeholders, especially users,[1] when planning services. Although the health authority had conducted the usual consultation surveys, it accepted the report's view that this had been neither substantial nor effective. As a result my colleagues[2] and I were approached in January 1995 by the health authority to find an effective way of engaging service users in each borough. In broad terms, the purpose of this project was as follows:

- to elicit users' views about current and future mental health services within each of the three boroughs covered by the trust
- to draw conclusions from this process which could inform strategies for improving involvement of, and collaboration with, service users in general.

Looking for the cracks

The three of us had all worked in adult mental health for some years and had seen changes that included the closures of the large hospitals, the move to care in the community and the introduction of the purchaser/provider split. While the old system had many flaws and there was much to be said for the potential of the new, we saw demoralized professionals struggling to manage a system that was under-resourced, finance-led, attacked by the press and in a state of flux and crisis. The system that had been established to contain disturbance was itself disturbed, and inevitably anxiety was rife.

As a system changes from one form to another, what has been a solid structure inevitably develops fissures. These will cause uncertainty and anxiety, but they can also be places where light gets in. Our central question was whether we could perceive cracks in the system as it changed that could be exploited to allow a more radical form of relationship between those who work in a service and those who use it.

We had all had considerable experience of 'user consultation' in the past, but this had been as service providers and had essentially consisted of 'us' (the professionals) asking 'them' (the users) what they thought of what we did. There were varying degrees of response, from the apathetic to the mildly interested to the belligerent. While small adjustments to the service might result from these consultations, it was usually a frustrating experience, never resulting in any fundamental shift in power relationships. Often the process itself quickly became institutionalized, and rarely did it feel that staff and clients were in any sort of genuine partnership. Those dependent on the service are unlikely to rock the boat too much, and those not using it are rarely asked. User consultation conducted by providers is valuable and should retain a place, but it has its limitations.

What interested us about this project was the fact that it was to be a piece of work conducted on behalf of purchasers rather than providers, and that it would be borough-wide rather than confined to one particular service. Could it be run as a way of offering a genuine challenge to the status quo? We were particularly concerned to establish whether the funders were prepared to move from consultation to partnership, and whether they would attempt to find ways of embedding the collaborative process into their systems.

The key figures in the health agency responsible for purchasing mental health services seemed keen to find a way of bringing users into the system as more than passive recipients of treatment. While they held many of the purse strings, they were aware that they had difficulty reaching the people on whose behalf they were spending money. The notion of forming a genuine link between themselves and the users had its attractions and they have remained committed to this process throughout, both by funding the work and by attending all meetings when requested to do so by users.

Power and the status quo

Having made it clear that we were concerned to facilitate a change in relationship from mere consultation to one of collaboration and partnership, we recognized that we were proposing a shift in the existing power relationship between provider and user. In planning the project, therefore, we focused on where power had lain historically and where it seemed to be moving in the current system. The following is necessarily a simplistic and brief overview of two important strands.

The medical model

Traditionally the medical model has been dominant in the definition and treatment of people with mental health needs. Rooted in physical medicine, the same fundamental precepts pertain when translated to disorders of the mind. The individual under consideration is defined as 'the patient' who is 'ill'. The origins of this illness are regarded as primarily organic and, therefore, so must be its treatment. The doctors who are trained in such treatments are 'well', and their job is to diagnose the illness and find its cure (see Chapter 1).

However, unlike most other branches of medicine, psychiatry has been consistently unsuccessful in developing these 'cures'. Medication may help to contain and subdue the more extreme symptoms of the defined illness, but the cost in terms of side-effects can be high and it is rare for the individual to be entirely rid of the original problem. In the process of treatment, the assumptions underlying this model perpetuate a relationship whereby the doctor retains ultimate power and responsibility, thus removing from patients authority over key aspects of their lives. Given that such authority is a central feature of mental health, the model can be viewed as working against its stated aims of helping sufferers to recovery.

The contract culture

The introduction of the purchaser/provider split has brought a different authority into the system – that of the marketplace. This is fraught with its own paradoxes and difficulties but also, perhaps, with some potential for positive change.

Within capitalism, business relies on the existence of customers with money who wish to buy what is produced. The working of market forces assumes that a variety of products is available for selection and the customer will choose that which they prefer and can afford. A company making shoddy, over-priced or unwanted goods will fail while others succeed. The 'good' becomes strong, and what is strong survives, so what survives must be good. There are, of course, a range of criticisms of such a system that suggest that, even in the field of commerce, it does not exactly work like that. But it is a system, and is consistent to some degree within its own context.

However, when such an ethos is imported into a service sector such as mental health provision, impossible anomalies occur. By definition, most of those who need the services have not got the money to buy them. The 'customers' have no cash and therefore have no direct power to affect what is made available to them. Purchasing departments are set up to buy on their behalf and are under pressure to spend with care and sparingly. 'Good' services can too easily become those that are cost effective (or cheap).

The increased pressure for accountability has had its positive effects in forcing organizations to address what they are funded to do, whether they are effective or not, and to tighten up on sloppy practice. However, a central difficulty remains. These institutions exist to serve distressed human beings and consequently the work is often messy, chaotic, unmeasurable and distressing. Where the emphasis is on cost effectiveness, it is hard to justify the time required for the building of relationships and the temptation is to go for the short, sharp solutions.

Purchasing departments, often staffed by people with little direct experience of mental health work, struggle to meet the requirements from the government, while uncertain about what it is they are trying to do. The fundamental contradiction is that, however well meaning the individuals in these purchasing departments are, they are not the ones who will use what they buy and are usually separated from those who will. Thus, we have a split customer.

An alternative to the medical model?

In considering the emerging scenario, our interest was in whether there was potential in the change and, in particular, how the entry of market forces onto the scene might alter existing power structures. Health trusts now have to compete with other service providers and are having to offer ways of working outside the hospital setting. If there is an easing of the grip of the medical model, can we find something constructive in the philosophical uncertainty remaining?

Each of us had worked in therapeutic communities and retained a commitment to the movement's philosophical ideals despite its fall in popularity in recent years. These ideals offered a challenge to the medical model by positing a spectrum of health/illness rather than a clear-cut divide. This challenge to the notion of a clean division between the 'ill' patient and the 'well' practitioner leads to a different way of thinking about the relationship between professional and client. The focus of 'treatment' within this model moves from 'cure' to the individual's gaining help in managing their own lives, and places relationship (especially that with the group) at the centre. It requires an acknowledgement of the 'illness' that may arise within the staff group, and a recognition and encouragement of the 'wellness' in the client. It is a difficult task, for there is an investment by both client and practitioner to maintain the divide so that clients can give up the responsibility for being 'well' and practitioners can avoid facing any 'illness' in themselves (Main, 1957; see also Chapter 1).

The four aspects of the therapeutic community proper as defined by Rapoport (1960) are *communalism* (the importance of individual and group relatedness), *democratization* (the sharing of power regarding decision-making), *permissiveness* (the toleration of a variety of behaviours but within set limits) and *reality confrontation* (the presentation to the individual of the effects of their behaviour on others). All these aspects depend on the belief that all members of the community, while having to manage personal mental health difficulties, also have the capacity to engage with others, to be well.

Therapeutic communities are usually restricted to a physical building. What happens if the philosophy is shifted outside such confines and applied to a community within a geographical location to form a 'therapeutic community *in* the community'? What sort of relationship between professional and client needs to develop which works to contain the illness and focus on the health of the client? How might individual users be supported so that they are able to manage the process themselves? What then becomes the professional's role and responsibility in facilitating this difference in relationship?

Certain key elements seemed essential in setting up a project if it were to model different ways of relating to and working with users:

- The project needed to be established in such a way that it was user-led from the start so that the users involved had a real – not token – say in the running of the project (democratization). Working as a group together (communalism) was central.
- As the 'professionals' facilitating this process, our own 'illness' (including anxiety, need for control, personal tensions, etc.) needed to be owned and contained.
- A degree of tolerance of the difficulties that individuals might experience (permissiveness) was needed, but where someone's behaviour adversely affected others, this might need challenging (reality confrontation).

We decided to run a series of search conferences in each borough, organized and run by a group of users who would be paid for their work at a realistic rate. Our role was to establish and facilitate the planning groups, and to act as a link between the service user planning group and those commissioning the project.

Four stages of the project

Initial research

This was to establish a basic understanding of the way that services were organized, and of general issues and practices related to user involvement in the area. We were also seeking out ways of making contact with users in the area who would be interested and able to join a planning group.

In all three boroughs there were considerable numbers from ethnic minorities and, although specific services were provided, the consultation system had been little used by them. We decided, therefore, to set up a cross-borough group to consult with users from black and ethnic minorities.

Planning

Having established a general picture, we then identified a group of users in each borough (between five and ten) to work with us towards setting up appropriate consultation events. We wrote a job description and criteria and spread these around as much as possible, inviting volunteers to contact us. The usual questions of representatives arose, but realistically the goal was to identify any user willing and able to support the scheme, and to try to ensure that a representative group of users attended the conferences.

The fact that we were paying users made a significant difference:

1   It was a direct incentive to be involved and it helped to overcome some early scepticism.
2   It encouraged users to treat their involvement in a business-like fashion, like a job.
3   It made them feel valued and valuable.

Nevertheless, a great deal of scepticism about the genuineness and likely effectiveness of this consultation process existed. Users felt that they had been asked to give their views many times over the years, but what they said seldom made much difference. They had a sort of 'consultation burnout'. As their capacity to network and enthuse others about the process was central to the project, generating enthusiasm required a good deal of explanation and honesty.

We spent far more time on this stage than we had budgeted for, but it was worth it. In each borough, it was evident how little users understood about how the system of care was financed and organized. While the structure of how their services were to be provided had undergone major changes, no one had explained it to them. We spent a considerable amount of time with each group defining the purchaser/provider split, care in the community and the differences between health agencies, health trusts and social services. These sessions underlined how, if any consultation process is to be effective, it must include a first stage of education. The importance of this work was obviously recognized as each group decided to include a similar instruction session at the start of each user conference.

After these initial sessions, each planning team met several times to define the conference programme and organize the venue, publicity, catering, transport, who would do what on the day, evaluation forms, and the like. Inevitably, as in any group of individuals working together to plan an event, there were differences of views about how things should be, not everyone always liked each other, and at times there were conflicts and clashes which had to be managed within the group.

The second area on which we spent time was that of training the members of the planning teams to develop skills in public speaking, chairing, facilitating and recording in groups. We ran a cross-borough training day. These joint meetings, as well as the planning sessions, helped to develop individual confidence and competence, but also gave people whose experiences had often left them feeling isolated and vulnerable a sense of connection and collective strength, a community that both supported and enabled them.

When the outline for the event had been decided upon and the publicity material produced, the groups went out networking. The planning teams identified places where users would meet and went to speak to groups. They achieved a level of contact, loyalty and trust from people who use mental health services which could never have been commanded by any group of professionals.

The user events

These events were certainly unlike any other conference we had attended. The prevailing mood was a combination of chaos, energy, creativity and realism. A room full of people with varying degrees of mental health needs at varying stages of health or ill health can be an unpredictable environment. The user-facilitators were undoubtedly anxious about their new roles and we had a 'run through' immediately before the doors opened. When the events began, things seldom ran smoothly. Timetables slipped as the conference organizers, with their newly acquired chairing and recording skills, struggled to contain the mass of views that poured forth once participants realized that there were no professional providers present, that the event was being managed by users, and that others were genuinely interested in what they thought. A wide cross-section of people attended. The energy and passion from the membership was exciting and a privilege to share, and it gradually focused into a range of highly positive and creative ideas.

There was anger, cynicism and resentment expressed, but it did not turn into the kind of destructiveness and negativity that can bedevil even the most sophisticated and highly controlled conferences. There was a realistic understanding of the political, social and financial context, and an honest recognition that the services were vital. Yet alongside this recognition was a frank appraisal of the limitations and shortcomings of these services. People were keen to forge alliances and partnerships with professionals. They were ready to acknowledge the skills and experience of the professionals. Could the professionals, in turn, acknowledge the unique skills, insight and understanding that had been gained at great personal expense by service users in the process of their careers as psychiatric casualties?

Feeding back

After each event, the notes taken by planning-group members were gathered together and a report was written. The first draft was always discussed among the planning teams and a final draft agreed. This was then distributed to all users who had attended and copies were sent to the purchasers and all providers in the borough.

The reports from each borough event were specific to that locality, but some prevailing themes were striking:

• We had been warned that, if asked, users would always demand more counselling for which little money was available. In fact, while there was indeed a call for more to be provided in the way of 'talking cures', the strikingly consistent theme was the *wish for relationship*. The commonest experience recounted was of ten minutes with a psychiatrist who moved on every six months or so, visits from a variety of community psychiatric nurses, and a vacuum where the social worker used to be. Many knew little or nothing about care plans and they frequently had no idea who their keyworker was supposed to be.

• Where they did come into contact with staff, especially in hospital, the experience too often described was of being treated with disrespect and in a patronizing manner. Good experiences were recounted, but so too were ones of abuse. Participants recognized the stress on staff, as well as the process of institutionalization which could result in exacerbating the terror that the individual can experience when hospitalized or treated involuntarily. A solution was sought through users becoming more involved in the training of staff at an early stage in their careers when they might still be open to a more empathic approach to patients.

• A worrying feature of the events was the extent of the feelings of power-lessness and fear that emerged. The anxieties expressed, and the need for reassurance that speaking up would not put them personally at risk, was too common to be put down merely to individual paranoia. People who have experienced compulsory admission to hospital, ECT and having to take medication that they have neither chosen nor understand, know what it is like to be subject to the power of the system and of another person. When recounting their experiences, participants understood the ill state that they had been in at the time and how alarming this might have been for others. However, the way that some of those in authority had managed this, and the legacy of fear this had left, was disturbing to us.

• A contributory factor in this experience of powerlessness was the lack of information given to users. Few knew much about the system they were in. There was a consistent call for better education for users concerning medication and its side-effects, as well as the opportunity for greater self-management.

• There was a consistent complaint that the system was run for the convenience and benefit of professionals rather than for the clients, resulting in the 9 to 5 nature of service provision outside the hospital. A need for more extensive crisis services was emphasized in all conferences.

- Time and time again came a strong call for the system to shift in order that the users themselves could have a greater say in how services were run. 'We may be ill but we're not stupid' was a common statement. The plea was to involve the people who knew the services from the inside to help spend the money most efficiently.

User/professional events

Up to this point, it was we who had provided the bridge between users and professionals. Now the planning teams and the conference participants wanted a direct communication with purchasers and providers who were invited to respond to the initial report. Because the report and the conference were sanctioned and commissioned by the purchasers, there was a commitment from senior representatives from social services, the health trust (providers) and the health authority (purchasers) to attend.

Again the conferences were organized and facilitated by the user planning teams. In a typical conference, key professionals were invited to respond to sections of the report to the large group. The second part of the conferences consisted of small groups on specific areas of concern, with reports back to the large group. In the final discussions, the central issue was how the process of user involvement in the decisions about the running of services would get embedded into the structure.

Outcomes

As this is an ongoing process, it is hard to be definite about the outcomes in terms of real changes to service provision, especially as these varied from borough to borough. At the time of writing, two of the three boroughs have had two further conferences where professionals have been pressed regarding the promises that had been made previously. In both boroughs, the process of involving users in the selection and training of staff is under way, as are structures for user participation in decision-making and planning. A user liaison post is already established in one borough and proposals for a similar post in the other two are under consideration. A two-day workshop to develop users' training skills has been run, and a group of user–trainers are establishing themselves to develop a training cooperative. In the third borough, as in the cross-borough black users group, things are moving more slowly.

One outcome which is harder to measure is the effect that the conferences themselves may have had in lessening the anxiety of professionals concerning working with users and shifting attitudes. It was always a service user in the chair, with the responsibility and authority to manage a group which included senior directors of social services, the trust and the agency. This meant that the conferences themselves modelled a way in which the balance of authority can alter without dire consequences.

Our role

Throughout this process, our role in facilitating the planning teams was a critical one which we needed to keep under close review. It is often difficult to surrender the control traditionally held by professionals and accept that, although the process may be different, the outcomes unfamiliar and some-times (in our eyes) flawed, it is necessary to allow people the freedom to develop their own solutions to problems. However, the wish to move from a position where we take too much responsibility, evoking dependency and resentment, can lead to moving too far in the opposite direction so that we become neglectful of users' genuine needs. Finding the correct mix between support and empowerment was always a complex balancing act, and there were times when we got it wrong. As the project progressed, the planning groups became more able to tell us when they required our specific skills and when we should back off.

Conclusion

While this project has not been perfect, there have been substantial achieve-ments both in the specifics of service provision and in the general culture in some areas. The key factors of particular significance where there has been success include the following:

- The project was commissioned and funded by the purchasers rather than the providers. This meant that there was the possibility of bringing together the two elements required if the ethos behind market forces is to have any meaning: the people with the money to buy, and those who need and use services. In this way a sort of *composite customer* was established, with us as the link. To continue to be effective into the future, this link is being formalized so that the relationship can be a direct one without the need for facilitators.

- While this facilitation role was required to form the link, it was impor-tant that we were independent of the service provision. This independence allowed for the necessary degree of trust in us to be estab-lished by both sides of this new partnership, the purchasers and the users. Where suspicion has been expressed, this has tended to come from providers. Within the triangle of purchaser, user and provider, where a partnership develops between the first two, the third has to move to a different position which may feel uneasy and uncertain. The suspicion is therefore understandable.

- The commitment of the health agency to the project allowed the space and time necessary for such work. A common shortcoming of attempts by professionals to consult with users is that the pace is too quick. In their own busy, pressurized, diary-dominated lives, professionals become frustrated by the time it takes to genuinely inform people not used to having things explained, to generate optimism in a climate of failure, and to work with the particularities of the mental health problems experienced by the people whom they apparently wish to shift from patients to partners. In response to this frustration, they often withdraw and call the experience a failure; at best a failure acknowledged as born of their own limitations, at worst as evidence that users are incapable of acting responsibly and should therefore continue to be recipients of treatment rather than being partners in a process of collaboration.

Because of the unique position we were in, we were able to take the time to build the relationships necessary for collaboration. This is a two-way relationship and time was therefore needed, not only to help and facilitate the development of capabilities in the thirty-odd users with whom we worked directly in the planning teams, but also to consider ourselves as the other side of the equation. This has meant facing some difficult truths about our own fears, prejudices and anxieties, and to learn to trust the users themselves to help us manage the process.

Notes

1 Throughout this project, concern has been expressed about the terminology in current use. I am aware that there are objections to the term 'user', but also that an acceptable substitute has not yet been found. I have therefore referred to those who have used psychiatric and mental health services as 'users' throughout the chapter for want of a preferable alternative.
2 This project was originally conceived and implemented by myself, Nick Benefield and Phil Russell. Once it was established as an ongoing process, I have continued to work as the sole consultant to the user planning groups. The others have ceased to have direct involvement due to changes in work and location, but continue their interest and support and have adapted many of the original principles to other projects.

References

Main, T.F. (1957) 'The ailment' (paper given to Medical Section, British Psychological Society), in J. Johns (ed.) (1989) *The Ailment and Other Psychoanalytic Essays*, London: Free Association Books.
Rapoport, R.N. (1960) *Community as Doctor: New Perspectives on a Therapeutic Community*, London: Tavistock.

16

Learning to keep one's head
Analysis of a training workshop[1]

Angela Foster and Lorenzo Grespi

Introduction

Implementation of the NHS and Community Care Act (DoH, 1990) put considerable strain on workers in health authorities, social service departments and voluntary sector agencies. The legislation was experienced as a form of managerialism which aimed to create and maintain structures at the expense of addressing the nature of the processes that occur within systems of care. Processes between people and between different parts of a system are both the cause and the product of anxieties experienced by users and workers. The skills needed to address process issues are the same therapeutic skills of containing, managing and metabolizing anxiety that one utilizes in client work. If anxieties remain unaddressed, then the system operates defensively, as depicted in Figure 16.1.

In order for this new market system of community care to be effective, workers need to be able to combine their therapeutically oriented management skills with their new business-oriented management skills (see Figure 16.2). With this in mind, the Adult Department of the Tavistock Clinic ran a ten-week pilot workshop on community care of the adult mentally ill with the aim of developing a safe setting that could contain the anxieties and provide experiential training in community care. This chapter examines the processes that took place within the workshop as we all struggled to keep in mind the

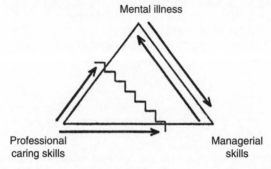

Mental illness

Professional
caring skills

Managerial
skills

Figure 16.1 A defensive system in which anxieties remain unaddressed

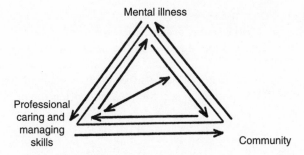

Figure 16.2 A system capable of addressing anxiety

demands and the difficulties of the task of providing community care for the mentally ill. It is interspersed with quotes from the written feedback of workshop members.

Planning the workshop

The task

The task was to provide a safe and constructive setting where the anxieties generated by community care of the adult mentally ill could be identified, addressed and thought about. The staff aimed to provide this containment through management, theoretical orientation and structure.

The management

The workshop was planned and managed by three psychotherapists; two were from a social work background and one was a psychiatrist. They were present throughout the entire workshop and were leaders of the three small groups within it. A fourth member of staff joined the workshop for the large group only and also acted as consultant to the other staff in a session that followed each meeting of the workshop.

Theoretical orientation

This was based on studies that examined the personally damaging, defensive, anti-task dynamics that occur within systems of care. In particular we had in mind the work of Menzies (1959) on social systems as a defence against anxiety; the work of Main (1975) on the temptation of both users and workers to project all the illness into the users and all the health into the workers; and the work of Woodhouse and Pengelly (1991) on how these same dynamics are often repeated between professionals engaged in work that requires inter-professional and inter-agency collaboration.

The adult mentally ill encounter enormous difficulty in negotiating and maintaining informal networks, and they often exert a disruptive influence on formally established systems of care intended to offer them support. This destructive behaviour can be mirrored in the behaviour of professional and non-professional carers. In addition, while the term 'community' may conjure up powerful fantasies of a nurturing environment, the reality is that relationships in the community are complex and often uncomfortable (see Chapter 2).

The structure

The workshop took place one morning a week for ten weeks. Each meeting began with three small, multidisciplinary groups, followed by the 'market-place' and finally by a large group involving all participants. The small groups had the following tasks:

- Working on case material which was to be provided by the members. The term 'case material' was used broadly to include presentations of any difficulties within particular systems of care.
- Developing multidisciplinary teamwork skills by reflecting together upon policies from the perspectives of the different participants.

The 'marketplace' was an informal gathering in a designated room where refreshments were available at the end of the small group. This unstructured space represented the open and fluid space that exists in the community at large in which we all live and need to survive as whole people in a variety of roles. It could also represent the market of community care in which people are expected to buy and sell as well as make collaborative contracts with each other.

The large group took place in the same room as the marketplace. It provided a setting where integration of the experience of the small groups and the informality of the marketplace could be attempted and in which we could all participate, witnessing the roles and relationships that existed and the processes between them. It was also a place where tensions could be held and addressed. In other words, this was a space in which developments might take place.

The membership

Membership of the workshop was open to representatives from statutory and voluntary agencies, and to carers. It included both people whose work brings them into direct contact with the mentally ill, and those involved with policy-making and implementation. Thirty people were recruited – twenty women and nine men. Five people left the workshop. One withdrew before the beginning, three left during the course of the workshop and one was unable to finish due to sickness. It is important to note that all these people were managers, which may be indicative of the difficulties that surround the task of management within community care (see Chapter 8).

Analysis of the processes within the workshop

The group processes are described as they developed, and are analysed using Kleinian theory of splitting and projection in the paranoid–schizoid position, and integration and ambivalence in the depressive position (see Introduction). Our intention was to attend to shifts in the course of the workshop between these two positions.

> A continuous movement between the two positions takes place so that neither dominates with any degree of completeness or permanence. Indeed it is these fluctuations that we try to follow clinically as we observe periods of integration leading to depressive position functioning or disintegration and fragmentation resulting in a paranoid–schizoid state.
>
> (Steiner, 1992: 48)

When functioning in the paranoid–schizoid position, we all use the mechanisms of splitting and projection and our focus is exclusively on our own relationships which are felt to be either good or bad. Relationships between others are not considered. Our concern is for personal survival, and our anxieties, if we stop to examine them, are about annihilation. It was assumed by the workshop staff that when this sort of activity was witnessed within and between groups, it was because the subject under discussion was disturbing and was increasing people's anxiety. It was also assumed that at such times the staff and the structure of the workshop were experienced as inadequate to the task of containing this increased level of anxiety.

On the other hand, when one is functioning in the depressive position, then it is possible to reflect thoughtfully on one's relationships with others and to observe and think about relationships between people other than oneself (i.e. find the third position – see Chapter 5). It is a mental state where concern can be felt for others.

The beginning: a desire to engage in the work

In the first session all three small groups began in a lively and open manner. Members were keen to offer to present their work for discussion and it seemed that the need to talk and share one's experiences outweighed any anxiety about what would happen if one did. The small groups focused on the needs inside the groups, locating conflict outside, either in another part of the workshop or outside the workshop altogether. This state of mind was highlighted in one member's description of a day centre which had 'pulled up the drawbridge', preferring to keep the status quo inside and to focus on that, rather than on what was happening outside or on what might have been happening in transactions between the centre and the community.

During this first meeting two senior managers, when introducing themselves to their small groups, indicated that they had no time to think while at work. It was possible to see that the disturbance was identified in the workers and the persecution was viewed as coming from the legislation, not from clients. The community, insofar as it featured, was the workshop which was there to support them. This was a dyadic system consisting of disturbed and needy carers and the caring workshop. Members needed to believe that the workshop was good and were prepared to split off the bad into more senior, absent parties. 'This reflects a measure of integration which allows a good relationship to a good object to develop by splitting off destructive impulses which are directed towards bad objects' (Steiner, 1992: 50).

In the second session, members were examining this dynamic in more detail in their small groups. One group talked about the difficulty that clients had in leaving a day centre. This presentation could be interpreted as an attempt to 'lower the drawbridge'. However, when another group member questioned what the centre actually achieved, this was experienced as a threat. The group had difficulty in ending and put off moving into the marketplace. Thus the difficulty of moving on, which had been the topic of this group, was acted out rather than managed by the group. This process highlighted a major area of vulnerability in community care, i.e. the difficulty in negotiating and managing the interface between institutional settings (represented by the small group) and the open space of the community (represented by the marketplace). Persecuting management entered this group via a comment that questioned the effectiveness of the day centre and this promoted an atmosphere of suspicion, rather than one that would contain anxiety and foster thinking about the difficulty of moving into the open space of the community. This reinforced a paranoid–schizoid mode of relating in the group. Members took on the roles of victims or persecutors and it became more difficult for them to expose themselves to the uncertainties and fears of the transition into the unstructured space of the marketplace.

Another group had a presentation from a manager who gave a coherent and articulate history of his community mental health centre but who lost confidence when talking about the present, becoming vague with little to say. This was a reflection of his experience of losing his mind in all the current changes and demands made on him at work, something that he was relieved to have acknowledged. The group took up where he left off, elaborating on various themes and planning some future sessions around others, demonstrating that it was possible to take risks, to contain anxiety, to think and plan.

The third group began with expressions of anger at the comments made by the consultant to the large group in the first week, along with doubts about the purpose of the large group. The group was then presented with a situation where a mentally ill person was picked up outside a hospital, taken to a police station where an approved social worker was called to see him, then taken back to the hospital. Here the group was struggling with the fine line between real care and the frustrating bureaucracy of care. Presumably, the same concerns were being expressed indirectly about the workshop. The fear was that the workshop member would be pushed around the workshop system only to end up where he or she had begun.

By this second week, the persecution located within the workshop could be seen as moving around the workshop system. Within this, managers were viewed as either disturbed or persecuting, the workers as either disturbed or therapeutic and the workshop as either persecuting or containing. This represented an initial move towards the depressive position, as we were beginning to experience ambivalence.

The middle: anxieties that hindered the work

The containment provided by the workshop was threatened in the third week by the arrival of members who had been unable to attend the earlier sessions, and by absences possibly related to the experience of the previous session. The topic brought for discussion in one small group was a day centre that was now required to take on more dangerous clients. This was making the staff angry and anxious and was affecting the quality of their work. The group, in acknowledging the physical danger that the presenter was in, shifted the focus of the discussion from persecuting and neglectful external managers to persecuting clients and neglectful internal managers. By this means the group expressed the need for effective management within the day centre, within the workshop, and within oneself in order to feel safe and effective in one's work.

Another group heard about the work of a church minister's wife who was attempting, as a counsellor and member of the community, to offer care to people who had spent most of their lives in psychiatric institutions. It was possible in this group to gain some understanding of these clients while simultaneously experiencing the unrelenting burden of such involvement for the lay worker, and recognizing that this is also a burden that community care places on the community. It was easy to see how one would want to resist taking it on.

By this stage, the membership of the workshop was clearly beginning to tackle some of the most disturbing aspects of their work. There was an awareness of the need for strong containing management, given the demands of the work. However, the boundaries and the structure of the workshop were more like those of a community – in which people come and go and move about – than those of a protected therapeutic setting. The large group, wanting to lay the blame for this disturbing experience on management, overlooked the management within the workshop, focusing instead on the manager who had left after the first week. The hostility and murderousness of the membership towards what was experienced as destructive, uncaring management could safely be directed outside the workshop. This was evidence of a move back towards a paranoid–schizoid mode of functioning, prompted by the fear that internal management was inadequate to the task of containing the anxiety about destructiveness within the group.

Fragmentation and amputation

In the following sessions, the degree of splitting increased to the extent that there was a danger of fragmentation as the workshop moved towards the more disturbed end of the paranoid–schizoid position. The anxiety felt by all groups arose out of an increasing recognition of the enormity of the task of community care. As one member put it, 'The burden and responsibility are so great it is exhausting to remain involved.' As we all became aware of this, we recognized the mental processes of amputating parts in order to make the task seem more manageable, and of clamping off one's feelings in order to make it feel more bearable.

The amputation theme was raised in an account brought to the large group by a carer. She described a homeless, mentally ill person who got the care he needed only after his legs were amputated because of frost-bite. This succinctly expressed the unconscious anxiety of the workshop that something vital might be lost through neglect and amputation.

Earlier that same morning, one small group was presented with an idea from the staff of a day centre who wanted to establish a service for black clients. The discussion, however, developed into an argument in which the roles of business management and professional management were split between the two protagonists. This conflict in the group enabled the participants to distance themselves from the disturbance – which is both their own and that of their clients – and the group discussion was impoverished as a result. This was an externalization of a conflict that is experienced by all managers as they struggle to integrate their professional skills within their new role as business managers. Often this struggle is felt to be impossible. The urgency of the business management tasks means that they take precedence, while time to think and reflect on process is felt to be, at best, a luxury and, at worst, a danger. This signalled a feeling of impasse in the workshop as a whole and highlighted a failure in the ability of workshop staff to provide a secure enough setting for disturbing voices to be heard and listened to. The theme continued the following week.

One small group heard about the frustration of being a mental health worker in a housing agency. As the other workers in the agency saw their task as housing rather than illness, the mental health worker felt isolated within the agency and alone with her concerns about some of the tenants.

When a tenant became disturbed and their behaviour stirred up anxiety in those living near to them, and in turn in the housing workers, the mental health worker could easily find herself marginalized by her colleagues as the person representing mental illness within a setting that did not wish to deal with disturbance but rather wanted it removed (see Chapter 2). The rage that one feels in such a situation, and the effort to achieve change, are so exhausting that this worker was in danger of clamping herself, shutting out her awareness in an attempt to make the situation more comfortable for herself. Others in the workshop could identlfy with this position.

The dangers of amputation, clamping and inaction

The awareness of danger in the community and the sort of tragedy that can arise when people put things out of mind instead of acting, came straight into the workshop in the sixth week in relation to the national news that a 2-year-old boy had been abducted from a shopping centre by two young boys and murdered. Members of the public had observed the 2-year-old's distress but had not intervened.

Not surprisingly, the large group now began to rise to the challenge of engagement, clearly acknowledging the destructive consequences that can occur through non-involvement and through pathological splitting, yet fearing the destructive consequences that might arise if people were to become meaningfully engaged with each other. Would the workshop be able to contain the rivalry, destructiveness and rage within it or would it be destroyed by it? Would the workshop staff be able to manage the *feelings* as well as the *business* of running the workshop?

This process signalled a shift back towards depressive-position functioning. The main anxiety was that the membership might destroy the authority that was necessary if any effective intervention was to take place. The large group expressed an urgent need for a form of management that could be authoritative, protective, in control and easily identifiable. The two policemen in the workshop were pulled into taking on this role.

The end: thinking and action

In the seventh session, it was possible to trace the beginnings of integration as the small groups began to face the enormity of the task of community care instead of retreating from it. One group heard about a community home for patients discharged from a long-stay mental hospital who had everything set up for them except the bus passes without which they could not move within their system of care. Group members could recognize within themselves a psychological stuckness and a feeling that something else was needed in order for them to function effectively within a community-based system of care.

Another group heard about an approved social worker who was surprised to note her ability to think clearly and act decisively while carrying out an emergency assessment in the community accompanied by several police. Far from feeling more anxious in this situation, she felt better contained here than amid the chaos and confusion of her agency. This group could then recognize the need for strong management and for the containment it provided, this being a necessary ingredient of community care. They wondered if it was possible to hold on to this awareness in the marketplace, i.e. that part of the workshop that represented the community as opposed to the institution.

The emergent meaning of the marketplace

The marketplace gradually acquired meaning as a place that represented both the chaos of the community – insofar as it threatens personal and professional boundaries – and the business place of the community where useful contacts can be made. It also represented the potential of the community to provide containment for mental disturbance.

As in any community, the marketplace was able to contain succesfully a certain degree of disturbance, while splitting off and leaving out feelings that were *too* disturbing. On the other hand, when the containment in the large group was experienced as inadequate, the marketplace seemed to offer a setting where members' personal and emotional needs might be met in an informal way by others. Thus the tripartite structure of the workshop slowly began to acquire a meaning for the membership of the workshop.

> In the marketplace the anxiety was stepped up a bit, but trading information, views, and talking to people who one liked or was curious about was useful.

> A place where new ideas could germinate.

> The marketplace was an opportunity for some to distance and retreat from others and from the community, perhaps to feel isolated and alone, or perhaps to reflect personally.

There was an increased awareness of the need for each person to own their own authority and behave less dependently.

> I felt I could have been more active as there were some people I would have liked to meet and talk to, however I did not feel inclined to break into their circle or approach them and introduce myself.

The carer in the group – who could be thought of as the person living in closest contact with mental illness – had initially sat alone in the market-place, possibly feeling marginalized. Over time, she began to feel much more at ease in this setting and this was due to more than simple familiarity. The marketplace of the community was beginning to work, and as communica-tion of differences between members increased, changes took place in the large group. The men took on more prominent roles and a form of creative intercourse began to emerge. Members began to think that if they could manage this sort of communication, they could manage community care.

Such hope was countered by an anxiety that it would not be possible to achieve this aim within the three remaining weeks of the workshop, and the fear of failure must have been a contributory factor in the eighth week when the absenteeism was greatest. Ten people were missing: five from one small group and five from another. While these groups struggled with a sense of failure, the third group, which was fully attended, also felt anxiety. Their discussion was about media attention to community care which put profes-sionals in the spotlight. This rekindled feelings of inadequacy and meant that members felt vulnerable, cautious and once again afraid of taking an authoritative stance in relation to their work.

The consultant to the large group was left sitting with an empty chair on each side of her and this could be seen as an indication of the desire of workshop members to keep a distance from the reflective task in order not to feel the pain of it or to experience failure. On examining this, members stated that the consultant had been given the name of Cruella de Vil. However, there was also evidence of a desire to take authority and find a voice that could express the vulnerability felt by members in relation to their work both outside and inside the workshop, and the police were relieved of carrying this function on behalf of other members.

The ninth session was about change. The staff member in the third group presented his consultancy work with community psychiatric nurses to good effect. The experience that management could participate in thinking about process as well as policy was liberating. Throughout much of the workshop, until this point, there had been a split between the management of policy – which was experienced as largely an economic concern – and the manage-ment of care – which was ostensibly what the policy was about.

Another group discussed residential work and noted how the apparent mindlessness and hopelessness of chronically dependent clients is catching and can affect one's functioning. To remain mindful of their plight and actively engaged in working with such clients is hard to bear. This may go some way towards explaining the preoccupation with organizational change within the new systems of care, as this enables managers to feel alive and active, but this is quite contrary to the way that many of their staff and clients feel. What is needed is a system in which it is possible to think about changes that might accommodate lack of change (see Chapter 1).

In the large group, the communication was lively as the enjoyment of the work was openly acknowledged for the first time. Members who had been largely silent now spoke up about their need for space and time to adjust to the demands being made on them. The staff of the workshop, as well as members, noted that they needed to be very robust if they were to survive both the attacks and the disinterest of others when struggling to make inroads in community care.

The final session was about self-management. Some members reported that they had been told by their colleagues that they had been functioning better since attending the workshop. Others identified the need for a setting that would help them get to grips with the new structures and with the demands of community care. For the first time the large group began with some members being unaware of the consultant's presence. The prospect of working without her was reported as both anxiety-provoking and exciting.

The movement over the ten weeks of the workshop along the continuum from the paranoid–schizoid position to the depressive position is represented in Figure 16.3.

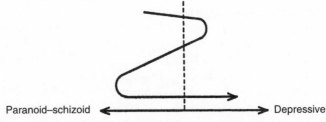

Figure 16.3 Psychic development within the workshop

Evaluation

Evaluation of the workshop from its members was provided through a follow-up session and written feedback.

The structure

Clearly the small groups represented multidisciplinary teams. This setting was valued by the majority of the membership.

> It felt quite comforting to hear so many people experiencing similar difficulties and somehow being able to acknowledge the reality and the enormity of the situation.

> The small group was definitely the most useful. I enjoyed thinking about common problems within a multidisciplinary group. It helped me challenge my own prejudices about other professions and gain a clearer idea of what their responsibilities and preoccupations were.

As a consequence of the small group I have altered my thinking on how
to consult and deal with very difficult problems that arise ... I have set
up a staff consultation/ discussion group that follows a similar format,
feedback from which has so far been very positive.

The marketplace had become a place both where commerce took place
and where the life and the history of a community acquired meaning. Here,
thinking coexisted in a dynamic relationship with splitting and projecting.
This setting had acquired a literal and symbolic meaning as the centre of the
community and the informal container of its tensions.

It remained to establish what the large group represented and what its
function had been.

The nature of the large group and my feelings in it made me reflect on
the lack of predictability and enduring systems in community care – all
the muddle and madness of the purchaser/provider split and the
constant state of change.

The large group demonstrated the nature of the wider community and
the problems that the various players have in communicating with one
another.

The large group represented the community which includes clients and
professionals with all our fears and defences in full swing.

The formality and structure of the large group provided an opportunity to
witness the mental disturbance and to work with the dynamic processes of
splitting and projection that take place in any community but which usually
remain unnoticed and unprocessed, with damaging consequences for all
of us.

I felt little optimism for the future but retained some hope – though felt
any real progress and application required long-term work between
professionals and members of the community.

Through listening to and thinking about the external and internal voices
of mental disturbance, the painful process of taking back projections and of
integration had eventually become possible in the large group. Managing
and caring at personal and institutional levels gradually came to be seen as
viable and coexistent ways of relating.

The willingness of the membership to own authority and engage in the
struggle was supported by the efforts of the staff whose collective management, while at times inadequate, had on the whole been 'good enough'.
Members wrote the following comments:

I now listen to staff and hear about the awfulness of the job in a way I never did. The workshop really helped me to progress both my thinking and understanding of my feelings in relation to the work and to bring the two together. I felt this integration was skilfully managed by the staff of the workshop.

It was the structure, and the staff, who for me seemed to have some understanding in mind, which enabled the chaos to be experienced. It is a space for being with the wider community to experience that chaos, to feel the anger and yet to come away feeling understood and held and able to think.

The workshop as a whole provided a place where it was possible to face the reality and the enormity of the task of community care.

Further developments

Similar workshops have been commissioned by employers who wanted to establish workshops within a particular locality for people working within the area. This increases the level of anxiety in the workshops because the tasks of understanding and appreciating the different roles of workshop members and of forming effective collaborative networks of care are performed in a real (as opposed to an 'as if') situation. In many cases, when a member of a small group brings a particular client or situation for discussion, others in that group are also working with the client or have some prior knowledge of the issues. While this makes group discussions more threatening, as each person worries about what others will think of their particular contribution, its advantages are self-evident as members, through examining the whole system of care, achieve greater insight into the situation. Particularly traumatic situations (for example, a very unpleasant compulsory admission) where it is evident that clients have suffered more distress than necessary due to ineffective inter-agency collaboration, are likely to be known to most workshop members. In these situations, the large group offers the possibilites of debriefing, of understanding how such a situation arose and how it might be handled better in future. In addition, the experience of getting to know each other and of working together within the workshop enhances the collaborative skills of workshop members.

A second development has been the establishment of forums for managers. The first one took place at the Tavistock Clinic and was established specifically to help managers to find an effective balance between the demands of business management and those of clinical management and supervision. The second of these was commissioned by an NHS trust. This took the form of a Providers' Forum with the dual tasks of: (a) providing managers (from a defined geographical area) with a place to meet together, to share information and concerns, to support each other, and to foster greater collaboration; and (b) the creation of an effective group for the purposes of liaising with the purchasers. Clearly, such a group of managers, from a defined geographical area, contains a lot of expertise and knowledge. The task was to harness this, enabling the group to become a potent representative body in discussions and negotiations.

In all these developments from the first workshop (described above), the structure has been maintained because, arising from our experience, we would argue that it proved a useful structure in that it facilitated successful achievement of the task – of providing effective containment for the anxieties generated by the implementation of a policy of community care for the mentally ill – and, in doing so, enabled participants to create effective networks of relationships. Such workshops are clearly in the spirit of the policy as outlined in the following quote and it is hoped that future developments of this model might attract an even wider range of participants.

> There is a very wide range of interests and agencies in the mental health field, from health and social services involved in purchasing and providing mental health services, and individual users of services and their carers, to the criminal justice system, benefits offices, and indeed the wider general public. To make community care for mentally ill people work, networks of relationships need to be developed.
>
> (DoH, 1995: (04))

Note

1 An earlier version of this chapter by A. Foster and L. Grespi entitled 'Managing care in the community: analysis of a training workshop' was printed in *J. Social Work Practice* 8(2), 1994. The authors wish to acknowledge the valuable contributions of Julian Lousada and Evelyn Cleavely who were the two other members of staff in the original workshop.

References

DoH (1990) *National Health Service and Community Care Act*, London: HMSO.
—— (1995) *The Health of the Nation. Building Bridges: A Guide to Arrangements for Inter-agency Working for the Care and Protection of Severely Mentally Ill People*, London: Department of Health.
Main, T. (1975) 'Some psychodynamics of large groups', in L. Kreeger (ed.) *The Large Group: Dynamics and Therapy*, London: Constable; reprinted in J. Johns (ed.) (1989) *The Ailment and Other Psychoanalytic Essays*, London: Free Association Books.
Menzies, I. (1959) 'A case study in the functioning of social systems as a defence against anxiety: a report on a study of the nursing service of a general hospital',

Human Relations 13: 95–121; reprinted in Isabel Menzies Lyth (1988) *Containing Anxiety in Institutions*, London: Free Association Books.

Steiner, J. (1992) 'The equilibrium between the paranoid–schizoid and the depressive positions', in R. Anderson (ed.) *Clinical Lectures on Klein and Bion*, London: Routledge.

Woodhouse, D. and Pengelly, P. (1991) *Anxiety and the Dynamics of Collaboration*, Aberdeen: Aberdeen University Press.

17

Space to play

Vega Zagier Roberts

Introduction

People working in the field of community care – indeed in health and social care generally – often experience their organizations as almost entirely crisis driven, so that they are constantly reacting to the latest emergency. This is already very anxiety-provoking for staff and managers who find it difficult to plan their workdays; in addition, the crises frequently lead to supervision sessions being cancelled or to people being unable to attend meetings that might afford time for reflection and planning. Yet it is supervision and calm time for thinking together that have traditionally provided much of the containment so necessary to this kind of work.

Requests for consultancy are too often made at a time of crisis. Anxieties in the client organization, together with the consultant's sense of pressure to be as helpful as possible as quickly as possible, may lead to very goal-oriented interventions. Alternatively, the consultant may be used as an auxiliary manager by staff who find their own managers either unavailable or unhelpful. In this chapter, I will first describe two situations where the presenting problem was a sense of imminent catastrophe, and where consultative interventions involving an element of play proved useful in shifting how people construed their difficulties, so that they could begin to think about how to address them. The third case study is of a team that was unable to engage in play, and illustrates how both consultants and managers sometimes need temporarily to relinquish their determined efforts to be helpful.

Case study 1: an external threat

Pathways was a small organization set up as a pilot programme within a housing trust to support homeless people in transition from psychiatric hospital to the community. When the project was first set up, it had been envisaged that the team would probably offer some counselling and other direct support, but its main task was to link users with statutory services in the area. Initial funding had been for three years, and I was called in just after the funders' two-year review which had indicated that the project was unlikely to be refunded at the end of the third year.

The team consisted of sixteen workers, five full-time and the rest part-time or sessional staff. I was invited to facilitate their annual awayday, to help them plan how they would work over the coming year, and to deal with their feelings about the unfavourable report from their funders. The staff were reportedly united in their outrage at the decision, blaming the funders for not giving more priority to the disadvantaged clients who depended on Pathways, as well as anxious about their own futures. Staff who had come from other parts of the housing trust were likely to be re-deployed, while those who had been recruited specifically for this project, mainly counsellors on time-limited contracts, would probably be made redundant. I was told that the funders, as well as the senior managers for the housing trust, felt that the project had not been successful in its core task – very few of their clients had been linked in to statutory services. Instead of focusing on short-term assessment and liaison work, the staff were using most of their time to provide long-term individual counselling for a relatively small number of people.

In the opening session of the day, I tried to open the way to explore different views among the staff in relation to their work generally and the funders' report specifically but, despite the apparent differences in how they worked and how they would be affected by the closing down of the project, it proved impossible to bring these into the open. Every comment was couched in terms of 'we' as if 'we' were an entirely homogenous group, very unfairly judged by a 'them' unable to appreciate the value of their work or indifferent to the fate of their clients. When I gingerly touched on the fact that some of them would have jobs and some might well not in a year's time, I was filled with a sense of having done something unnecessarily nasty for which I might be severely punished.

To me, it seemed likely that I was picking up something in the room – a feeling that there was something that needed to be addressed but which was too dangerous to put into words. So in the next session I engaged them in an exercise. Participants were divided randomly into three groups, one to speak as the senior management and funders, the second as the Pathways staff, and the third as the people for whom the service had been set up (i.e. both current and potential users). Each group was to prepare a statement to present to each of the other two groups. The 'managers' group was predictably critical and the 'staff' group predictably defensive. The 'users' group, however, were very energetic in criticizing the service for being 'glossy', hard to access, and not really helping them effectively.

Up to this point, the value of the service had been treated as a given, the identified problem being that the people proposing to discontinue the project cared only about numbers and could not appreciate the real needs and difficulties of the client population. However, for the group standing in the shoes of the users to have voiced their scepticism so quickly suggested that there were depressive anxieties within the team about the value of what they were offering, very near the surface but not possible to talk about, and therefore not addressed. Their offices were indeed unusually glossy for this inner city area and the type of work being done there; their caseloads were light compared to their counterparts in statutory services; their waiting list was long. And, most painful of all, even the clients with whom they had worked in depth over considerable periods of time had made few major changes in their lives.

Self-doubt and self-blame had been projected upwards and outwards. The proposed cutting of the service, which at an unconscious level may have felt like a deserved punishment, served to shift the team from feeling guilty to feeling persecuted, that is, from depressive to paranoid anxieties. As a result, instead of being able to consider ways of improving their service, or to negotiate effectively with their managers and funders, they had resorted to splitting and projection, banding together to blame their problems on outside enemies. This then made it extremely dangerous for group members to express – or even hold – different views: the pressure to be united was intense, and this in turn made learning from experience almost impossible. The shock of recognition resulting from the role-play made available and public those thoughts that had previously been suppressed, and thus constituted a first step towards planning how to face the future.

Case study 2: an internal threat

Champion Hill was one of several residential units in an organization set up for the re-settlement of people leaving long-stay mental hospitals to live in the community. It consisted of a block of twenty flats in a pleasant suburb, each flat providing independent accommodation for one or two tenants. A team of twelve staff were available to help the tenants develop independent living skills, for advice and counselling, and for a range of other services designed to help the tenants make the transition from the institutions where most had spent many years, to 'normal' life in an ordinary community. When I first heard about Champion Hill I thought it sounded like a dream come true: there was 24-hour staff cover and support, yet tenants had the same privacy and freedom of choice as any other member of the community.

I was asked to consult to the Champion Hill team some two years after the project opened. My brief was for five days' work comprising team-building, a review of service aims, and establishing objectives for the coming year. In my preliminary meeting with the managers, I was told that the team seemed to be in disarray. Morale was low, and there was considerable disagreement and uncertainty within the team about what they were trying to achieve and how they should work with tenants. The managers were dissatisfied with the quality of the service, although they could not specify what was wrong, and were perplexed by the high levels of staff stress and sickness. Sleeping in was experienced as extremely onerous. Although all the staff were experienced residential workers, well accustomed to being on duty alone at night, they apparently found sleeping in at Champion Hill frightening. They were aware of tenants' distress and isolation at night, but had no way of checking on their state of mind or even their safety, since respect for tenants' privacy was the foundation-stone of the team philosophy. Staff entered the other flats only when invited, or when there was actual evidence of danger to tenants' safety. It was as if distress and even madness hung in the night air or oozed through the walls into the staff flat, disturbing their sleep but too intangible to deal with. By day, there was often uncomfortably little to do, since tenants rarely approached staff directly for help and the team considered it inappropriate to interfere with how tenants chose to manage their day or how they used the staff on duty.

Having been led to expect considerable resistance to the consultation, I was pleasantly surprised by my first meetings with the team. They seemed to be very pleased to have the opportunity to review their service, and engaged with me warmly. Bit by bit we began to build up a picture of what they hoped they could offer their clients, and of some of the strengths, shortcomings and dilemmas of the work at Champion Hill. But something was missing. The staff distress which had been described to me so vividly was not coming into the consultation. Indeed, in some fundamental way, the tenants were not coming into the consultation either. So I began our third meeting by inviting the team to participate in a role-play. I handed out short briefings to four team members. The scenario was that a prospective tenant, accompanied by a social worker, was visiting Champion Hill for an informal meeting with two current tenants. The 'visitors' were asked to prepare questions which would help them decide whether they wanted to pursue arrangements for the prospective tenant to be referred to Champion Hill. The 'current tenants' were asked to answer questions truthfully, one emphasizing all that was positive and the other all that was negative in their own experience of life in the flats.

I had designed this exercise in the hope that it would provide a relatively safe way for the team to express their concerns about weaknesses in the service and to criticize it openly without worrying too much about shaking the new sense of team cohesiveness that we had achieved. But the outcome took us all by surprise. It was not the negatives but the positives that proved most disturbing. The tenant who extolled the virtues of life at Champion Hill described how he was allowed to watch television all night and to sleep all day, that he was not forced to eat proper meals at set times but could live on 'junk food' if he wished, that there were no obligatory group activities or therapy, and that he hardly ever needed to leave his flat. There was no mention of staff being available for advice and support, nor of the communal activities on offer at Champion Hill, let alone of taking advantage of opportunities in the community outside. It was appalling and compelling. This man had described a life as narrow as the one he had had in hospital; the only change was the absence of rules to govern his days and nights. His praise seemed to make a mockery of the team's mission statement, which was to provide tenants with opportunities to develop their potential and to become integrated into the community.

In the debriefing following the role-play, and in our subsequent work on re-examining the purpose of the service, this aspect of the tenants' experience came to be referred to as 'the empty core'. For the first time, the real implications of long-term mental illness were discussed in the team and taken into account in service planning. In particular, the hands-off approach which had always been taken for granted was reviewed. As part of a new, more proactive approach to their work, the team developed a structured day with regular appointments three times a week to meet with each tenant. This served both to contain their own anxieties and to facilitate the tenants' making more use of the considerable staff resources which had previously been so grossly under-utilized.

Containing anxiety in organizations

According to Bion (1967), the capacity to think, or even to distinguish reality from fantasy, is severely compromised by 'primitive' anxieties (anxieties about survival, physical or psychological). Thinking depends on what he called 'alpha-function' which transforms sense impressions into usable thoughts or alpha-elements. When anxiety is not contained, other mental contents, which Bion called beta-elements, cannot be thus transformed, but can only be evacuated as violent projective identifications. In the earliest months of life, babies communicate anxiety using projective identification. Maternal containment, or reverie,

> permits the infant to project a feeling, say, that it is dying, into the mother and to reintroject it after its sojourn in the breast has made it tolerable to the infant psyche. If the projection is not accepted by the mother, the infant reintrojects, not a fear of dying made tolerable, but a nameless dread.

> (Bion, 1967: 116)

The mother can fail to contain the infant's anxieties in a number of ways: she can be too preoccupied to hear the infant's distress, or she may pick him up dutifully while conveying 'I don't know what is the matter with this child', or the intensity of her own anxieties may render her incapable of 'metabolizing' the projection, so that it is returned unchanged or made yet more dreadful, into a fear of utter annihilation.

In organizations, the containing function which makes thinking possible normally comes from the management of the system, from firm boundaries and from the support and supervision that managers provide. These days, however, such sources of containment are often inadequate or unavailable. Boundaries are increasingly unreliable, as organizations undergo constant change (see Stokes, 1994), and managers themselves are less able to provide containment since they are caught up in similar anxieties themselves. Obliviousness to need, or the 'I don't know what is the matter with you' response is all too common.

When there is breakdown of containment within an organization, consultants may well be brought in to provide the lost function. However, what is presented to the consultant or manager is usually not a request for containment but a 'problem' requiring a 'solution'. In order to contain organizational anxiety, it is crucial that they contain their own anxiety to be seen to be doing a good job by responding too promptly to the presenting request. What is needed is a state of mind or an intervention that can transform the immobilizing dread into a worrying but tolerable and nameable difficulty which can be thought about. Once the capacity to think has been restored, the presenting problem can often be 'handed back' to the team or organization to find a solution. However, both managers and consultants are also under pressure to do as good a job as possible as quickly as possible. They may well respond to the presenting problem by 'taking it away' to solve, thereby implicitly (sometimes explicitly) confirming staff's self-doubts about their competence, rather than looking for ways to help their staff feel more contained and thereby more able to think.

The formal briefing for the consultancy work at Pathways was to design and facilitate their annual review. From the first session, it seemed to me that there was something going on about which it was not possible to talk or think. Instead of seeking information, the agency was lost in a fog of supposition and speculation. The unfavourable report from their funders had excited a flurry of activity focused on fighting an external enemy, making critical self-review impossible.

At Champion Hill my brief was to help the team to address the apparent lack of effectiveness of the service in enabling clients to live more fulfilling lives in the community. Their complaints about sleepless nights and anxious days were treated almost dismissively as an unfortunate hindrance to service development. However, my early encounters with the team gave me the impression that their dogged adherence to established routines, however unsatisfactory, and their repetitive arguments over details and rules, were obsessional defences against being flooded by the tenants' distress. Like the Pathways team, they were locked into defensive positions, unable to think. In both cases, it was imperative to find a way to help participants stand back from the pressure to act, and to look at their situation from a fresh perspective.

Play and the capacity to be surprised

When people in organizations are locked into a particular defensive position as described above, I often find it very useful to introduce an element of play into the consultative intervention. At Pathways, the group was stuck in an entrenched us-and-them polarization. The exercise was designed to help them shift out of this by introducing a third position, namely that of the users of the service. In addition, inviting two-thirds of the participants to step out of their everyday work roles and to stand for a while in others' shoes, so to speak, was intended to provide them with a playful opportunity to think about their situation from an unaccustomed vantage point.

The exercise as a whole, based on a design by Eric Miller, offers a kind of transitional space where issues get highlighted very quickly because the element of play temporarily removes participants from the immediacy of their anxieties and the pressure to find solutions. When the three groups come together to exchange the statements that they have prepared, everyone has a chance to hear something new. Specifically, in this instance, the design made it safe enough for the 'users' to articulate what, at some level, everyone knew but had been unable to acknowledge: that Pathways had failed to provide a service that felt relevant to the users they intended to serve. Had this observation been put to them from outside – by a manager, or a colleague in another agency, or by the consultant – there is little doubt that it would have been rejected. Since, however, it came from within the team, the statement evoked a shock of recognition, and made available a crucial insight. It then became possible for them to begin to think about alternative ways of providing a more efficient and effective service.

Winnicott (1971) makes two statements about playing which seem relevant here. One is that playing has a place and a time, the place being neither inside oneself nor outside in the repudiated world, but rather in what he calls the 'potential space' between child and mother, self and other. The other statement is that 'the significant moment [of play] is that at which the child surprises himself or herself' (1971: 59).

So, too, the design of an intervention involving play is about providing a place – one that is neither 'real' nor 'not real' but rather intermediate between the two – *and* a time for playing. Place and time together provide a container for anxiety, and can create a space where it is possible for the players to surprise themselves. This is quite different from being surprised by someone else, for example by a clever interpretation from the consultant. The crucial function of the consultant is to manage the boundary conditions needed to provide a dependable setting where play and discovery can happen. The 'as-if'-ness of the situation also means that insights occur when the players are ready for them, and not before.

At Champion Hill, the design of the role-play allowed team members to put aside their preoccupation with what to *do* (for example, whether to knock on doors at night). Instead, they stood in the tenants' shoes and discovered the power of the 'institution within'. The largely unconscious anger and anxiety that they had felt at not being approached more often for help, which had made them feel useless and rejected, gave way to recognition that being given a key to their own front door was not enough to liberate the tenants, nor were respect and opportunities for self-development enough to fill the 'empty core'. Their decision to be more proactive meant that they would have to struggle constantly with the tension between, on the one hand, drawing their clients out of their locked worlds and, on the other, respecting their right to choose what they made of the opportunities offered. This fundamental and inevitable tension in the work was one that the team had been evading. Once they faced this dilemma, they became more able to use expertise within the team, to go out and learn from others, and also to use their own managers as a resource – less anxious that displaying a need for help would lead to their being 'put away' again and losing their cherished autonomy.

However, as Winnicott also points out, playing is inherently precarious. The necessary space between me and not-me, between fantasy and external reality, can be eroded when the contents of the fantasy too closely approximate what is feared and repudiated in the outside world. In this case, playing becomes impossible or is spoiled. Indeed, the capacity for playing is itself a sign of health. I would now like to consider an example of a group that was unable to play.

Case study 3: when play is not possible

Queen's Lane was a large bungalow on the outskirts of London, staffed by a team of residential social workers and providing accommodation for eight elderly men and women, most of whom had spent several decades in psychiatric hospitals. The team's philosophy was very similar to that of the team at Champion Hill, and I had a similar brief, to assist them in reviewing their service and drawing up new aims and objectives. There was considerable conflict in this team, often quite bitter, which centred on opposing views about whether staff should be doing as much as possible to care *for* the residents, given how profoundly disabled they were by age, ill health and having spent most of their lives in institutions; or whether the main emphasis should be on supporting residents to do as much as possible for themselves. There were constant complaints against managers, frequent formal grievances and high absenteeism.

Since I thought that some of the difficulties were similar to those at Champion Hill, I decided to use the same role-play here, in the hope that the service users' views would introduce the missing 'third position'. Initially, several team members refused to participate, saying that the role-play was disrespectful of the residents. However, eventually they went through the motions of cooperating, although without any enthusiasm. Each player responded quite briefly and blandly, and as far as I could see the exercise was a total failure. I felt baffled by the antagonism that the team had shown towards the exercise, and quite stuck as to how to proceed. It felt as if every idea or intervention I introduced was killed off so that nothing new could emerge. Presumably the team were unconsciously communicating to me what it was like for them to work at Queen's Lane, by ensuring that I too had the experience of feeling that nothing I did was of any use in bringing about change. But this thought was of no help to me in planning how to proceed, and I was quite relieved when our next meeting was cancelled because over half the team were unable to attend.

For various reasons there was then a long hiatus before another meeting could be scheduled, and in the interim I met only with the team and service managers. They too felt rejected and useless, and expressed some irritation at the constant barrage of complaints from the team about their management style, their disrespect for others' rights and views, and so on. At one point, the service manager said that perhaps the rest of the consultation should be cancelled, since the team was refusing to make use of this expensive resource, and my services could then be offered to another team that was asking for consultancy.

Up to this point, our conversation had felt rather desultory, with a similar sense of disengagement as had characterized my earlier work at Queen's Lane. This last remark, however, was said in a way that felt aggressive and punitive towards the team. I fell silent, musing as to where this dissonant note was coming from. Until now, we had been bending over backwards to be understanding and patient, and now, suddenly, there was an opening to 'get back' at this group of ungrateful people. The idea was rather appealing, not least because it offered an acceptable way for me to get out of an unusually onerous piece of work.

I found myself thinking of the residents I had seen in the lounge, their bleak faces and grudging greetings. Surely the staff must sometimes long to get back at *them* for making the work so cheerless. Yet they were unfailingly kind and friendly to the residents, reserving their aggression for the managers. When I shared my thoughts with the others, a stream of associations followed, of gifts offered and rejected, and of other cruel attacks by the clients on staff members' self-esteem. The service manager recalled an incident from many years before, when she had been working in another residential unit with a similar client group, of being presented with an elaborately wrapped and be-ribboned gift on Christmas Day, only to find that the contents were human excrement. The horror, pain and hate of that long-ago event were palpable in the room.

Suddenly we all seemed to have come alive and were able to think again. The discussion shifted to some of the socially sanctioned ways that staff use to express aggression towards patients in traditional institutions; for example, how nurses can be 'too busy' to respond to a patient who needs help to get to the toilet, or can punish uncooperativeness by refusing to give out cigarettes. I recalled Winnicott (1947) referring to the end of the psychoanalytic hour as a permitted way for the analyst to express hate towards the patient. At Queen's Lane, none of these were possible. Indeed, it had been set up to prevent just such abuses of power by care staff. Always there must be respect, treating all with dignity, so that cruel withholding of cigarettes or of help with toileting could not happen. Nor was there an end of the hour: a shift was many hours long. Suddenly it seemed obvious that the team's determination to respond unstintingly to clients' demands was a defence against unbearable hate and rage. With nowhere else for these unacknowledged feelings to go, was it any wonder that they found their way into endless carping at management, formal grievances and high absenteeism?

My own inability to think about this until now was, I believe, an indication of how powerful the defences were in this organization against recognizing these unacceptable feelings. The role-play in this case had probably been too close to the psychic reality of life at Queen's Lane, so that the team's defences became more rigid than ever, making playing impossible. It was too dangerous to run the risk of being surprised. Perhaps I too had unconsciously avoided surprise by using a role-play that had worked well elsewhere, rather than devising a new one based on my experience of this particular team, as I normally would. My meeting with the managers away from the rest of the team had given us a space where we could recover our own capacity for play, this time with ideas.

One outcome of our discussion was that the managers decided to set up a series of team meetings to review each client in detail, with particular attention to the feelings that the work stirred up in the workers. They hoped that if they as managers could openly acknowledge their own negative feelings towards the clients, this would free their staff to face feelings that *they* had previously denied. When I next met with the team some two months later, the atmosphere was completely different. The managers had been able to give a lead in the task of rewriting the aims of the project, and the team had been able to accept and use the proffered guidance, instead of rejecting it as they had before. This enabled us to make optimal use of the little time remaining, identifying priorities and strategies for the coming year, and the entire team participated in this task with energy.

Conclusion: playing with ideas

In this last example, it was the period of more random free associating that made it possible for us to be surprised and to discover something new and useful. Winnicott (1971) regards all cultural and creative activity, and also free association as used in psychoanalytic work, as adult forms of playing. Like playing, he locates them in the intermediate area between me and not-me. And like playing, they require trust in a dependable setting. Excessive anxiety, and also excessive purposiveness, make all of these activities impossible, since they erode the space within which to be surprised.

Achieving this relaxed, non-purposive state is difficult. In my consultancy work with individual managers, I find that with some we never get past the struggle to find better ways of addressing their presenting problems. While this can be very useful, it is quite different from my experience with those where we find a way to play with ideas. For example, in a session with the director of an organization working with people with severe learning difficulties, a chance remark of his about a staff member's apparent stupidity led to an hour of random associations to the meaning for him, for his management team and for the different residential projects across his organization, of intelligence and stupidity. For a time, we both wondered if we were not straying rather far from the point, for he had brought an urgent difficulty in one of the units to the session. It was within the last quarter hour of the session that all the apparently random bits fell into place. He left in a very different state of mind than that in which he had arrived, feeling able to handle the crisis, without my having made any specific suggestion about it.

In staff support groups and other agenda-less group meetings, a degree of free association and playing with ideas is possible. When time is very limited, or there is particular pressure to 'get somewhere', to sort out a crisis or solve a problem, it can be very difficult to preserve a space for play. It is in these situations that I am likely to design into my intervention an element of play, usually in the form of an exercise that involves participants taking on roles related to, but different from, their usual ones. While these 'role-plays' fall far short of true playing in Winnicott's sense, they are often very useful in reducing anxiety and the pressure towards purposive problem-solving. By serving as a temporary 'container' for anxiety, the design provides opportunities for participants to recognize in the here-and-now previously unconscious aspects of their experiences at work. One outcome can be the re-framing of the presenting problem in such a way that new and creative responses become possible.

The word 'play' is often used to mean the opposite of work. As used in this chapter, it is not about parties and outings – although these have importance in the workplace too. It is about a special kind of work requiring particular conditions which enable participants to banter, to free associate, to muse, to play with ideas. Managers have a crucial role in safeguarding and sanctioning the space for this kind of play – both for themselves and for those they manage. Ideally, there will be a time and a place where they can play together.

References

Bion, W.R. (1967) 'A theory of thinking', in *Second Thoughts: Selected Papers in Psychoanalysis*, London: Heinemann Medical; reprinted (1984) London: Maresfield Reprints.

Stokes, J. (1994) 'Institutional chaos and personal stress', in A. Obholzer and V.Z. Roberts (eds) *The Unconscious at Work: Individual and Organizational Stress in the Human Services*, London: Routledge.

Winnicott, D.W. (1947) 'Hate in the counter transference', in (1958) *Collected Papers: Through Paediatrics to Psycho-Analysis*, London: Hogarth Press and the Institute of Psychoanalysis.

—— (1971) *Playing and Reality*, Harmondsworth: Penguin.

18

From understanding to action

Angela Foster and Vega Zagier Roberts

In today's mental health services – indeed, throughout the human services – the pressure towards action is enormous. In most teams and organizations, we hear the cry: 'We have no time to think.' Even those most committed to the idea that reflection is essential to effective work are prone to cancelling supervision sessions and other 'thinking' forums. Others, from front-line staff up to executive directors, may regard such forums as time taken away from the already short supply of time available to meet clients' needs. The connection between 'understanding' and 'action' therefore needs to be examined.

It is a well-recognized phenomenon in the public sector that when the failings of all or part of the system become impossible to ignore, one of the commonest 'solutions' is to restructure. Yet, as Hinshelwood points out in Chapter 1, to set up new structures without sufficient understanding of the causes of the earlier failings will 'drive us forward blindly', with the result that the new structures are likely to repeat some of the very problems that they are designed to remedy.

A second favoured 'solution' is to enforce tighter controls, for example setting more explicit service standards and performance targets, requiring additional documentation, and so on. While these can be very useful when they provide greater clarity about key issues such as task, role, authority and accountability, they can – and often do – fail to achieve the desired improvement in effectiveness or client satisfaction. They can also add to staff stress, distress and disaffection.

Obholzer (1994), writing about health care systems, says:

> In the unconscious, there is not such concept as 'health'. There is, however, a concept of 'death', and, in our constant attempt to keep this anxiety repressed, we use various unconscious defensive mechanisms . . . Indeed, our health service might more accurately be called a 'keep-death-at-bay' service.
>
> (Obholzer, 1994: 171)

By analogy, we could say that there is no concept in the unconscious of 'mental health' but only of madness and the associated anxiety about having our capacity to think annihilated. The client's capacity to think – to make links between different aspects of their internal and external experience – is under constant assault from within, and the impact of the work involves a barrage of projections such that madness gets into the worker and into the system. Before we can act rationally we need to contain the anxieties stirred up in mental health work (both by the nature of the work itself, and by the external pressures on workers) so as to recover the capacity to think.

Menzies' ideas about how organizational systems evolve in ways that serve to defend against primitive (life and death) anxieties are referred to repeatedly throughout this book. A counter-argument to these ideas is that it is not anxiety that produces counter-productive organizational systems, but rather 'that it is badly organized systems that arouse psychotic anxieties' (Jaques, 1995: 343; see also page 218 below). Both arguments have validity: it is not a matter of either/or but of both/and. In the next section, we examine some of the uses, and also some of the misuses and limitations, of the kind of psychoanalytically informed understanding used in this book. This is followed by some brief comments on the relevance of psychoanalysis as a method.

Psychoanalysis as a source of understanding

Some uses of psychoanalytically informed understanding

Some concepts have not only repeatedly proven their value to us as consultants and trainers, but have also been particularly useful to our consultancy clients in helping them to take up their management roles more effectively. The first of these, already referred to above, is Menzies' (1959) concept of *social systems as a defence*. Consultancy clients might, for example, be invited to explore the particular anxieties inherent in the nature of their own work, and how their workplaces and practices are structured to defend against these. This includes attention to unconscious aspects of design as discussed by Colman (1975), of which perhaps one of the most often cited examples is of the general hospital that was built – after extensive consultation with a vast range of professionals as well as members of the local community – without a mortuary, as if death were to have no place in the new building.

Projective identification and splitting

Here the invitation is to think in terms of what 'gets into' the organization and its members from the clients, and from staff into managers. For example, the deputy manager of a hostel for disturbed adolescent girls was at his wits' end as to how to manage staff who were constantly late to work, leaving their jobs without notice, smoking cannabis at hostel parties and engaging in other delinquent behaviour. He found himself becoming increasingly authoritarian and was uncomfortable with this 'new' side to himself, as well as angry with his manager for being so placatory with the staff and therefore popular and idealized, while he himself was increasingly marginalized. He found the concepts of splitting and projection enormously helpful. He shifted the focus of group supervision, for which he was responsible, to discussion of the feelings evoked by encounters with the girls. The staff became more reflective, their need to 'discharge' their feelings in the same ways as their clients diminished, and they began to experiment with different approaches to the work. As the deputy became more 'understanding', the manager and the staff became less permissive, and the tensions in the team as a whole between these two attitudes became less extreme.

Valency

This refers to the particular availability or vulnerability of an individual to attract and identify with certain projections rather than others. Our consultancy clients often find it illuminating to consider what unconscious needs they are seeking to meet through choosing their particular job or type of work, and how these feed into both the strengths and the problems of their organizations. Thus, in the above example, the deputy came to see how he and his manager both contributed to the particular ways in which they were 'used' and split by their staff. This kind of understanding can considerably reduce scapegoating and related processes which lock particular individuals into dysfunctional roles.

The self-assigned impossible task

This term, first used by Roberts (1994), is not, strictly speaking, a psychoanalytic concept but rather refers to a constellation of defences which arise in response to the anxiety and guilt stirred up when reparative efforts in helping organizations prove disappointing or threaten staff with a sense of failure. These defences include denial, omnipotence, idealization (including self-idealization) and denigration of others. For example, an outreach team of six social workers was set up with the plan that they would eventually carry a caseload of fifty clients. For the first year, however, their task was to provide very intensive support for six frail, elderly clients recently resettled in independent flats after decades of psychiatric hospitalization. When the time came to extend the service, the team leader was struck by the team's apathy. It seemed that they had assigned themselves the impossible task of doing as much for the new clients as for the original six because not to meet their new clients' needs in the accustomed ways felt unbearable. This insight freed the team leader to stop 'volleying back' the projections and blame that were flying around, but rather to contain them. Over time, the team became very creative in deploying their limited resources to optimal effect.

Some misuses of psychoanalytic understanding

Any concept, however valuable, can also be misused. In reviewing our experiences of our own work and that of colleagues and of our consultancy clients and students in applying ideas drawn from psychoanalysis, we identified two major sources of such misuses. The first comes from taking the view that defences are something to get rid of, or evidence of 'pathology' to be cured: for example, telling people to stop being so dependent and to take more responsibility for themselves. Such an approach is likely to be counterproductive.

The second is closely allied to the first: to regard unconscious processes as something that happens in other people and then to see others as 'putting things into us'. Thus, for example, the disquieting report from a team manager of his having told his staff that they had been projecting their anxieties into him and needed to 'take these projections back'. When we forget that we are all subject to unconscious processes and that they *are* unconscious, we are tempted to use concepts like projective identification to 'explain away' our own discomfort and our mistakes.

Words like 'defences' readily suggest something wrong that needs to be corrected. In fact, we all need defences against anxiety – without them we would be utterly overwhelmed. The question is whether the defences operating – in individuals or in the collections of individuals that comprise our organizations – are helpful and necessary, or have become counterproductive. Where the defences themselves are adding to stress and distress, and/or undermining the aims of the service, then alternatives need to be found.

Some limitations of psychoanalytic understanding

The reason we have bad or dysfunctional organizations is . . . that there has never been an adequate foundation of understanding of organizations *per se*. We have simply not yet learned how to construct adequate organizations. . . . The main source of psychological stresses that then arise, lies in our failure to clarify and specify the requirements of the roles in our major organizations. We get gross mismatches between the difficulty of roles and the capabilities of their incumbents. Or we fail to specify the accountability and authorities in role relationships, and leave it up to the individuals to exercise personal power or otherwise manipulate each other in order somehow to get things done. It all becomes an unpleasant paranoiagenic zoo.

(Jaques, 1995: 344)

At a minimum, besides clarity about tasks, roles, relationships and account-ability, and a match between the amount of responsibility and the degree of authority given to people at each hierarchical level, organizations need to provide adequate opportunities for participation and contribution, and a system of remuneration and reward that is experienced as fair (Obholzer, 1994; Jaques, 1989). These are rarely all present in our organizations. Jaques argues that until faulty structures are put right, attempts at understanding are misguided. The case study in Chapter 3, for example, demonstrates clearly the limitations of understanding when the fundamental basis on which a service has been set up is faulty. If this is the case, then no amount of consultancy aimed at understanding can put it right. One might even argue that, in such situations, consultancy may serve to obscure political and policy issues beyond the immediate client system which desperately need to be confronted. However, the same case study suggests that, even then, understanding can help – albeit to a limited extent – by containing some of the surplus anxiety washing around the system, and by leading to small local changes in both structure and attitude.

Psychoanalysis as a method

Psychoanalytic theory provides a method for investigating unconscious psychic processes, and as such can be applied to a number of situations involving human beings, including – as argued in the preceding section – to the understanding of unconscious processes in organizations. Psychoanalysis is also a therapeutic technique, and this cannot legitimately be applied beyond the confines of the therapist–patient(s) encounter in the consulting room. This book is most definitely *not* about putting organizations (or their members) 'on the couch'. However, there are some essential elements of psychoanalytically informed treatment methods that *are* transferable.

At the heart of any psychoanalytic treatment method is the *provision of a container* – a safe space where the patient can dare to explore the uncon-scious connections and meaning that have given rise to their symptoms. The safety comes first from having a dependable, regular time and place in which to do the exploratory work. It comes also from the availability of the thera-pist/analyst for projections from the patient, his or her capacity to take in the projections and 'metabolize' or 'digest' them so that they can then be returned to the patient in a less terrifying form. This containing function is similar to the one that a mother performs for her child (Bion, 1967a). A mother overwhelmed by her infant's distress, or too preoccupied by her own concerns, cannot be sufficiently psychologically available to do this. Neither can overwhelmed or over-stressed mental health workers do this for their clients, nor mental health service managers for their staff. These ideas have been referred to repeatedly in this book.

Containment in organizations

Let us revisit the word 'dependable'. The patient needs the therapist to be dependable – to *be* both physically and emotionally present. Part of the dependability comes from the predictability of the structure of therapy sessions: held in the same room, at the same set times. How can this be transferred to organizational life, where structures as well as physical spaces for the work keep changing, and where the only certainty seems to be constant change and uncertainty about tomorrow? Indeed, the very suggestion that dependability is desirable implies that dependency is legitimate, and this idea is currently being seriously challenged.

Halton (1995), in his discussion of the positive inspirational aspects as well as of the dangers and negative aspects of the dependency culture prevailing in the United Kingdom from the Second World War until the 1980s, writes:

> In its attack on the negative features of a national dependency culture, particularly a parasitic reliance on the all-providing welfare state, the government prescribed its remedy: market values . . . seen as benefiting the individual psychologically by encouraging self-reliance and productivity through stimulating survival-anxiety. . . . To treat passive dependency with a dose of survival-anxiety seems a reasonable proposition. It gets out of hand when a culture contaminated by the delusion of total social provision is transformed into one affected by the opposite delusion, that of alienated self-sufficiency.
>
> (Halton, 1995: 189)

He goes on to point out that while, for certain organizations (say, in commerce and industry) that use conflict and competition as a means of achieving their primary goals, this kind of fight/flight culture can be effective, for organizations in health care and education this attack on dependency is at such variance with their primary task as to put the task seriously at risk.

> In these organizations there should be a degree of healthy competition for scarce resources and in the pursuit of excellence, but it should be managed and contained so that it does not interfere with the interprofessional collaboration and trust necessary for the provision of care. . . . Market structures, which aim to benefit the self, do not match the primary task of caring for others . . . nor do they affirm the vocational motivation of practitioners.
>
> (Halton, 1995: 190)

How is the competition for and anxiety about scarce resources to be managed and contained? This, clearly, is a central challenge to everyone involved in mental health care – whether practitioners, managers or policy-makers. When anxieties are not contained, they are likely to be 'discharged' in the form of action (hence the psychoanalytic term that has now entered popular language: 'acting out'). This can take many forms at work, from delinquency to negligence and other forms of professional misconduct. It can also take the form of anxiety-driven decision-making. If we are to move on from the 'when in doubt, restructure' or the 'what we need is tighter management' solutions referred to in the opening section of this chapter, it is imperative that we enhance the capacity both of individuals and of systems to learn from experience – their own and one another's.

Learning from experience

Bion identified two states of mind in groups: *work mentality* where members stay in touch with the primary task of the group, take reality into account and are capable of learning from experience; and *basic assumption mentality* where the primary function of the group behaviour appears to be to defend members from anxiety. In this state of mind, produced by excessive (uncon-tained) anxiety about survival, there is likely to be an absence of scientific curiosity about the group's effectiveness, an inability to think about or learn from experience, and great difficulty adapting to change (Bion, 1961). In his later work, Bion explored the intrapsychic processes of thinking in more detail, and notes the dangerous effects of a state of mind where 'emotion is hated ... [and] felt to be too powerful to be contained'. These include 'the disturbance of the impulse of curiosity on which all learning depends', and attacking the linking function of emotion on which thinking depends, so that 'the links surviving are perverse, cruel and sterile' (Bion, 1967a: 108–9). He subsequently elaborated on the connection between these phenomena and a failure of breakdown in containment: it is containment that makes linking, thinking and learning from experience possible (Bion, 1967b).

> For the container to have the best chance of containing and metabo-lizing the anxieties projected into it, it needs to be in a depressive position mode, which means it has a capacity to face both external and psychic reality. For organizations, this requires ... remaining in touch with the nature of the anxieties projected into the container, rather than defensively blocking them out of awareness. In order for a system to work according to these principles, a structured system for dialogue between the various component parts is necessary. This depends on all concerned being in touch with the difficulties of the task.
>
> (Obholzer, 1994: 172–3)

Throughout this book, we have tried to demonstrate ways of *attending to experience* differently, since this kind of attention is a necessary precursor to learning from experience, and to shifting from a culture of blame and persecution to one of curiosity and collaborative enquiry. This needs to happen at a number of different levels:

- *Individual experience.* Through examining their emotional responses to particular clients, and the impact of the work on their feelings and behaviour, and by using these emotional responses as data, individual workers can deepen their understanding of their clients. This can happen in supervision, but also in other settings. It is dependent not only on the availability of supervisors in a suitable frame of mind (that is, who are themselves sufficiently held so that they can be emotionally available to their supervisees), but also on a system that values and supports this kind of reflection.
- *Experiences within a team.* Sharing their different responses to a particular client or situation, and piecing these together, can help members of a team to make sense of the work in a new way. Different ways of encouraging and supporting this kind of reflective work are described throughout this book. These include staff support (or staff dynamics) groups, in-depth case discussions and team debriefings. (See, for example, Chapters 11 and 12.) Senior management teams, too, need 'an adaptable and *collaborative* reviewing capacity' (Amado, 1995) where they can attend to their emotional experience as well as to 'external reality'. This reflective work makes possible more informed action planning, no longer so 'blindly driven'.
- *Experiences across hierarchical levels.* The widespread use of splitting as a defence has been vividly illustrated in many of the case studies in this book. This can be particularly entrenched between different levels of an organization (and between different agencies – see below) where face-to-face contact is infrequent and there is not the daily experience of shared work. In our experience, senior managers are rarely as out of touch with the stresses of the face-to-face work, nor practitioners as out of touch with the realities of financial constraints, as each would like to believe the other group to be. Nonetheless there is a reluctance on both sides to get too close to the particular anxieties and preoccupations of the other and we must bear in mind that their staying apart serves a defensive function which – provided it is not too extreme – is not entirely negative. However, when staff can take time to think about needs, demands and difficulties relating to the task, instead of feeling ignored, resentful and powerless they feel more in touch with their expertise. All staff have information and knowledge that their managers do not hold and most managers are pleased to receive proposals for service developments which team members would like to operationalize. This approach can lead to joint consultation and the possibility of radical change.

- *Experiences across different agencies.* Here again, geographical distance can reinforce splitting which then makes 'the other' a repository for negative projections. However, where different organizations are providing different 'bits' of the 'care package' to the same clients, reflection and review of experience and collaborative learning are crucial. Case conferences and inter-agency meetings such as CPA reviews can be forums for this, but are all too rarely used in this way, not least because of the pressures to arrive at decisions as speedily as possible. Some of the costs of this splitting and examples of consultative interventions to enhance collaboration are described in Chapter 10.

The provider forum described in Chapter 16 enabled managers from a range of different provider organizations to gain a better appreciation of the function performed by each agency and of the demands, constraints and frustrations experienced by people in different roles. Through this empowering process they were able to identify and sort out a number of inter-agency difficulties as well as to help each other with information.

In addition they were able to collectively voice their concerns about service provision to members of the joint planning team (purchasers from health and social services) whereupon it became evident that the agendas of these two groups were sharply divergent, the providers wanting to put additional funds into improving existing services and the purchasers wanting to fill gaps in provision by creating new services. The need for better communication between these two groups had become obvious and the provider forum took on an enhanced role as an advisory body to the joint planning team.

In all these situations, the time for reflecting together is not about the pursuit of understanding as an end in itself, but as a *prerequisite for action.* Reflection (and consultancy directed at enhancing the capacity for reflective self-review) is neither self-indulgent nor aimed at 'keeping the workers happy (or quiet)', but rather it is a central part of the primary task of mental health work. Reflection, reviewing what has been learned and decision-making (action planning) need to be part of an ongoing cycle (see Figure 18.1).

Only when such a system is built in and effectively managed can there be true learning from experience.

Some reflections on management

The title of this book, 'Managing mental health in the community', reflects a key preoccupation everyone in the field, from policy-makers and executives to front-line staff. But what is management?

The most usual answer to this question relates to functions that ensure that the core product or service is delivered. In open systems theory, this is

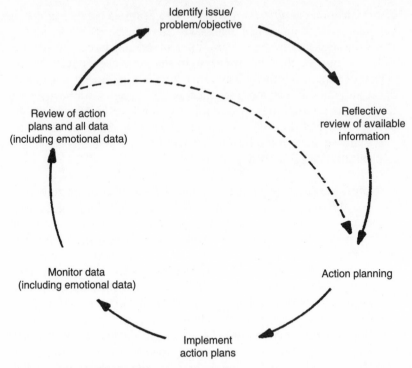

Figure 18.1 The cycle of reflection and action

called the 'primary task', defined as the task that the group or organization must achieve in order to survive (Rice, 1963). In simple terms, an organization has inputs – say, raw materials – and has to convert these into outputs. In manufacturing, these would be the saleable products. In human service organizations, the inputs are people in a certain state, and the outputs are these same people in a different state. For example, a hospital could be said to take in people who are ill and 'export' some proportion of people who are well (or less ill).

In Figure 18.2, the box in the middle represents the system of activities required to perform the task of converting the inputs into outputs. Around it there is a boundary separating the inside from the outside, across which the exchanges with the environment take place. These exchanges need to be regulated in such a way that the system can achieve its task, and therefore there needs to be *management of the boundary*, represented by M. In more complex systems, there is a boundary around the whole as well as around each subsidiary system, and each of these boundaries needs to be managed so that all the parts function in a coordinated way (Miller and Rice, 1967). In Figure 18.3, the smaller boxes represent discrete task systems, each with a boundary managed by m1, m2, etc. In conventional organizational terms, M is the line managers of the four m's.

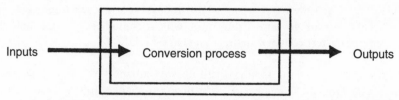

Figure 18.2 Schematic representation of an organization as an open system[1]

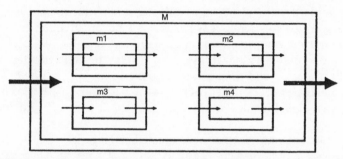

Figure 18.3 Management of multiple systems of activity within an organization

Note The smaller boxes represent discrete task systems, each with a boundary managed by m1, m2, etc. The larger box represents the overall enterprise, managed by M. In conventional organization terms, M is the line manager of the four m's.

The managers at each level need to ensure that the necessary conditions prevail which make it possible for the staff to carry out their task, for example that staff have the necessary resources (time, tools, skills, clarity about what is expected of them, relevant information about what is happening outside their system, and so on) to do their work effectively. They also need to ensure that the boundaries of the systems that they manage are appropriately permeable so that information flows across the boundary inwards and outwards – or, in conventional hierarchical terms, downwards and upwards – in the right degree. (While it is often said that 'information is power', excessive amounts of information that cannot be absorbed and used can be highly persecuting.)

But these management functions are not enough. Reed and Armstrong point out some of the limitations of attending only to questions of effective service or product delivery. They suggest that good management requires two different kinds of thinking:

(Grubb Institute, 1991: 10–11)

1   *Purposive systems thinking.* This focuses on what the organization's stakeholders seek to achieve. Here the organization is regarded as a piece of sophisticated social engineering designed to use resources to achieve a specific purpose.

2   *Containing systems thinking.* This focuses on patterns of customs, beliefs, meanings and behaviours which characterize what actually happens, irrespective of defined aims and intentions.

They and others at the Grubb Institute subsequently elaborated on these ideas, evolving the concept of 'organization-in-the-mind' – 'the mental picture of the institution in its context which is informing the managers' experience, shaping their behaviour and influencing their relations, both overtly and covertly' (Hutton, Bazalgette and Armstrong, 1994: 185–6). They argue that this requires a particular kind of attention to one's own emotional experience, and that 'understanding the emotional experience of living and working within an institution is key to understanding what its primary process is and what has to be done to manage it' (*ibid.*: 200). The effective manager needs to get back in touch with those aspects of his or her own beliefs and longings which may have been split off and located in others.

But it is not only people in designated managerial posts who have to manage. As has been said before (Chapter 4), we all have to manage ourselves, that is, we have to manage our own boundary which separates inside (our intrapsychic world) and outside, if we are to be effective (or sane). We could substitute for 'management' the word 'containment', which – as discussed in the preceding section – is a necessary condition for thinking and effective action to take place. Without containment – whether within an individual or in a work system – there is a chaotic flow of information across the boundary, so that the internal and external get mixed up. For the individual, this produces a psychotic state. It also produces mad (chaotic) systems.

Conclusion: empowerment and change

> In 1990 community care was predicted – by the editor of the magazine of the same name – to be a 'policy set to advance from anarchy to chaos without the redeeming interregnum of rational thought'.
>
> (Philpot, 1990: 13)

This pessimistic comment is quoted by Tudor (1996) who goes on to say:'community care has unfortunately fulfilled such predictions and warnings and indeed has provoked the abandonment to objective, regulatory models of disease and mental illness of both individuals and of notions of positive mental health care within the community' (1996: 108).

In relation to Tudor's views on a radical approach to these issues, this book addresses some of the reasons that rational thought is so difficult, and seeks to identify ways in which it can be reinstated, leading us, we hope, to a position (on top of the hill rather than buried under the rubble) from where it becomes possible to see and to think anew about the nature of the needs, the demands and the difficulties. This then enables us to consider what actions we would wish to take (rather than rushing into reactions).

We need to develop appropriate and flexible systems of care that can be solid, dependable and containing for people who are feeling fragile, disturbed, afraid of their own state of mind, afraid of what they might do, and desperately needy. That is, we need community asylum (Tomlinson and Carrier, 1996). These same systems need to be capable of empowering people who are feeling stronger and healthier (both clients and workers). This can only be done through careful consultation, and through collaboration among the different professionals involved.

However, good collaboration is difficult to achieve unless the practitioners themselves feel well held and managed. There is a need for much more work to integrate services provided by different agencies – health, social services, voluntary sector organizations, the police, housing organizations and others. Integrated management structures (not subsumed under health alone, as this increases the risk of over-medicalizing social care) – based on shared definitions of core purpose and values – facilitate interprofessional collaboration. They would also be able to provide the joint funding necessary for consultancy and joint training initiatives.

It has been said that a good manager is someone who has their feet on the ground and their head in the clouds, that is, who is simultaneously in touch with the reality (including the emotional reality) of the work at ground level and is capable of vision. The same image might be used for a healthy system: that those with responsibility for strategy and those working directly with clients need to be connected into an organic whole. But how far is this possible in community care today? The 'head' is constantly assaulted by the hail and meteorites of competing visions, escalating and often contradictory demands by purchasers, policy-makers and the public, while the 'feet' are awash with the projections of madness. The task of staying in touch with both is enormous. The search for ways of containing anxiety so as to support connections – the capacity for linking, thinking and informed action – is a major challenge for us all. This book has been about some of the steps that might take us nearer to meeting it.

Note

1 Figures 18.2 and 18.3 were previously published in Roberts (1994), and are updated from Miller and Rice (1967).

References

Amado, G. (1995) 'Why psychoanalytical knowledge helps us understand organizations; a discussion with Elliott Jaques', *Human Relations* 48(4): 351–8.

Bion, W.R. (1961) *Experiences in Groups*, New York: Basic Books.

—— (1967a) 'Attacks on linking', in *Second Thoughts: Selected Papers on Psychoanalysis*, London: Heinemann Medical; reprinted (1984) London: Maresfield Reprints.

—— (1967b) 'A theory of thinking', in *Second Thoughts: Selected Papers on Psychoanalysis*, London: Heinemann Medical; reprinted (1984) London: Maresfield Reprints.

Colman, A.D. (1975) 'Irrational aspects of design', in A.D. Colman and W.H. Bexton (eds) *Group Relations Reader 1*, Washington, DC: A.K. Rice Institute Series.

Grubb Institute (1991) 'Professional management', notes prepared by the Grubb Institute on concepts relating to professional management.

Halton, W. (1995) 'Institutional stress on providers in health and education', *Psychodynamic Counselling* 1(2): 187–98.

Hutton, J., Bazalgette, J. and Armstrong, D. (1994) 'What does management really mean?', in R. Casemore, G. Dyas, A. Eden, K. Kellner, J. McAuby and S. Moss (eds) *What Makes Consultancy Work: Understanding the Dynamics*, London: South Bank University Press.

Jaques, E. (1989) *Requisite Organization*, Arlington, VA: Cason Hall.

—— (1995) 'Why the psychoanalytical approach to understanding organizations is dysfunctional', *Human Relations* 48(4): 343–9.

Menzies, I.E.P. (1959) 'The functioning of social systems as a defence against anxiety', *Human Relations* 13: 95–121; reprinted in Isabel Menzies Lyth (1988) *Containing Anxiety in Institutions: Selected Essays*, London: Free Association Books.

Miller, E.J. and Rice, A.K. (1967) *Systems of Organization: The Control of Task and Sentient Boundaries*, London: Tavistock.

Obholzer, A. (1994) 'Managing social anxieties in public sector organizations', in *The Unconscious at Work: Individual and Organizational Stress in the Human Services*, London: Routledge.

Philpot, T. (1990) 'Comment. April fooled', *Community Care*, 26 July: 13.

Rice, A.K. (1963) *The Enterprise and its Environment*, London: Tavistock.

Roberts, V.Z. (1994) 'The self-assigned impossible task', in A. Obholzer and V.Z. Roberts (eds) *The Unconscious at Work: Individual and Organizational Stress in the Human Services*, London: Routledge.

Tomlinson, D. and Carrier, J. (1996) *Asylum in the Community*, London: Routledge.

Tudor, K. (1996) *Mental Health Promotion: Paradigms and Practice*, London: Routledge.

Index